# FROM
# EDEN
# TO
# BABYLON

# FROM EDEN TO BABYLON

*The Social and Political Essays of*
*Andrew Nelson Lytle*

*Edited and with an Introduction by*
*M. E. Bradford*

REGNERY GATEWAY
*Washington, D.C.*

Copyright © 1990 by Andrew Nelson Lytle

Library of Congress Cataloging-in-Publication Data

Lytle, Andrew Nelson, 1902–
    From Eden to Babylon : the social and political essays of Andrew
Nelson Lytle / Andrew Nelson Lytle; Edited by M. E. Bradford.
        p.      cm.
    ISBN 0-89526-548-6
    1. Southern States—Rural conditions.    2. Lytle, Andrew Nelson,
1902—Political and social views.    I. Title.
HN79.A13L98    1989
307.72'0975—dc20                                                    89-38147
                                                                         CIP

Published in the United States by
Regnery Gateway
1130 17th Street, NW
Washington, DC 20036

Distributed to the trade by
National Book Network
4720-A Boston Way
Lanham, MD 20706

Manufactured in the United States of America

10   9   8   7   6   5   4   3   2   1

*To my sister Polly Lytle Darwin
and to the memory of our Aunt
Mary Greaves Nelson*

# ACKNOWLEDGMENTS

The editor acknowledges the indispensable assistance of Professor George Core and Mr. Don Keck DuPree. The publisher is grateful for permission to reprint the following:

**"The Hind Tit"** originally published in *I'll Take My Stand: The South and the Agrarian Tradition,* by Twelve Southerners, New York: Harper and Brothers, 1930; reprint by Baton Rouge: Louisiana State University Press, 1977. Copyright 1930 by the authors. Copyright renewed 1958 by Donald Davidson. Reprinted by permission of Harper & Row, Publishers, Inc.

**"The Small Farm Secures the State"** originally published in *Who Owns America?,* edited by Herbert Agar and Allen Tate, Boston: Houghton Mifflin, 1936; reprint by Lanham, Maryland: University Press of America, 1983.

**"John Taylor of Caroline"** originally published as "John Taylor and the Political Economy of Agriculture" in *The American Review,* III (September 1934), 432–37, III (October 1934), 630–43, and IV (November 1934), 84–99.

**"The Backwoods Progression"** originally published in *The American Review,* I (September 1933), 409–34.

**"R. E. Lee"** originally published in *The Southern Review,* 1st ser., I (July 1935), 411–22.

**"John C. Calhoun"** originally published in *The Southern Review,* 1st ser., III (Winter 1938), 510–30.

**"A Hero and the Doctrinaires of Defeat"** originally published in *The Georgia Review,* X, No. 4 (Winter 1956), 453–67. Copyright 1956 by The University of Georgia. Reprinted by permission of *The Georgia Review.*

**"A Retrospect on *Bedford Forrest and His Critter Company"* originally published as the Introduction to the fifth edition of *Bedford Forrest and His Critter Company,* by Andrew Nelson Lytle, New York: McDowell, Obolensky, 1960; first edition, New York: Minton, Balch and Co., 1931.

**"How Many Miles to Babylon"** originally published in *Southern Renascence: The Literature of the Modern South,* edited by Louis D. Rubin, Jr., and Robert D. Jacobs, Baltimore: The Johns Hopkins Press, 1953.

**"A Christian University and the Word"** published by the University of the South, Sewanee, Tennessee, November 1964 for complimentary distribution.

**"The Search for Order in American Society"** originally published in *The Southern Partisan,* II (Fall 1981) 21–24, 29.

**"The Momentary Man"** is an original piece by the author for this collection of his essays.

**"Semi-Centennial: An Agrarian Afterword"** originally published as "Afterword: A Semi-Centennial" in *Why the South Will Survive,* by Fifteen Southerners, Athens: University of Georgia Press, 1981. Published here with a revised conclusion.

**"A Myth in a Garden"** originally published in *Chronicles,* June 1987, 11–14.

**"A Journey South"** originally published in *The Kentucky Review,* I (Spring 1980), 3–10.

**"The Abiding Mystery"** originally published as "The Momentary Man" in *The Hillsdale Review,* I (Spring 1979), 4–11.

**"They Took Their Stand: The Agrarian View After Fifty Years"** originally published in *Modern Age,* XXIV (Spring 1980), 114–20.

**"Monteagle—1983"** originally published as "Andrew Nelson Lytle: An Exclusive Interview" by James B. Graves in *The Review of the News,* August 31, 1983, 39–57.

**"A Conversation with Madison Smartt Bell"** originally published as "Andrew Lytle Talks to Madison Smartt Bell" by Madison Smartt Bell in *Chronicles,* September 1988, 9–13.

While every effort has been made to secure permissions, some copyright holders may not have been traced. We apologize for any apparent oversight.

# CONTENTS

PART IV
# TWO INTERVIEWS   231

# INTRODUCTION

THE publication of the social and political essays of Andrew Nelson Lytle is an occasion for rejoicing and special celebration. To have these pieces presented as a set, in company, is to put in perspective the scope of Mr. Lytle's overall achievement, the larger resonance of historic vision which stands behind his career as artist and sage—as teacher, editor, critic, and keeper of the communal memory. Even though we know better than to anticipate what he may yet have to say, such a collection, published in Mr. Lytle's 87th year, with only Robert Penn Warren of his original companions in the making of *I'll Take My Stand* remaining with him on this side of the river, is a kind of completion for the witness of a lifetime, the fulfillment of a promise made long ago when he first began to speak his mind concerning the right order of Christian civilization; or rather, to bespeak as much of that order as can expect a hearing, given the modern dispensation. These essays, written over the course of half a century, give us Andrew Lytle as citizen and public man, as commentator on Southern history and the general secularization of what once was Christendom, in roles which he has played throughout his adult life. There are, of course, social and political materials in most of his critical essays. Furthermore, a version of what has happened in the history of the West, to replace the old covenant, since Machiavelli, Luther, and Columbus ushered in a triumph of the will, is at work in most of his fiction in the enveloping actions which contain the lives of individual men and women as they interact in particular fables. Even so, the social and political essays illuminate not only one another but the entire Lytle canon, objectifying the oneness of his total performance.

The seventeen essays and two interviews gathered here present to us Andrew Lytle as preeminently a social being, the same person we recognize in his extraordinary family chronicle, *A Wake for the Living* (1975), and in numerous public readings and addresses, as an individual and immediate presence, even when he appears in print. For however deliberate his manner or weighty the subject with which he is engaged, the voice to be heard in a Lytle essay is one that is never far removed from speech. It was out of a social, personal circumstance, a speaking relation with other Vanderbilt graduates and professors, that in 1930 he came to contribute to *I'll Take My Stand*. Though a fledgling playwright and actor, his views on the value of a distinctive Southern identity were known and very much in place *before* he began to discuss with other Agrarians the embattled status of their region. As a planter's son, he recognized the plight of the Southern farmer and had in 1925 to 1926 made a crop on Cornsilk, his family's place near Guntersville, Alabama, in the Tennessee River Valley. Moreover, though still a young man, he had seen what was happening in the great world beyond Middle Tennessee, had studied in France, at Oxford and Yale, and had performed on the Broadway stage. Living outside the South, he had come to understand the threat to the familiar ordering of life that belonged to him by inheritance, gathering just beyond the boundaries and intellectual fortifications of that old and established regime. Therefore, after becoming a member of the continuing conversation of the Agrarians, it was inevitable that Lytle contribute to their manifesto, that he would play a role in the activities following their fierce collective reaction to the predominant current of American history flowing through their place and time. Like his hero, General Nathan Bedford Forrest, he "bought a one-way ticket" to these wars, and from the position to which they committed him he has not retreated.

Indeed, the immediate and practical origins of Mr. Lytle's Agrarian essays are in his biography of the "wizard of the saddle," *Bedford Forrest and His Critter Company* (1931). Work on this book, for which he commenced his research in 1928, led Lytle to ask what sort of men made up the Confederate army, why they were eager to serve there, and why they continued to remember Forrest with affection fifty years after their amazing and high-spirited performance under his command. The answers to these questions, which he discovered among the people of the Middle South, pointed to the importance of the small freeholder in embodying the character of the larger Southern community. Forrest drew to the cause of the Confederacy the plain people, the self-sufficient farmers who saw the War Between the States as a struggle with a self-righteous invader. In outrage, they sent their sons to turn away that invader and preserve the freehold by fighting under a commander whose view of the conflict was essentially their own.

When the Agrarians took their stand, the patriarchate, the traditional society of independent Southern families living in a precapitalist fashion on the land, on mortgage-free holdings not subject to the vagaries of the market, was still intact; though frail, still as it had been more than a century before. As Mr. Lytle has recently observed, the prophecies of the Agrarians were so little heeded by their original audience because no one could imagine how quickly the old familiar society that "lived by the farm" could disappear, particularly the small holder of that society—once the majority of Southerners and the backbone of the region's independence of spirit. A culture "composed of families with real property" or with a private business or craft necessary to the communal life around them cannot be easily transformed into a "servile state." Such a culture locates the blood and gives a continuity to the life of corporate man—a creature who is better identified by his history as part of a group situated in a place than by his limitless future. For, as Mr. Lytle has also observed, "It is the family's sense of itself which gives freedom." And that sense lives "somewhere, or in some familiar task."

Andrew Lytle wrote his Agrarian essays "The Backwoods Progression" and "The Hind Tit" to maintain that "the small farm upholds the state"—the kind of polity brought into being by the American Revolution. Since the Republic had its origins in reaction to remote, arbitrary, and potentially unfriendly power, he has persistently rejected the argument of those savants who believe we should re-create that power in our day and surrender our destiny into its keeping. To give up that individual responsibility for the ordering of one's private life which is (apart from the restraints of nature) characteristic of the small subsistence farmer (who grows or makes most of what he needs) is "to surrender that delicate balance of order which alone makes the state a servant and not the people the servant of the state."

These essays are also full of aesthetic celebration, even in the exposition of old John Taylor. They are spun out in the spirit of "hard pastoral," in praise of a vigorous rural life as demanding of strength as it is physically and morally wholesome. This life, says Lytle, is both free and responsible: suited to preserving the "manliness of men." Within its context, the public and the private things were once kept apart. Furthermore, by its seasonal patterns the spirit of man was rejuvenated and reminded of his creaturehood. Thus the Agrarian life is a more inclusive trope than might seem obvious at first glance. But Lytle *meant* his metaphor; and contrary to those who see in Agrarianism only a literary construct, he still does.

In style, Lytle's Agrarian essays are dramatic, direct, and often admonitory—concerned with contemporary Southern affairs. These essays advance a position and suggest a policy. The writings which follow in *From Eden to Babylon* are very different in content and purpose, treating as they do of the antecedents of present difficulties and the causes of historical change and military defeat. The Andrew Lytle who both wrote and taught history speaks here. Certainly the Agrarian vision of the good society has not been left behind, or the commitments implicit in it. But Lytle writes of Freeman's biography of Lee or Styron's life of Calhoun in order to measure and understand these worthies. He writes again about Forrest in exploration of the full implications of that heroic career not clearly visible to him when he was composing his Forrest biography. Here his objective is expository and interpretive, an accounting of what has transpired: he aims to get the story straight.

What the novelist has learned about the rendering of character is sometimes visible in these meditations and in the cryptic and foreboding "How Many Miles to Babylon." This transitional essay is reaching after that broad context where cultural analysis and moral philosophy merge in an apocalyptic overview of what will be the final costs of modernity, of its encouragement to the vanity of mortal men. What comes is the end of civilization as we have known it since Charlemagne was crowned Emperor of the West.

Mr. Lytle agrees with the theory that what chiefly characterizes modern man is his Faustian worship of power—a worship, Lytle would add, that is incompatible with the truth about finitude and our need for the grace of God, both in this life and at its conclusion. Progress, finally, cannot take the place of Christian consolation, for it is purely material and is promised only by those who desire power. Neither can the priest rightfully usurp the divinely ordained obligations of the secular authorities—princes and magistrates. In such definitions concerning the providentially intended relation of all temporal regimes to the always unrealized City of God there are more important political distinctions than what we are to think of the haughtiness of Andrew Jackson or of the failure of Jefferson Davis to bring unity to an embattled Southern nation. More important, but not unrelated. For the action begun in the Garden is continuous, and, though it will eventually come to an end, repetitive.

The Lytle essays written in the last three decades, the works of his full maturity, range far afield and in almost every case articulate that long, reflective view of their subject which made its initial appearance in "How Many Miles to Babylon." Three of these pieces look back directly on the Agrarian experience of 1930 to 1938. Mr. Lytle had contributed to *Who Owns America?* and to various issues of the *American Review*. When the Agrarians met in person, he was likely to be there; or else he served (with his father) as the host who presided at Cornsilk, a proper setting for their deliberations. But in the late 1930s his career as artist—as the maker of fictions—began to gather a momentum of its own. Thus from 1939 to 1958 he wrote little social and political commentary. But as he began to plan out *A Wake for the Living*, the mood of retrospection came over him: a disposition which has continued to provide the dominant motif— the sense of loss—in much of what he has written after *The Velvet Horn* (1957). Andrew Lytle remembering, in an elegiac vein looking back over the years of his teaching and writing, listening to friends when they were young and to other neighbors and relations now long since dead, introduces a third voice into this collection, a persona of incredible charm and good humor. What he has written in these later years is graceful in a nonpareil fashion, informed with an air of assurance and unchallenged authority; and, I believe, also satisfying to its author, since the role he plays there so well suits his disposition, never tempting him, staunch champion of orthodoxy that he is, toward despair. For to look back to Eden and forward to Babylon is to recall Who is in charge of the play—and how He expects it to conclude.

Yet, though in Christian hope Lytle accepts what must be seen as mysterious by those who inherit the West in its "Satanic phase"—that "the gates of hell will not prevail"—his reiterative subject is declension and how it has been accomplished since Columbus made such "a hole in Christendom as can never be plugged." The worship of Power, Mass, and Speed is apostasy. The idea that we may have something for nothing, that there is a shortcut to Paradise, is "the first article in the constitution of hell." It is written just above the article about man in the state of nature which equates the "abstract idea democracy with the abstract idea equality" and which promises absolute freedom—"a condition which history has shown us no man can stand." For Mr. Lytle, the source of this confusion lies in the fact that modern man "lost his faith in the divine order of the universe." Therefore, his sense of the obligation to keep his place, to match his estate and function and thus hold the body of this world in "fee simple," has been much attenuated. The contemporary political absolutes of which Mr. Lytle speaks ironically in the passages just quoted are those which have no incarnation in historical experience, which can have no incorporative standing until finally located in institution and prescription—the elements of customary life. These essays which take a long view naturally pose the generic questions. They look out at the contemporary world from the perspective of a wise and thoughtful man born out of his time, at a world changed more in one lifetime than between the reign of Henry VII and 1900. Mr. Lytle talks of being more a man of the eleventh century than a citizen of what his country has become; and although he has never taken lightly his obligations as a public figure, he is probably correct in his comparison. How then could he be less than troubled by what we do, or other than confident with what the Lord may accomplish, working with the detritus of our free agency?

Apart from the Agrarian afterthoughts, the other essays included in this last group of papers under the heading of "The Long View" are concerned with myth and its value in reducing human experience to perennial and repetitious patterns such as are invaluable in describing and summarizing our common nature and destiny.

These patterns of action, once discovered in the flux of time, are as useful for the cultural historian or the political philosopher of a traditionalist persuasion as they are to the novelist. Ancient myth defines as action the essence of our experience as God's creatures, made in His image and possessed of one great gift from His nature, the ability to imitate the original creative act. By submitting to the materials of their subject they may discover in them a significant form—as in Mr. Lytle's "A Journey South." In this narrative Lytle remembers Odysseus, another widely travelled fellow. At the age of 25, Lytle encounters Circe in her New York lair and then, with Allen Tate, Caroline Gordon Tate, and (for a time) Robert Penn Warren, goes to visit battlefields in Pennsylvania, Maryland, and West Virginia. This exercise is, of course, reminiscent of Odysseus in his consultation with the dead in Book 10 of the *Odyssey*. After the military tour was over, the larger journey to recover a patrimony and enact the imperative it contained "was underway; but if we called up the dead to lap blood, it brought Allen finally home to Ithaca." The time of this reportage is 1927 and the home of which Lytle writes is not Benfolly (Tate's home) but the traditional civil and religious order of the South which the Agrarians had to understand from the inside, in all of its fullness, before they could come together in the wake of the Scopes trial and oppose the concerted efforts being made to subvert the mind and spirit of a homeland no longer sure of itself. Here myth and Agrarian retrospect come together in one action which is both singularly evocative of the larger events in which Mr. Lytle participated and true to the details of his memory. It is a small masterpiece, which can with equal justice also be said of several other chapters in this book.

Though the narratives in Genesis and the classical story of the underworld journey are important to Lytle, the myth most frequently suggested in his work is that of the young man growing up, the archetype of the painful, problematic, and necessary education in human limitation and the fragility of all civilized life. This process occurs both in the university (where the issue is language—calling things by their proper names) and in the world of action (where prudence becomes a practice, even a habit). It is a nurture which goes to the formation of young people who have seen enough, and read and heard enough, to know that, though life is a splendid gift, nothing and no one can ensure that they will "live as do the gods." That is, unless the self-elevating metaphor, as in fighting the Puritan temptation to self-contempt, implies the most distant of analogies. The kind of education which Lytle defends discursively is the old training in letters which from its first appearance in a European context was designed to impart an understanding of men and manners—and particularly of the boundaries of our common condition, the value of our liberty inside a contingent state, and the reason why it is sometimes better to risk death than to live under degrading circumstances. This education in Lytle's formulation is a preparation for responsibility in the various estates and conditions, grounded in a reasonable ontology that is neither passive and fatalistic nor too aggressive, too Faustian, in its effect on human conduct. One hopes the products of such nurture will know themselves as "Christian ladies and gentlemen," as Lytle specifies in his "The Christian University and the Word." At their best, they should be capable of acting on a grand stage, out of a memory larger than their own. In submitting to the given materials of their lives and culture, they should find the form of their vocation implicit there, the form which determines their role in society. Even as the Agrarians found their roles in keeping alive the mythopoeic vision of the world as a mysterious, *a priori* given. They have become exemplars of the essentially submissive attitude toward the providential things—a commonplace among poets who wrote before the end of the Renaissance and also at the heart of most prerevolutionary or antirevolutionary politics.

What is to be said first of all about the Nashville Agrarians is that they were, along with some Neo-Humanists and old-fashioned Constitutional lawyers, the bridge between the limited-government, anti-ideological conservatives of the early Republic and those intellectuals and journalists who orchestrated a general revival of conservatism after 1945. Andrew Lytle, when he writes of himself and his compatriots in that heroic interval, speaks always in full awareness of their contribution to the larger enterprise of American conservatism and to the old order of the Western world. Hence, his emphasis on Southerners and Europeans of earlier generations. It has been the fashion to ignore the role of the Agrarians in holding up the banner of traditionalist conservatism in an American context. Instead, in most cases we are offered for a conservative patrimony elaborate genealogies which attempt to run from the strong-government men in the Philadelphia Convention to the High Feder-alists, Whigs, and Abraham Lincoln. This tradition, extended from 1865, is in its turn represented by a series of "responsible Republicans"—conservative centralizers and egalitarians on every subject but money. The appearance of *From Eden to Babylon* reminds us that there is another American conservatism, one which the Framers would have recognized. According to this tradition, the defeat of the South in 1865 destroyed "not only the South but the initial sense of itself that describes the federation of the states and society after the American Revolution." The vision of the Agrarians did not presume a culture or a politics "poured in from the top." The virtue of private property is not wealth but its capacity to resist Leviathan and to secure the "peace of the family." Because of Southerners like Andrew Lytle, *this* understanding of conserva-tism still survives among us in a dark, utilitarian time.

So much in summary of one of the most powerful and consistent conservative voices to be heard in our day. As becomes obvious while reading through these essays as a sequence, Mr. Lytle has with the passage of years become more and more convinced that all the great questions are at bottom theological in nature. Indeed, *From Eden to Babylon* is an unfolding which works from the topical to the histori-cal to the anagogical. But that does not mean that this Tennessean in looking upward, in searching for a long view of modern history, has ever ceased to pay attention to the details of the contemporary scene. To the contrary, the impressions from the one reinforce and supply informative substance to the other. To demonstrate that interaction, the fine interview with Jim Graves has been included. As an action, it puts the reader directly in the personal, proprietary presence of the Andrew Lytle who is, in a circle of friends or students, a precise illustration of the virtues of which he writes. And this is even more the case with the concluding conversation with Madison Smartt Bell. The richness of his discourse, his piety and felicity, are there to be resolved in a feast, which is an apt description for this book. At least for those who live somewhere between Eden and Babylon, the Land of Nod, and Heaven's Gate.

—M. E. Bradford
Irving, Texas
July 1989

# PART I

# AGRARIAN ESSAYS

# The Hind Tit

I

WHEN we remember the high expectations held universally by the founders of the American Union for a more perfect order of society, and then consider the state of life in this country today, it is bound to appear to reasonable people that somehow the experiment has proved abortive, and that in some way a great commonwealth has gone wrong.

There are those among us who defend and rejoice in this miscarriage, saying we are more prosperous. They tell us—and we are ready to believe—that collectively we are possessed of enormous wealth and that this in itself is compensation for whatever has been lost. But when we, as individuals, set out to find and enjoy this wealth, it becomes elusive and its goods escape us. We then reflect, no matter how great it may be collectively, if individually we do not profit by it, we have lost by the exchange. This becomes more apparent with the realization that, as its benefits elude us, the labors and pains of its acquisition multiply.

To be caught unwittingly in this unhappy condition is calamitous; but to make obeisance before it, after learning how barren is its rule, is to be eunuched. For those who are Southern farmers this is a particularly bitter fact to consider. We have been taught by Jefferson's struggles with Hamilton, by Calhoun's with Webster, and in the woods at Shiloh or along the ravines of Fort Donelson where the long hunter's rifle spoke defiance to the more accelerated Springfields, that the triumph of industry,

3

commerce, trade, brings misfortune to those who live on the land.

Since 1865 an agrarian Union has been changed into an industrial empire bent on conquest of the earth's goods and ports to sell them in. This means warfare, a struggle over markets, leading, in the end, to actual military conflict between nations. But, in the meantime, the terrific effort to manufacture ammunition—that is, wealth—so that imperialism may prevail, has brought upon the social body a more deadly conflict, one which promises to deprive it, not of life, but of living; take the concept of liberty from the political consciousness; and turn the pursuit of happiness into a nervous running-around which is without the logic, even, of a dog chasing its tail.

This conflict is between the unnatural progeny of inventive genius and men. It is a war to the death between technology and the ordinary human functions of living. The rights to these human functions are the natural rights of man, and they are threatened now, in the twentieth, not in the eighteenth, century for the first time. Unless man asserts and defends them he is doomed, to use a chemical analogy, to hop about like sodium on water, burning up in his own energy.

But since a power machine is ultimately dependent upon human control, the issue presents an awful spectacle: men, run mad by their inventions, supplanting themselves with inanimate objects. This is, to follow the matter to its conclusion, a moral and spiritual suicide, foretelling an actual physical destruction.

The escape is not in socialism, in communism, or in sovietism— the three final stages industrialism must take. These change merely the manner and speed of the suicide; they do not alter its nature. Indeed, even now the Republican government and the Russian Soviet Council pursue identical policies toward the farmer. The Council arbitrarily raises the value of its currency and forces the peasant to take it in exchange for his wheat. This is a slightly legalized confiscation, and the peasants have met it by refusing to grow surplus wheat. The Republicans take a more indirect way— they raise the tariff. Of the two policies, that of the Russian Soviet is the more admirable. It frankly proposes to make of its farmers a race of helots.

We have been slobbered upon by those who have chewed the mad root's poison, a poison which penetrates to the spirit and rots the soul. And the time is not far off when the citizens of this one-time Republic will be crying, "What can I do to be saved?" If the farmers have been completely enslaved by that time, the echo to their question will be their only answer. If they have managed to remain independent, the answer lies in a return to a society where agriculture is practiced by most of the people. It is in fact impossible for any culture to be sound and healthy without a proper respect and proper regard for the soil, no matter how many urban dwellers think that their victuals come from groceries and delicatessens and their milk from tin cans. This ignorance does not release them from a final dependence upon the farm and that most incorrigible of beings, the farmer. Nor is this ignorance made any more secure by Mr. Haldane's prognostication that the farm's ancient life will become extinct as soon as science rubs the bottle a few more times. The trouble is that already science has rubbed the bottle too many times. Forgetting in its hasty greed to put the stopper in, it has let the genius out.

But the resumption by the farmer of his place of power in the present order is considered remote. Just what political pressure he will be able to bring upon the Republicans to better his lot is, at the moment, unknown. Accepting the most pessimistic view, the continued supremacy of this imperialism and his continued dependency upon it, his natural enemy, the wealth-warrior who stands upon the bridge of high tariff and demands tribute, he is left to decide upon immediate private tactics. How is the man who is still living on the land, and who lives there because he prefers its life to any other, going to defend himself against this industrial imperialism and its destructive technology?

One common answer is heard on every hand: Industrialize the farm; be progressive; drop old-fashioned ways and adopt scientific methods. These slogans are powerfully persuasive and should be, but are not, regarded with the most deliberate circumspection, for under the guise of strengthening the farmer in his way of life they are advising him to abandon it and become absorbed. Such admonition coming from the quarters of the enemy is encouraging to the landowner in one sense only: it assures him he has something left to steal. Through its philosophy of Progress it is committing a mortal sin to persuade farmers that they can grow wealthy by adopting its methods. A farm is not a place to grow wealthy; it is a place to grow corn.

It is telling him that he can bring the city way of living to the country and that he will like it when it gets there. His sons and daughters, thoroughly indoctrinated with these ideas at state normals, return and further upset his equilibrium by demanding the things they grew to like in town. They urge him to make the experiment, with threats of an early departure from his hearth and board. Under such pressure it is no wonder that the distraught countryman, pulled at from all sides, contemplates a thing he by nature is loath to attempt . . . experimentation.

If it were an idle experiment, there would be no harm in such an indulgence; but it is not idle. It has a price and, like everything else in the industrial world, the price is too dear. In exchange for the bric-à-brac culture of progress he stands to lose his land, and losing that, his independence, for the vagaries of its idealism assume concrete form in urging him to over-produce his money crop, mortgage his land, and send his daughters to town to clerk in ten-cent stores, that he may buy the products of the Power Age and keep its machines turning. That is the nigger in the woodpile . . . keep the machines turning!

How impossible it is for him to keep pace with the procession is seen in the mounting mortgages taken by banks, insurance companies, and the hydra-headed loan companies which have sprung up since the World War. In spite of these acknowledged facts, the Bureau of Agriculture, the State Experimental Stations, farm papers, and county agents, all with the best possible intentions, advise him to get a little more progressive, that is, a little more productive. After advising this, they turn around and tell him he must curtail his planting. They also tell him that he (meaning his family) deserves motor-cars, picture shows, chainstore dresses for the womenfolks, and all the articles in Sears-Roebuck catalogues. By telling him how great is his deserving, they prepare the way to deprive him of his natural deserts.

He must close his ears to these heresies that accumulate about his head, for they roll from the tongues of false prophets. He should know that prophets do not come from cities, promising riches and store clothes. They have always come from the wilderness, stinking of goats and running with lice and telling of a different sort of treasure, one a corporation head would not understand. Until such a one comes, it is best for him to keep to his ancient ways and leave the homilies of the tumble-bellied prophets to the city man who understands such things, for on the day when he attempts to follow the whitewash metaphysics of Progress, he will be worse off than the craftsman got to be when he threw his tools away. If that day ever comes, and there are strong indications that it may, the world will see a new Lazarus, but one so miserable that no dog will lend sympathy enough to lick the fly dung from his sores. Lazarus at least groveled at the foot of the rich man's table, but the new Lazarus will not have this distinction. One cannot sit at the board of an insurance company, nor hear the workings of its gargantuan appetite whetting itself on its own digestive processes.

He must close his ears because an agrarian culture and industrial warfare are sustained through the workings of two different economies. Nothing less than confusion can follow the attempt of one economy to react to the laws of another. The progressive-farmer ideal is a contradiction in terms. A stalk of cotton grows. It does not progress. In 50,000 years it may evolve into something different, but for us and our four score and ten, it grows.

This error is also seen in the works of those highly respectable historians who, pointing to the census returns and the mounting wealth of the industrial states during the early decades of the nineteenth century, declared that the Southern culture was then already doomed, and that the Civil War merely hastened its demise. This view holds that industrialism is *manifest destiny*, that it would have supplanted agriculture in the South even if the Confederacy had maintained its withdrawal from the already disrupted Union. It strangely argues that the victorious planter and the small yeoman farmer would have abandoned what they had waged a desperate war to preserve from others; and what, in spite of defeat, survived in its essential features until the second decade of the twentieth century; and what still possesses sufficient strength to make a desperate fight for its inherited way of life.

If an abundance of those things which a people considers the goods and the riches of the earth defines wealth, then it follows that that particular culture is wealthy in proportion to the production and distribution of just those things and no others; and it does not depend upon what another people may consider the goods and riches, no matter how greatly those things have multiplied for them, nor how many individuals they have to possess them. What industrialism counts as the goods and riches of the earth the agrarian South does not, nor ever did.

It is true that the planting aristocracy bought freely from England and the North. It is also true that the Cotton Kingdom was hastened into being by the invention of the cotton gin, an apparatus of the Machine Age; but because of this, it did not assume the habits and conduct of a factory town. Stocks and bonds and cities did not constitute wealth to the planter. Broad acres and increasing slaves, all tangible evidence of possession, were the great desiderata of his labors; and regardless of their price fluctuation on the world market, if they were paid for, their value remained constant in the planting states.

But the farming South, the yeoman South, that great body of free men, had hardly anything to do with the capitalists and their merchandise. In the upland country, the pine barrens, in the hills and mountains, and interspersed between the large plantations or lying on their fringe, and in the bad-road districts wherever they lay, communication with the main arteries of trade was so difficult that the plain people were forced into a state of self-sufficiency. And those who could reach the main turnpikes or the rivers and those who owned a few slaves in the planting districts, when they sold their cotton in New Orleans, were even less dependent than the planters, for they kept their looms going and fed their stock home-grown feed. Even the planters were beginning to say in the middle 'fifties that horses do not fatten on bought corn.

By 1860 these broad, as yet somewhat flexible, outlines marked the structural formation of the Confederacy: belonging to the planting body, in round numbers, 3,000,000; slaves and free negroes, 4,000,000; townsmen, 1,000,000; plain people, including those who owned a few slaves, 4,000,000. By 1830 the lower South, leavened by Tennessee and Kentucky, became dominant in the agrarian stronghold below the line; and the lower South at this time was largely the plain people. From them the planter class was made.

After 1860 there would have been no fundamental economic rivalry between the yeoman farmer and the great landowner. The struggle before that time had been to determine who would rule, and the planters who emerged had done so because they were the more vigorous, the more intelligent, the more fortunate—the strong men of their particular culture. Jackson, demanding for the talented obscure the chance to grow rich and distinguished, expressed their demands politically. Jacksonian Democracy was, therefore, no Democracy; and although it claimed to be sired by Jefferson, his self-sufficient republic of freeholders did not contemplate any such leadership. "Down here, men like me and Gineral Jackson and Colonel Davy Crockett always demands our rights; and if we don't git 'em, somebody else is mighty liable to git Hell!" is not the assertion of one contented to live easily and at peace on a fifty-acre steading. Cotton had changed the connotation of the demand.

In a society which recognizes the supremacy of nature and man's frailty each individual enjoys or subdues nature according to his capacity and desires, and those who accumulate great estates deserve whatever reward attends them, for they have striven mightily. This is the common way a ruling class establishes itself. The South, and particularly the plain people, has never recovered from the embarrassment it suffered when this class was destroyed before the cultural lines became hard and fast.

The Whig Party was evidence of the painful readjustment between the static East and the dynamic West, and it pointed to the metamorphosis of the two into Calhoun's Feudal Aristocracy. It is significant that when the Western states were changing their constitutions to deliver universal suffrage into the hands of the farmer and artisan, Dew from Virginia and Harper from South Carolina were publishing tracts defending the strictest sort of society.

The force of Jackson's character introduced tragedy into the drama. His fight with Calhoun divided the house with an internecine struggle and so confused the agrarian states that they were unable to stand united before the irrepressible conflict. Calhoun, a philosopher as well as a logician, could see beyond his times the conclusion to the premises; but Jackson and Clay, men of action, one a soldier, the other a politician, could only act the parts their periods gave them. It was impossible for them, living pleasantly on their country estates, to foresee the impending dominion of technology.

The story of these strong men and their negro slaves has been told and mistold; but the farming South has had few to tell of its virtues, and it has left fewer written records to tell its story. Oblivion has almost covered it in a generation. The planters whom it looked to in the days of its strength to defend their common life have busied themselves after the migration to the towns with a defense of their own part in the story, ignoring or referring to the yeomanry as the pore white trash.

Travellers have remembered the bedbugs, greasy food, rough cribs found in some places, and all those disagreeable elements which in the midst of the fatigues and worries of travel over-emphasize the virtue of clean sheets and native food. Fresh linen has too often been mistaken for culture by people who scrub all the oil from their skins in the articles of the plumbing industry.

The most unique example of a garbled interpretation is found in the journals of one Olmsted, who traveled through the South in the early 'fifties. In the hill country he called to a young ploughman to inquire the way, and when not one, but several, ambled over and seemed willing to talk as long as he cared to linger, his time-ordered attitude was shocked at their lazy indifference to their work. Others who were mixed in their geography, who thought, for example, that New York lay to the south of Tennessee, amazed him. Although he could never know it, it was the tragedy of these people that they ever learned where New York lay, for such knowledge has taken them from a place where they knew little geography but knew it well, to places where they see much and know nothing.

This will be the most difficult task industrialism has undertaken, and on this rock its effort to urbanize the farm will probably split— to convince the farmer that it is time, not space, which has value. It will be difficult because the farmer knows that he cannot control time, whereas he can wrestle with space, or at least with that particular part which is his orbit. He can stop, set, chaw, and talk, for, unable to subdue nature, it is no great matter whether he gets a little more or a little less that year from her limitless store. He has the choice of pleasant conversation, the excitement of hunting, fishing, hearing the hounds run, or of the possibility of accumulating greater spoils. Olmsted's young ploughmen did well to stop and talk with the "quair strangy"; ask "whare he's bin"; "whare he's aimin' to go"; and "air he bin to see his kin in Texas?" for by so doing they exchanged an uncertain physical satisfaction for a certain mental pleasure.

But those records which have been left, some few in writing, some through the patronage of journalists like Olmsted, through folk-games, songs, and ballads, particularly in the bad-road districts, and scattered more generally than is supposed upon the farms of the South, make it clear just how Southern life, and that part of it which was the plain people, was crystallizing when the war came.

One of these records comes from C. C. Henderson's *Story of Murfreesboro*. Martin Van Buren, when he was Chief Executive, made a speech from the court-house balcony. Everybody who could travel was there, for no Southern man ever missed, or misunderstood, a speech. Among those who had come to town that day was one Abner L., a squatter living on a large farm near the town. The landowner had promised Abner that he would introduce him to the President. After the speaking the planter moved through the crowd to keep his promise. This gentleman understood thoroughly the honor he was about to receive. In a becoming, if somewhat nervous, manner he received the hand of the New-Yorker, squeezed it damply, then turned and presented Abner. Unlike the planter, Abner stepped up with perfect composure, pressed His Excellency's hand deliberately down, and said in a calm, even tone:

"Mr. Buren, the next time you come down here I want you to come out my way and ra'r around some with us boys."

This man worked a little truck patch on somebody else's land; hunted at night for pelts; fished in Stone's River; and ra'red around when he was a mind to. He possessed nature as little as possible, but he enjoyed it a great deal, so well that he felt the President might be satisfied with what hospitality he had to offer. Whenever a society has at its base people so contented with their lot, it may not be perfect ideally, but it is the best politicians will ever effect and maintain.

When Confederate defeat destroyed the planter as a class, it upset the balance of the whole. The yeomanry, who had had little to do with the money crop before, moved down from the hills and bought for a song the planter's dismembered plantations. As this was done, it only prepared the way to undermine the Southern culture, for the destruction of the rulers did not mean its destruction. The plain man brought from his isolation his ways and habits, and the impoverished state which had fallen upon the country after war and reconstruction forced him to rely upon home manufactures. In the great exodus to Texas in 1873 all the emigrants wore homespun. It looked as if conditions were preparing to produce another set of rulers.

Unfortunately, the plain man did a thing which prevented this. When he took over the planter's land, he took over the worst of his habits, the furnishing system. Whereas with the planter it had been the factor of the great ports, with him it became the merchant of the county towns, the villages, and even the crossroads. The high price of cotton was responsible for this. When the prices broke in 1870, the small farmer was faced with a new experience: his reliance upon a money economy made him responsible to its laws. So long as they paid him well for his labors, it was profitable; but he learned that there was no assurance that this would continue. Something he could not understand was beginning to control his life. He could only hope for better days, and in the meantime mortgage next year's crop. Because it was the money crop, the merchant forced him to grow only cotton and buy the feed for his stock. This caused over-production, a drop in prices, more mortgages, and still greater over-production.

Such conditions broke many, and for the first time in the Cotton Kingdom, white tenantry developed. This was a definite social loss. With an entirely different race to serve the rich men as in slavery, the small white man could feel no very strong social inequality, and those who lived in isolation none at all. Now, economic dependence brought about social lines drawn, not upon a comparative use and enjoyment of nature, but upon a possession of cash.

This turned the plain man, for he had lost his independence, into something he had never been before, the pore white, the hook-wormed illiterate. Formerly, no matter how wealthy or how powerful a neighbor might grow, or how many slaves he might own, the small farmer who lived next to his plantation was still a free man so long as he paid his taxes and provided his family with food, clothes and shelter. He was economically and politically independent.

The uses of fertilizers, making for a quicker maturity, spread cotton culture northward and into Texas. Railroads ended the isolation of those places which bad roads had cut off from the markets, and the plain people who remained at home were brought into the money economy. The Cotton Kingdom before 1860 was supported by black backs. It now changed its nature. The small white farmer, from raising 12 per cent gradually worked and picked the greatest part of the crop. This spread of cotton meant the spread of a false set of economics.

He had been misled, and he was to wander farther afield under false doctrine. His former leaders, the generals and colonels and lawyer-statesmen, moved into the towns and cities and entered the industrial world. This move deprived them of any right to lead or rule the farmer, for no longer would his problems and theirs be the same. Nevertheless, for a long time after the war, from habit and affection, and because of the menace of the free negro, they still followed the counsel of these men. The time came when they realized their betrayal, for railroad and corporation presidents as they spoke of chivalry and pure womanhood did not put sow-belly in the pantry, nor meal in the barrel. This protest expressed itself politically through Private John Allen from Mississippi, Tom Watson in Georgia, and Bob Taylor in Tennessee, and farmer candidates everywhere.

But he had listened too long. He himself began to think more and more of money, and his inability to take much of it from the industrial scheme produced a feeling of moral defeat. His ambitious sons, instead of becoming the leaders of the farm communities, went North and West and to the growing Southern cities to make their fortunes, and as they left he did not protest. Those who remained, caught by the furnishing system, could not rise to lead. They were bound hand and foot—so firmly bound that the high price of cotton during the World War led them deeper into the money economy instead of freeing them.

As a result, up to the entrance of the United States into this war the farmer was trying unconsciously to live by two antithetical economies. In spite of his dual existence he managed to secure many good things from the soil, for his life was still largely ordered after his agrarian inheritance. The next, the fatal step, is to become a progressive farmer, for then he must reverse this dualism and think first of a money economy, last of a farmer's life. The new emphasis puts him in a critical condition; the precedence of the money economy means the end of farming as a way of life.

## II

On a certain Saturday, a group of countrymen squatted and lay about the Rutherford County court-house yard, three-quarters of a century after Abner L. extended his invitation to Van Buren. One remarked to the others that "as soon as a farmer begins to keep books, he'll go broke shore as hell."

Let us take him as a type and consider the life of his household before and after he made an effort to industrialize it. Let us set his holdings at two hundred acres, more or less—a hundred in cultivation, sixty in woods and pasture, and forty in waste land, too rocky for cultivation but offering some pasturage. A smaller acreage would scarcely justify a tractor. And that is a very grave consideration for a man who lives on thirty or fifty acres. If the pressure becomes too great, he will be forced to sell out and leave, or remain as a tenant or hand on the large farm made up of units such as his. This example is taken, of course, with the knowledge that the problem on any two hundred acres is never the same: the richness of the soil, its qualities, the neighborhood, the distance from market, the climate, water, and a thousand such things make the life on every farm distinctly individual.

The house is a dog-run with an ell running to the rear, the kitchen and dining-room being in the ell, if the family does not eat in the kitchen; and the sleeping-rooms in the main part of the house. The dog-run is a two- or four-crib construction with an open space between, the whole covered by one roof. The run or trot gets its name from the hounds passing through from the front to the rear. It may or may not have a floor, according to the taste or pride of the occupant. This farmer will have it floored, because his grandfather, as he prospered, closed in the dog-run with doors, making it into a hall; added porches front and rear, weather-boarded the logs, and ceiled the two half-story rooms. His grandfather belonged to that large number of sturdy freemen who owned from three to five hundred acres of land and perhaps a slave or two in better days. But owning a few slaves did not make him a planter. He and his sons worked alongside them in the fields. Of farmers so situated in the South there was one to every twelve and one-tenth of free population.

There is a brick walk running from the porch to a horse block, lined on either side with hardy buttercups. From the block a road marked off by tall cedars goes out to the pike gate, two hundred yards away. The yard is kept grazed down by sheep, and occasionally the stock is turned in, when the pastures are burned in a drought. The house needs paint, but the trees are whitewashed around the base of the trunks to keep insects off and to give a neat appearance to the yard.

Over the front doorway is a horseshoe, turned the right way to bring luck to all who may pass beneath its lintel. The hall is almost bare, but scrubbed clean. At the back is a small stairway leading to the half-story. This is where the boys sleep, in their bachelorhood definitely removed from the girls. To the left is the principal room of the house. The farmer and his wife sleep there in a four-poster, badly in need of doing over; and here the youngest chillurn sleep on pallets made up on the floor.

The large rock fireplace is the center of the room. The home-made hickory chairs are gathered in a semicircle about it, while on the extreme left of the arc is a rough hand-made rocker with a sheep-skin bottom, shiny from use, and its arms smooth from the polishing of flesh, reserved always for "mammy," the tough leather-skinned mother of the farmer. Here she sets and rocks and smokes near enough for the draught to draw the smoke up the chimney. On the mantel, at one end, is dry leaf tobacco, filling the room with its sharp, pungent odor. A pair of dog-irons rests on the hearth, pushed against the back log and holding up the ends of the sticks which have burnt in two and fallen among the hot ashes. The fire is kept burning through the month of May to insure good crops, no matter how mild and warm its days turn out to be. The top rock slab is smoked in the middle where for generations the wind has blown suddenly down the chimney, driving heavy gusts to flatten against the mantel and spread out into the room. A quilting-frame is drawn into the ceiling, ready to be lowered into the laps of the womenfolks when the occasion demands, although it is gradually falling into disuse. Beneath it, spreading out from the center of the floor, a rag rug covers the wide pine boards which, in turn, cover the rough-hewn puncheons that sufficed during the pioneer days. From this room, or rather, from the hearth of this room, the life of the dwelling moves.

If this is the heart of the house, the kitchen is its busiest part. The old, open fireplace has been closed in since the war, and an iron range has taken its place. This much machinery has added to the order of the establishment's life without disrupting it. Here all the food is prepared, and the canning and preserving necessary to sustain the family during the winter is done.

The cooking is a complicated art, requiring mastery over all its parts to burden the table with victuals that can be relished. Each meal is a victory over nature, a suitable union between the general principles of cookery and the accident of preparation. The fire must be kept at the right temperature (without a thermometer), or the bread won't rise; too much lard, or too little, will spoil the pastry; and since the test of all cooking is the seasoning, which can never be reduced to exact rules but is partly intuitive, too many pinches of salt may ruin the dish. The farmer's wife learns to satisfy the tastes of her particular family, but she can never set two meals on the table exactly alike. She never overcomes nature; her victories are partial, but very satisfying, for she knows her limitations.

The kitchen leads out to the back ell-shaped porch. Upon its banister, or, if there is no banister, upon the wash-table, a bucket of water and its gourd, a tin pan, soap, and towel wait to serve the morning toilet. The towel will hang on a folding rack fixed to the wall. This rack may also serve long strings of red peppers drying in the air. A bell-post rises up near the kitchen to ring the boys in from the fields at dinner-time. In the back, behind the kitchen, is the smokehouse and several outhouses. Iron kettles for washing tilt to one side in the ashes of an old fire, some distance away. An ash-hopper made from a hollow log, no longer in use, lies up against the buggy-house, having gone the way of the kitchen fireplace. The lye for soap- and hominy-making is now bought in town.

Convenient to the kitchen is the woodpile, made of different-sized sticks, some for the stove, split and cut to the right length, and some for the fireplaces, back logs and front sticks. The wood has been cut in the early fall, just as the sap begins to go down, not too early and not too late, but just at the right time, so that the outer surface will be dry and will catch quick, while the inside remains sappy and hard, burning slowly. It takes a great deal of study and intelligence to keep the fires going steadily.

Before dawn the roosters and the farmer feel the tremendous silence, chilling and filling the gap between night and day. He gets up, makes the fires, and rings the rising bell. He could arouse the family with his voice, but it has been the custom to ring the bell; so every morning it sounds out, taking its place among the other bells in the neighborhood. Each, according to his nature, gets up and prepares for the day: the wife has long been in the kitchen when the boys go to the barn; some of the girls help her, while the farmer plans the morning work and calls out directions.

One or two of the girls set out with their milk-pails to the barn, where the cows have been kept overnight. There is a very elaborate process to go through with in milking. First, the cow must be fed to occupy her attention; next, the milker kneels or sits on a bucket and washes the bag which will have gotten manure on it during the night (she kneels to the right, as this is the strategic side; the cow's foot is somehow freer on the left). After the bag is clean, the milking begins. There is always a variation to this ritual. When the calf is young, the cow holds back her milk for it; so the calf is allowed to suck a little at first, some from each teat, loosening the milk with uniformity, and then is pulled off and put in a stall until his time comes. There is one way to pull a calf off, and only one. He must be held by the ears and the tail at the same time, for only in this manner is he easily controlled. The ears alone, or the tail alone, is not enough.

This done, the milking begins. The left hand holds the pail, while the right does the work, or it may be the reverse. The hand hits the bag tenderly, grabs the teat, and closes the fingers about it, not altogether, but in echelon. The calf is then let out for his share. If he is young and there are several cows, it will be all that is left, for careful milkers do not strip the cow until the calf is weaned. The strippings are those short little squirts which announce the end, and they are all cream.

The milk is next brought back to the house, strained, and put in the well to cool. This requires a very careful hand, because if it happens to spill, the well is ruined. The next step is to pour up the old milk and let it turn—that is, sour—for churning. Some will be set aside to clabber for the mammy whose teeth are no longer equal to tougher nourishment. What she does not eat is given to the young chickens or to the pigs.

After breakfast the farmer's wife, or one of the girls, does the churning. This process takes a variable length of time. If the milk is kept a long time before it is poured up, the butter is long in coming. Sometimes witches get in the churn and throw a spell over it. In that case a nickel is dropped in to break the charm. The butter, when it does come, collects in small, yellow clods on top. These clods are separated from the butter-milk and put in a bowl where the rest of the water is worked out. It is then salted, molded, and stamped with some pretty little design. After this is done, it is set in the well or the spring to cool for the table. The process has been long, to some extent tedious, but profitable, because insomuch as it has taken time and care and intelligence, by that much does it have a meaning.

Industrialism gives an electric refrigerator, bottled milk, and dairy butter. It takes a few minutes to remove it from the ice to the table, while the agrarian process has taken several hours and is spread out over two or three days. Industrialism saves time, but what is to be done with this time? The milkmaid can't go to the movies, read the signboards, and go play bridge all the time. In the moderate circumstances of this family, deprived of her place in the home economy, she will be exiled to the town to clerk all day. If the income of the family can afford it, she remains idle, and therefore miserable.

The whole process has been given in detail as an example of what goes on in every part of an agrarian life. The boys, coming in to breakfast, have performed in the same way. Every morning the stock must be fed, but there is always variety. They never shuck the same ears of corn, nor do they find the mules in the small part of the stall, nor the hogs in the same attitudes, waiting to be slopped. The buckets of milk did not move regularly from cow to consumer as raw material moves through a factory. The routine was broken by other phenomena. Breakfast intervened. One morning the cow might kick the pail over, or the milkmaid might stumble over a dog, or the cow come up with a torn udder. It is not the only task she performs, just as feeding the stock is not the only task done by the boys. The day of each member of the family is filled with a mighty variety.

After the morning work is over, the family gathers about the breakfast table. Thanks are returned and the meal is served, one of the daughters or the mother waiting on the table; and then, without undue haste, the men go to the fields and the women about their dishes. If it is spring, the women can be of great help in the garden. Very likely the cut-worms will be after the young corn. The cut-worm does not like heat. If some one gets into the garden before the sun gets hot, the worm can be found under a clod near the top of the ground and mashed. In another hour he will have gone far below the surface. It is imperative to go at the right time, for of all the thousands of insects and varmints on the land, he has the distinction of his own habits. By learning these habits, and not those of some other pest, can he be overcome.

Before going to the fields the farmer consults the signs. If the smoke from the chimney is blown to the ground, there will be rain. Lightning in the north early in the night means rain before morning. If there is enough blue in the sky to make the Dutchman a pair of breeches, the weather will turn fair. Lightning in the south is a sign of drought. If the moon lies on its back, it is holding water; if it is tilted so that the water can run out, the season will be dry. Charms, signs, and omens are folk attempts to understand and predict natural phenomena. They are just as useful and necessary to an agrarian economy as the same attempts which come from the chemist's laboratory in an industrial society, and far wiser, because they understand their inadequacy, while the hypotheses of science do not.

According to these signs the work is hard or leisurely. If the fish are biting, the boys might knock off a day and go fishing, or hunting. Their father has not begun to keep books, so their time is their own.

At eleven o'clock the dinner bell rings. The ploughmen take out and come to the house. So regular is this ritual that a mule on the farm of Gen. Joseph E. Johnston's quartermaster used to square his feet in the furrow and answer the bell with a long, loud bray. Nor was anybody ever able to make him, by beating or pleading, plough a step farther. The teams are watered and put into their stalls, where so many ears of corn are shucked into the troughs, and a section of hay is thrown into the racks.

If the corn is low in the crib, the boys are likely to shuck carefully, keeping their eyes open for the king snake. This snake is worth ten cats as a ratter, and careful, economical farmers always throw one in their cribs if one is to be found. But not only as a ratter is he valuable. He makes war on all poisonous snakes and drives them from his presence. His invincibility is believed to be due to his knowledge of snake grass, an antidote for poison; for after bouts in which he has been bitten by venomous snakes, he has been seen to wiggle toward this grass and chew it. There is only one time of the year when he is to be avoided. He goes blind in August; and, feeling his defenseless condition, he will leg you—that is, charge and wrap his strong body about your leg, squeezing and bruising it.

The midday meal, like all the meals in the country, has a great deal of form. It is, in the first place, unhurried. Diners accustomed to the mad, bolting pace of cafeterias will grow nervous at the slow performance of a country table. To be late is a very grave matter, since it is not served until everybody is present. But only some accident, or unusual occurrence, will detain any member of the family, for dinner is a social event of the first importance. The family are together with their experiences of the morning to relate; and merriment rises up from the hot, steaming vegetables, all set about the table, small hills around the mountains of meat at the ends, a heaping plate of fried chicken, a turkey, a plate of guineas, or a one-year ham, spiced, and if company is there, baked in wine. A plate of bread is at each end of the table; a bowl of chitterlings has been set at the father's elbow; and pigs' feet for those that like them.

And they eat with eighteenth-century appetites. There is no puny piddling with the victuals, and fancy tin-can salads do not litter the table. The only salad to be seen on a country table is sallet, or turnip greens, or if further explanation is necessary, the tops of turnips cut off and cooked with a luscious piece of fat meat. It has the appearance of spinach; but, unlike this insipid slime, sallet has character, like the life of the farmer at the head of the table. The most important part of this dish is its juice, the pot licker, a rich green liquid, indescribable except as a pot-licker green. Mixed with corn bread, it has no equal. Particularly is it fine for teething babies. If the baby is weaned in the dark of the moon and fed a little pot licker, he will pass through the second summer without great trouble. This will not relieve the pain of cutting. To do that a young rabbit must be killed, its head skinned, and the raw flesh rubbed on the gums. If this fails, tie a spray of alderberries around its neck, or hang a mole's foot. But sallet will do everything but cut the pain.

His table, if the seasons allow, is always bountiful. The abundance of nature, its heaping dishes, its bulging-breasted fowls, deep-yellow butter and creamy milk, fat beans and juicy corn, and its potatoes flavored like pecans, fill his dining-room with the satisfaction of well-being, because he has not yet come to look upon his produce at so many cents a pound, or his corn at so much a dozen. If nature gives bountifully to his labor, he may enjoy largely.

The dishes of food are peculiarly relished. Each dish has particular meaning to the consumer, for everybody has had something to do with the long and intricate procession from the ground to the table. Somebody planted the beans and worked them. Somebody else staked them and watched them grow, felt anxious during the early spring drought, gave silent thanksgiving when a deep-beating rain soaked into the crusty soil, for the leaves would no longer take the yellow shrivel. A townsman can never understand the significance of rain, nor why an agrarian will study the signs with so much care and often with so much pain, for to him it has no immediate connection. The worst it can do him is to interrupt a picnic, and the best to beat from the asphalt of its streets and its tall buildings for a few moments the enervating heat peculiar to such places. The fullness of meaning that rain and the elements extend to the farmer is all contained in a mess of beans, a plate of potatoes, or a dish of sallet. When the garden first comes in, this meaning is explicit. If the yield has been large and rich, it will be openly and pridefully commented upon; if the garden has burned and it has lost its succulence to the sun, some will remark that sorrier beans have been seen, while others, more resentful of nature's invincible and inscrutable ways, will answer that better, also, have been seen. But aside from some such conservative expression, in its formal tone masking a violent passion, no other comment will be made. And as the enjoyment of the garden's produce becomes more regular, this particular meaning which the dishes at a country table has for its diners settles into the subconscious and becomes implicit in the conduct of the household.

The description of this particular board is by no means general. Just as no two farms are managed alike, so no two tables will be set alike. It is better than most, and slightly changed from ante-bellum days. It is more stable, as it has had a century in which to harden its form. But this form, troubled by the dualism, is less strict than it would have been if nothing had happened to disturb the direction of its growth. This farmer, being a Tennessean, perhaps has some advantage over other Southwesterners except Kentuckians of a tradition less shaken during the hard years. Tennessee has never been given over to any one money crop. It has looked upon its land to sustain its culture, and from the beginning has diversified according to its needs. Serving as a furnishing state to the cotton regions, when these regions were overturned, it naturally stood the shock better than they. In consequence the table will be more formal, its meals better, than in those places where the small upland farmer moved down upon the segments of the broken plantations. He can never have the same respect for the sow-belly and corn-meal furnished him by the merchant, and actually a large body of these farmers in Alabama, Mississippi, Georgia, South Carolina, and West Tennessee did not vary a great deal this diet, as he could for the vegetables and meat brought to the table by his own hand.

After the midday meal is over the family takes a rest; then the men go back to the fields and the women to those things yet to be done, mending clothes, darning, knitting, canning, preserving, washing or ironing or sewing. By sundown they are gathered about the supper table, and afterward set before the fire if it is winter, or upon the porch in warmer weather. One of the boys will get out his guitar and play "ballets" handed down from father to son, some which have originated in the new country, some which have been brought over from the Old World and changed to fit the new locale. Boys from the neighborhood drop in to court, and they will jine in, or drive away with the gals in hug-back buggies. If they are from another neighborhood, they are sure to be rocked or shot at on the way over or on the way home.

If the gathering is large enough, as it is likely to be when crops are laid by, it will turn into a play-party.[1] Most of these games practiced by the plain people have maintained the traditions brought from England and Scotland, while the townsmen lost their knowledge of them in a generation. For example, "The Hog Drovers" is a version of the English folk-game, "The Three Sailors." The Southern country, being largely inland, could only speculate upon the habits of sailors, but they knew all about the hog drovers. Every year droves of razorbacks, with their eyelids sewed together to hinder them from wandering off into the woods, were driven ten or eleven miles a day toward the Eastern markets. They would be stopped at private farms along the route, where pens had been put up to receive them, to feed. The drovers, nomadic and as careless as sailors, could not be made to keep promises. Parents, therefore, were careful of their daughters.

The game comes from, and is a copy of, the life of the people. A boy seats himself upon a chair in the middle of the room with a gal

[1] The play-parties were to be found in operation much later in Mississippi and Arkansas than in Tennessee.

in his lap. He is the head of the house, and she is his daughter. The
other gals are seated around the walls, waiting their turns; while the
boys, representing the hog drovers, enter two abreast in a sort of a
jig, singing the first stanza:

> "Hog drovers, hog drovers, hog drovers we air,
> A-courtin yore darter so sweet and so fair,
> Can we git lodgin' here, oh, here,
> Can we git er-lodgin' here?"

They stop in front of the old man, and he answers:

> "Oh, this is my darter that sets by my lap,
> And none o' you pig-stealers can git her from pap,
> And you can't git lodgin' here, oh, here,
> And you can't git er-lodgin' here."

The boys then jig about the chair, singing:

> "A good-lookin' darter, but ugly yoreself—
> We'll travel on further and sit on the shelf,
> And we don't want lodgin' here, oh, here,
> And we don't want er-lodgin' here."

They jig around the room, then return. The old man relents. Possibly it has as its genesis a struggle between greed and the safety of his
daughter's virtue:

> "Oh, this is my darter that sets by my lap,
> And Mr. *So-and-so* can git her from pap
> If he'll put another one here, oh, here,
> If he'll put another one here."

The boy who is named jigs to one of the gals, brings her to the old
man, takes his darter to the rear of the line, and the game starts
over. After every couple has been paired off, they promenade all and
seek buggies or any quiet place suitable for courting.[1]

---

[1] A complete version and account of the Hog-Drovers game song will be found in
A. P. Hudson's *Specimens of Mississippi Folklore*.

This and other games, "Fly in the Buttermilk," "Shoot the Buffalo," "Under the Juniper Tree," will fill an evening and break the order of their lives often enough to dispel monotony, making holidays a pleasure; and not so frequent nor so organized that they become a business, which means that games have become self-conscious, thus defeating the purpose of all playing. As they play they do not constantly remind one another that they are having a good time. They have it.

Besides these play-parties people pleasured themselves in other ways. There were ice-cream socials, old-time singings, like the Sacred Harp gatherings, political picnics and barbecues, and barn dances. All of these gatherings which bring the neighborhood together in a social way are unlike the "society" of industrialism. Behind it some ulterior purpose always lurks. It becomes another province of Big Business and is invaded by hordes of people who, unable to sell themselves in the sterner marts, hope to catch their prey in his relaxed moments and over the tea tables make connections which properly belong to the office. This practice prostitutes society, for individuals can mingle socially from no motive except to enjoy one another's company.

The songs of the Sacred Harp, like negro spirituals, are without accompaniment. The tune is pitched by the leader in the neighborhood schoolhouse under the shadows of oil-lamps. There is a grand meeting at the county seat once a year, and here the neighborhoods sing against each other and in unison under one general leader, who always remembers to turn the meeting over to each district leader for one song. This is a privilege jealously looked after; and if anyone is by chance overlooked, he will rise and make himself known. These songs of the Sacred Harp are songs of an agrarian people, and they will bind the folk-ways which will everywhere else go down before canned music and canned pleasure.

At the square dances, unlike round dancing, the stage is set for each individual to show the particularity of his art. Each couple is "out" in turn, swinging every other couple separately, ending up at "home" when the whole line swings "partners," then "corners." In this way a very fine balance is reached between group and individual action. Everybody is a part of the dance all the time, but a very particular part some of the time. There are no wall-flowers, no duty dances, no agonizing over popularity, and the scores of such things which detract from free enjoyment at the round dancings. "First lady out" means that she must step, cheat, and swing and show her superiority over the ladies who will follow; and likewise with the gentlemen. And the prompter, the one who calls the "figgers" (which happens still to be the proper English pronunciation of figure), is an artist and wit whose disappearance will leave the world much the poorer. Such calls as

> "Swing the gal you love best;
> Now cheat and swing."

> "Partners to yore places
> Like mules to the traces."

and from Mississippi,

> "Women swing hard, men swing harder,
> Swing that gal with the buckskin garter."

are metaphors and imperatives with full connotation for the dancers, and in an agrarian society will be as applicable a hundred years hence. But so will the fiddlers' tunes, "Leather Breeches," "Rats in the Meal Barrel," "Frog Mouth," "Guinea in the Pea Patch," "Arkansas Traveler," "Cotton-eyed Joe," "No Supper Tonight," "Hell Amongst the Yearlings," "Got a Chaw of Tobaccy from a Nigger," "All My Candy's Gone," and "Katy, Bar the Door." With a list of such dances as a skeleton, if all other records were lost, some future scholar could reconstruct with a common historical accuracy the culture of this people.

Before the farmer decided to keep books, the structure of his neighborhood culture had not been moved, and his sons and daughters, and he and the old woman, were a part of these things. Even mammy, if the rheumaticks had not frozen her jints, would put on her hickory-staved bonnet, a fresh-starched apron, and mount the waggin with the rest and drive to the singing and lift her cracked voice as the leader "h'isted" the tune, or at the barbecue pat her feet in time with the whining fiddle and think of better days when she and her old man balanced to "Cairo ladies, show yoreself," or "Jenny, the Flower of Kildare," until the sweat poured from her

strong back, gluing the gray linen dress to her shoulders and bal-
looning it in places with air caught in the swing.

### III

The Agrarian South, therefore, whose culture was impoverished
but not destroyed by the war and its aftermath, should dread industrialism like a pizen snake. For the South long since finished its
pioneering. It can only do violence to its provincial life when it
allows itself to be forced into the aggressive state of mind of an
earlier period. To such an end does bookkeeping lead. It is the
numbering of a farm's resources—its stacks of fodder, bushels of
corn, bales of cotton, its stock and implements, and the hundreds of
things which make up its economy. And as the only reason to
number them is to turn them into cash—that is, into weapons for
warfare—the agrarian South is bound to go when the first page is
turned and the first mark crosses the ledger.

The good-road programs drive like a flying wedge and split the
heart of this provincialism—which prefers religion to science,
handcrafts to technology, the inertia of the fields to the acceleration
of industry, and leisure to nervous prostration. Like most dema-
goguery, it has been advertised as a great benefit to the farmer. Let
us see just what the roads have done and who they benefit? They
certainly can be of no use to the farmer who cannot afford to buy a
truck. He finds them a decided drawback. The heavy automobile
traffic makes it hazardous for him even to appear on the main
highways. But if he has the temerity to try them, they prove most
unsatisfactory. Besides being a shock to his mules' feet, it is difficult
for the team to stand up on the road's hard, slick surface.

The large farmers and planting corporations who can afford to
buy trucks are able to carry their produce to market with less wear
and tear than if they drove over rougher dirt pikes. But this is a
dubious benefit, for the question is not between trucks on good or
bad roads, but between teams on passable roads and trucks on
arterial highways.

But in any case the farmer receives few direct profits. Asphalt
companies, motor-car companies, oil and cement companies, engi-

neers, contractors, bus lines, truck lines, and politicians—not the farmer—receive the great benefits and the profits from good roads. But the farmer pays the bills. The states and counties float bonds and attend to the upkeep on the highways and byways, and when these states are predominantly agricultural, it is the people living on the land who mortgage their labor and the security of their property so that these super-corporations may increase incomes which are now so large that they must organize foundations to give them away.

But the great drain comes after the roads are built. Automobile salesmen, radio salesmen, and every other kind of salesman descend to take away the farmer's money. The railroad had no such universal sweep into a family's privacy. It was confined to a certain track and was constrained by its organization within boundaries which were rigid enough to become absorbed, rather than absorb. But good roads brought the motor-car and made of every individual an engineer or conductor, requiring a constant, and in some instances a daily, need for cash. The psychological pressure of such things, and mounting taxes, induce the farmer to forsake old ways and buy a ledger.

The great drain continues. The first thing he does is to trade his mules for a tractor. He has had to add a cash payment to boot, but that seems reasonable. He forgets, however, that a piece of machinery, like his mules, must wear out and be replaced; but the tractor cannot reproduce itself. He must lay aside a large sum of money against the day of replacement, whereas formerly he had only to send his brood mare to some jack for service.

The next thing it does, it throws his boys out of a job, with the possible exception of one who will remain and run it. This begins the home-breaking. Time is money now, not property, and the boys can't hang about the place draining it of its substance, even if they are willing to. They must go out somewhere and get a job. If they are lucky, some filling station will let them sell gas, or some garage teach them a mechanic's job. But the time is coming when these places will have a surfeit of farmer boys.

He next buys a truck. The gals wanted a car, but he was obdurate on that point, so he lost them. They went to town to visit kin, then gradually drifted there to marry or get a job. The time comes when the old woman succumbs to high-pressure sales talk and forces him to buy a car on the installment plan. By that time he is so far gone that one thing more seems no great matter.

He then has three vehicles which must be fed from the oil companies, several notes at the bank bearing interest, and payments, as regular as clock strokes, to be made on the car.

He finds his payment for gasoline, motor oil, and power for his tractor is tremendously higher than the few cents coal oil used to cost him. Formerly he bought it by the lampful; he now buys it by the barrelful. In fact, he no longer uses coal oil for lighting. He has installed a Delco-plant. Besides giving illumination it pumps his water, turns the churn, washes the clothes, heats the iron to press them, and cooks the victuals. If his daughters had not already moved away, he would have had to send them, for Delco has taken their place in the rural economy. The farmer's wife now becomes a drudge. As the mainstay of the structure she was content to bear the greatest burden, but now she grows restive. She has changed from a creator in a fixed culture to an assistant to machines. Her condition is miserable because her burdens are almost as great without the compensation of the highest place in the old scheme. Her services cannot be recompensed with gold, and gold has become the only currency.

Gradually the farmer becomes more careless of his garden. Each year he cuts down on the meat—the curing takes too much time. He may finally kill only a hog or two, and, under the necessity of paying interest, sell all his cows but one.

He has concentrated on the money crop, and as bought fertilizers and war-time prices have brought cotton to Tennessee, he chooses cotton. This sinks him deeper into the money economy. He must buy highly productive, and also highly priced, seed, and artificial fertilizers. He used to haul manure from the barns, but this is too slow and too unscientific now. But the outlay of money is not ended. There are fertilizer-distributors, cultivators, and improved ploughs of all kinds, with a value arbitrarily inflated by the tariff. He is now as completely on the money basis as a farmer can ever get, and each day he buys more and more from the town and makes less and less on the farm.

Being in the race for wealth, he begins to learn that a farmer can only make war successfully by beating his ploughshare into a sharp-cutting weapon. He cannot match the plough against the wheel.

When he bought the various machines which roll where the mules stood and shivered the flies from their backs, he was told that he might regulate, or get ahead of, nature. He finds to his sorrow that he is still unable to control the elements. When it fails to rain and his fields are burning, he has no God to pray to to make it rain. Science can put the crops in, but it can't bring them out of the ground. Hails may still cut them down in June; winds may damage them; and a rainy season can let the grass take them. Droughts still may freeze and crack the soil. Dry weather does not greatly injure cotton, but if this farmer had happened to become a dairyman, his withered pastures and dry springs would have made him suffer.

The pests and insects are still with him. He may partially control them by poison: the army worm—possible; the boll weevil—evade by putting in early; flea—impossible! Neither can he control the tariff, nor a complete crop failure, nor a drop in prices. Since he cannot control these variables, his crop is not predictable; therefore his income is uncertain. But debt, the price of machinery, repairs, merchandise are all certain and must be met, if not by his crops, then by his land.

It is true that labor-evicting machines will give a greater crop yield, but a greater yield does not necessarily mean a greater profit. It means over-production and its twin, price deflation. Those who insist on the progressive-farmer ideal realize this, and for a long time the Federal Bureau of Agriculture and other agencies have insisted that he diversify his crops. In many instances this has brought relief, but it is not permanent. The diversification is always the money crop. The farmer is no better off when he has two or three money crops, if they are all over-produced, than he is with one. He has three crops, instead of one, to worry with.

There are farmers who manage to remain in the race, but they are few who actually make fortunes. When the land is very rich, the direction good, and the economy frugal, this is possible. Those places situated close to cities and towns may be turned very profitably into dairy, or poultry, farms; or a few acres may be turned advantageously into trucking. But where there is one like these there are thousands of others, one-horse, two-horse, or four-horse men, who suffer from these progressives who have made good.

Another way of growing rich on the land is to develop a new seed. Les Bedezer[1] is an example of this. A few make enormous returns

on their outlay; others hear of their success, study the methods, and
slowly make the effort to do likewise. By the time their crop is ready
for the market there is too great an abundance, a fall in price, and
the distress it always brings with it. Such farmers are enemies to the
agricultural body. The horse-cropper, in attempting to follow their
ways, puts his entire acreage in this crop, buying his feed elsewhere
on credit at exorbitant interest. In Alabama 20 per cent is the usual
demand. When the time comes to settle up, if he makes any money,
it goes for luxuries instead of discharging his debt. He is always
optimistic and hopes that next year will be as good, and on this wish
he gives a lien on his land, which under such circumstances means a
sale.

But even for those who succeed the disadvantage is too great, and
for the less fortunate who enter the conflict without the advantages
of science, it is overwhelming. At the outset there is the great
burden of direct and indirect taxation. Because land cannot be
hidden away in strong boxes it bears the greatest part of the national, state, and county expenses. According to Governor Lowden,
a considered authority on taxation and the farmer's problems, real
property, which is largely farmlands or property dependent upon
farming produce, bears 90 per cent of the taxation and receives 10
per cent of the income. Since Wilson's administration gave way to
Harding's normalcy, taxes have been increased on land four times
and decreased on great wealth four times, making a ratio of sixteen
to one against the farmer. The tariff, which he has borne a century,
grows heavier rather than lighter, and apparently the Republicans
have every intention of further increasing it.

The factory can close down to meet over-production and feed the
market with its stock on hand; but the farmer is unable to do this
because of the perishable quality attached to everything but cotton,
tobacco and sugar; and when he sells these crops, he is an individual
competing with large organizations.

Thanks to applied science, the factory can concentrate stupen-
dous power in one place and fabricate its commodities serially; that
is, a hundred yards of cloth can be reproduced exactly as a previous
hundred yards, or a hundred Ford cars with the same uniform
strokes, but the product of the farm cannot be so reproduced.

---

[1] A Japanese Clover, splendid as a land builder, excellent for pasture or hay.

There can be but approximate, and very general, organization to agriculture. Certain seasons require certain kinds of work: there is a breaking season, a planting season, a cultivating season, a laying-by time, and a marketing time. This very loose organization is determined by nature, not by man, and points to the fundamental difference between the factory and the soil. When the farmer doubles his crop, he doubles his seed, his fertilizer, his work, his anxiety . . . all his costs, while the industrial product reduces in inverse ratio its costs and labor as it multiplies. Industrialism is multiplication. Agrarianism is addition and subtraction. The one by attempting to reach infinity must become self-destructive; the other by fixing arbitrarily its limits upon nature will stand. An agrarian stepping across his limits will be lost.

When the farmer, realizing where all this is leading him, makes the attempt to find his ancient bearings, he discovers his provincialism rapidly disintegrating. The Sacred Harp gatherings, and to a less extent the political picnics and barbecues, have so far withstood the onslaught; but the country church languishes, the square dance disappears, and camp meetings are held, but they have lost their vitality. Self-consciousness has crept into the meetings, inhibiting the brothers and sisters and stifling in their bosoms the desire to shout. When shouting ceases and the mourner's bench is filled up by the curious from the rear, the camp meeting may count its days, for they are numbered.

He finds that there is a vast propaganda teaching him, but particularly his children, to despise the life he has led and would like to lead again. It has in its organization public schools, high schools, the normals, and even the most reputable universities, the press, salesmen, and all the agents of industrialism. It has set out to uplift him. It tells him that his ancestors were not cultured because they did not appreciate the fine arts; that they were illiterate because their speech was Old English; and that the South will now come to glory, to "cultural" glory, by a denial of its ancestry.

This is the biggest hoax that has ever been foisted upon a people. It is nothing but demoniacally clever high-pressure sales talk to unload the over-producing merchandize of industrialism on the South. New England began it with her carrying trade. The shrewd Yankee skippers realized that if they could persuade prospective buyers that the bric-à-brac which they had brought from the Orient and elsewhere was "culture," their cargoes would fetch a fancier price. This brought about the overthrow of their own theocracy by 1830; but so long as the South had the planters for defenders the peddlers made no great headway. But now, in the hands of the industrialists everywhere, it is making very great headway.

And unless the agricultural South, like this farmer, wakes up to the fact that he is swapping his culture for machine-made bric-à-brac, there will be an absentee-landlordism far worse than that which afflicted the continent at the breakdown of mediaeval society. When the nobility flocked to the court of Louis XIV, leaving the tenants the burden of land without the compensation of local government, conditions were bad enough, precipitating the French Revolution. But, even so, the French nobility retained certain ties to their estates. They were descendants of men who had ruled there.

But what of this absentee-landlordism of capitalism? Mortgage companies, insurance companies, banks, and bonding-houses that are forced to take over the land of free men . . . what will be the social relationship? What can an abstract corporation like an insurance company, whose occupation is statistics and whose faro-bank can never lose, know of a farmer's life? What can their calculations do before droughts, floods, the boll weevil, hails, and rainy seasons? What will be the relationship between tenants who formerly owned the land and their abstract selves?

To avoid the dire consequences and to maintain a farming life in an industrial imperialism, there seems to be only one thing left for the farmer to do, and particularly for the small farmer. Until he and the agrarian West and all the conservative communities throughout the United States can unite on some common political action, he must deny himself the articles the industrialists offer for sale. It is not so impossible as it may seem at first, for, after all, the necessities they machine-facture were once manufactured on the land, and as for the bric-à-brac, let it rot on their hands. Do what we did after the war and the Reconstruction: return to our looms, our handcrafts, our reproducing stock. Throw out the radio and take down the fiddle from the wall. Forsake the movies for the play-parties and the square dances. And turn away from the liberal capons who fill the pulpits as preachers. Seek a priesthood that may manifest the will and intelligence to renounce science and search out the Word in the authorities.

So long as the industrialist remains in the saddle there must be a money crop to pay him taxes, but let it occupy second place. Any man who grows his own food, kills his own meat, takes wool from his lambs and cotton from his stalks and makes them into clothes, plants corn and hay for his stock, shoes them at the crossroads blacksmith shop, draws milk and butter from his cows, eggs from his pullets, water from the ground, and fuel from the woodlot, can live in an industrial world without a great deal of cash. Let him diversify, but diversify so that he may live rather than that he may grow rich. In this way he will escape by far the heaviest form of taxation, and if the direct levies grow too exorbitant, refuse to pay them. Make those who rule the country bear the burdens of government.

He will be told that this is not economical, that he can buy clothes for much less than he can weave them, and shoes for half the labor he will put into their creation. If the cash price paid for shoes were the only cost, it would be bad economy to make shoes at home. Unfortunately, the matter is not so simple: the fifteen-hundred-dollar tractor, the thousand-dollar truck, the cost of transportation to and from town, all the cost of indirect taxation, every part of the money economy, enters into the price of shoes. In comparison, the sum he hands over to the merchant is nothing more than a war tax.

So long as he lives in a divided world he is rendered impotent in the defense of his natural economy and inherited life. He has been turned into the runt pig in the sow's litter. Squeezed and tricked out of the best places at the side, he is forced to take the little hind tit for nourishment; and here, struggling between the sow's back legs, he has to work with every bit of his strength to keep it from being a dry hind one, and all because the suck of the others is so unreservedly gluttonous.

As for those countrymen who have not gone so deeply in the money economy, let them hold to their agrarian fragments and bind them together, for reconstructed fragments are better than a strange newness which does not belong. It is our own, and if we have to spit in the water-bucket to keep it our own, we had better do it.

# The Small Farm Secures the State

FOR the first time since the great war of the sixties there is official political recognition that agriculture must have equal consideration with the other powerful interests. This is a step toward a sensible political economy. It is a return to older policies and natural alliances. Mr. Roosevelt, better than all those in authority now, unless it is Senator Bankhead or Secretary Wallace, recognizes this. In his Chicago speech before the American Farm Bureau Federation (December 9, 1935) he says that it is "necessary to bring agriculture into a fair degree of equality with other parts of our economic life. For so long as agriculture remained a dead weight on economic life, sooner or later the entire structure would crash."

This is true; it has always been true; and, as long as man may hunger, it will remain true. For agriculture, to paraphrase another great ruler, Napoleon, is the life of the people, industry is its comfort, and commerce its luxury. When this relationship is upset, we must expect the mechanics of civilization to come to a dead stop, as they did on March 3, 1933.

To recognize agriculture as a great business interest, trading its commodities for the goods and services of other interests, is a policy the soundness of which cannot be questioned by rulers who have the common well-being at heart. But this policy does not go far enough. *Agriculture* is a limited term. A better one is *farming*. It is inclusive. Unlike any other occupation, farming is, or should be, a way of life. Its business side is important surely, and in the modern world it has reached a degree of consideration never before seen in Christendom. Perhaps this is inevitable. But it is also inevitable that the State, to endure, must have internal security; and this security is best maintained when its citizens have a stake in the commonwealth; and the lasting kind of stake is property, and the most durable kind of property is a small farm.

There are many reasons why, from the point of view of a stable society, the small farm is necessary. It is the norm by which all real property may be best defined. The basis of liberty is economic independence. And in what other occupation is there so much independence? The man who owns a small farm has direct control over the life-giving source, land. The three prime necessities, food, shelter, and clothing, he may command because he has a small inexhaustible capital. The fact of possession gratifies his sensible demands, and because of the nature of his occupation his home and his living are combined in the same physical surroundings. Since the family's living is made by the family for itself, the small-farm economy, unlike the larger commercial farm, has less to do with the forces of trade. And yet it shares in the general practices of the trading world.

It is a form of property, therefore, that the average man can understand, can enjoy, and *will defend*. Patriotism to such a man has a concrete basis. He will fight for his farm in the face of foreign or domestic peril. And if a man has nothing to fight for, he has little to live for.

The kind of farm which must be kept in mind is not the amphibian of Mr. Henry Ford, where the family works part of the time in the factory and part of the time on the land. Such an arrangement is industrial. It is an attempt to better factory labor's condition, and as such there is much to be said for it. But it is not farming. Nor can the subsistence farms being established by government agencies, such as the T.V.A., be rightly called farming. A bad odor attaches itself to the word *subsistence*. It implies a lower standard of living in relation to what an American might be expected to demand. It has many of the marks of a desperate and temporary expedient to be indulged until the industrial mechanism of the country becomes readjusted to the 'highest standard of living the world has ever seen' of the twenties. Indeed, it is a form of dole. This is said in all due respect to those experiments which are proving themselves in many ways successful. They are a move in the right direction, but how timid and coy are their steps! And this is because the people responsible for the experiments have chiefly the commercial aspect of farming in mind: the swapping of the goods of the great industries for their mutual benefit. As has already been said, this parity between agriculture and industry is fairer and better than the old relationship when the earth and its cultivators were the contemptible but useful sources of a legal peonage. But it fails to recognize that too much commercialism has bankrupted agriculture and deprived farming of its freedom.

Our hope for the betterment of country life demands that these casual experiments be turned into a real offensive. And the offensive must be carried on primarily by those of us who live upon the land, well supported by our Government. Any life which has the vitality to endure must move from the *inside out* and not from the *outside in*. The moral and spiritual centers of a way of life will decide what kind of house, for example, a man will build for himself, how he will conduct himself in all his relationships: they will, in short, determine the cultural values of the community. These cannot be brought in as "uplift."

Let us look at the proper sort of small farm, a plain man's home and the good citizen's seat. A type will be aimed at, but with the understanding that where farming is concerned, there is no type. Just as liberty presupposes equality of opportunity and inequality of function, so does farm life expose wide differences. This is its chief virtue; and this makes for its stubborn resistance to regimentation. It is the agricultural corporation that sacrifices the security and the benefits of country living for the factory method, the money crop, the bank lien, and, inevitably, the sheriff's sale.

Let the real farm be called, for the want of a more descriptive name, the livelihood farm. The word is old and in good standing. It goes far back in the history of our common culture. Livelihood: to give the means of living. But what is it to live? It is to eat surely, but is that all? The economy of modern times—and how short and modern they are when we relate them to the centuries which enclose Western culture—has assumed that the greatest good lies in the alternate stuffing and purging of a man's belly. Well may a hearty meal seem to the hungry the whole purpose of living. But famine and want, except as occasional features, do not appear in a healthy society. And surely it is the healthy society that the great body of Americans would like to see again. For what is health? When we are sick, we know what it is. When a man is abed, all his natural action is stopped. He cannot eat well; he cannot work. His senses live on a fever. He cannot move about as he is accustomed. And when society is sick, all things are out of joint.

And when we are sick, what do we do? We look for somebody or something to make us well again. Sometimes we are desperate and we listen to quacks, especially if we are impatient to get up. And like men, society may listen to quackery. But a better way is to follow the course of nature and assist it with a few long-tried and simple remedies. And is there a better remedy than setting up conditions where life will be free? I do not think so. Nor does the history of human conduct show any other way.

The livelihood farm has those simple features which will secure to the simple man as good a living as he is able and willing to stand. First of all, it allows him to make his bread by the grip of his hands, the bent of his will, and the sweat of his brow. These are no new-fangled principles. They are habits that experience has proved good. And they find their surest expression in working the land with the knowledge that the harvest will be gathered and stored away in cribs and barns against the barren winter. Such a farmer should have as many acres as will keep him in comfortable circumstances. This will vary according to the location, the richness of the soil, and the size of his family. He must have fields for cultivation, land for woodlots, and for pasturage. The farm should not be so large that he cannot know the fields intimately, nor so small that he will fear want. He must work hard without becoming a slave to the earth.

Removed from the public thoroughfare, upon a good situation, in a grove of trees if they are available, his house will stand. If it is a new one, it should not bear the stamp of a typical architecture. It should fit the local traditions or be adapted to them. The early American builder considered the demands of climate, taste, and needs, using the materials to be found easiest to hand. The dwelling should not be built hastily but to last. This is one of the surest signs of a conservative people. Thus will the physical and spiritual demands of a home be gratified. The farmer has no rent to pay and no fear of having his family thrown out on the big road because some new machine has taken his job away. Only death can do that; even then the man is removed, and the job remains for the son and heir. This is the security of shelter.

Then there is the security, already spoken of, against hunger. Near the kitchen the garden will lie. In the spring, summer, and fall it fills the pots and supplies the table always with fresh, crisp vegetables. The surplus, and there is always a bountiful surplus in a well-tended garden, may be put away in cans and jars. But even after the frosts fall, the farmer's wife may follow the path toward the richest spot of ground on the place and pick collards and greens. High mounds of potatoes, both kinds, will rise under dirt and leaves to fall gradually before the coming of spring; and turnips, if there is a taste for them. The canning is no easy job, coming as it does in the hottest weather. It might be simpler to buy the cans from the nearby town, except that this will involve the budget and endanger the family's security. It will also force upon the family a lower standard of living, for goods put up for the general public cannot consider special tastes. And it is this very matter of seasoning and taste which defines, in cookery, the special quality which makes for high living. Food must not only be nourishing; it must also be palatable.

Back of the house the farm orchard will spread its branches, shake out the first blooming of spring, slowly bud; and, as the season turns, hang red with cherries, the furry peach, the heavy apples and the russet pears. The vineyard may cover the walk to the well, or it may line the garden fence. But, wherever set, the fresh fruits will fill out the plainer diet of the garden and the surplus go into jellies, preserves, cider, vinegar, and the heady wines. In the fence corners, harboring birds, the wise farmer will let the native fruits grow wild, or he may cultivate the blackberry, the strawberry, the cantaloupe, the melon, the quince, and somewhere the classic fig.

There can be meats according to the family's likes and dislikes: chickens, broilers and frying size; fattened hens that are outlaid by the pullets; and all the year their fruit to make bread and cakes and desserts, or come to the table scrambled, fried, or in omelet. For the three summer months, if the neighborhood is established in its practices, twelve farmers may form a beef club (there is one in Middle Tennessee a hundred years old, whose membership has jealously descended from father to son). Once a week a fat beef is killed and divided into twelve parts. The parts go to the members by progression so that, beginning with the head, the family by the time summer is ended, has eaten a whole cow. Then, if this is not enough meat, the farmer may raise in the proper season sheep for lamb and mutton, guineas, turkeys, ducks, and geese to vary the diet. And with the cold weather comes hog-killing time, the rich surfeit of the greasy meat for a short spell, the salting down, the hanging in the smokehouse, and the long curing. As a by-product the stands of lard will take their places in the pantry; and if there is more than can be used, it may be turned into cash.

But we must not forget the spring house and the dairy nearby, for the choicest possession of the livelihood farm will be its milk cow or cows. They must be bred with care, so that always the milk will flow from bountiful udders and, sweet and sour, stand in the high pitchers with rich yellow pats of butter lying between. This will take good management, to have a fresh cow coming in as the old one goes dry. The young bull calves can be fattened and turned into beef; and if the heifers are promising, they can be kept for milkers. Thus the physical necessities of the farm family are supplied in the most direct way. It is well housed and well fed. For the cover of clothing the small money crops may be sold and exchanged with the output of the factory.

But it must be understood that the supply of physical needs is no easy matter, nor can it always be of the same degree of excellence. There are two things which qualify the degree of plenty: the imagination and will-to-work of the farmer and the exigencies of nature. It seems almost a waste of type to reaffirm such old and stubborn truths, but the fact is that we are like drunkards who must reassure themselves that the sidewalks really lie solid underfoot, that in the morning the lamppost that is swaying like an elephant's snout will be found upright and immovable. These truths give the assurance, when a farmer fails, that his failure is his own, that in the conflict with natural forces either his manhood has been found wanting, or in the inscrutable ways of Providence he has been marked for special disaster. In either case he has no complaint to make of society. But under present conditions great injustice is done the competent, those who hunger after living, for it is impossible to separate these men from the dullards and the shirkers. Those who have been deprived of their birthrights and those who never had any are lumped together through the necessities and fears of an artificial deprivation of occupations.

This loss of occupation among the many is the most damning

betrayal of all. To take away bread and meat is to deny life, but to take away a man's occupation is to deny the desire and the joy of living. And in the consideration of a remedy for this condition of affairs the small livelihood farm offers the easiest and the surest way out, at least for a large fraction of the population. The act of providing the security of shelter and the security against hunger passes beyond the care for material needs. In the back of the farmer's mind is the knowledge that he must furnish the physical necessities; but unconsciously, for he is not a man of many words, he gets great joy in the doing of it.

He does not suffer the spiritual sterilization, and often the physical, which comes from the modern technique of factory and city labor: the dissociation between work and the life of the senses, where work is a necessary evil, and pleasure is to be bought with a part of its wages. What does the farmer feel when he begins the day's work? He is not rudely startled from sleep by the strident factory whistle or the metal whang of the alarm clock. At break of day he is found sleeping beside his wife in that deep and resting sleep which only the combined fatigue of the body, the mind, and the senses can induce. At first, the night turns blacker and the air grows chill with such a chill as settles the last of the frosts deep upon the low grounds, thinly skimming the high places, softening the earth for the spring's breaking. This holds for a short spell; then gradually the darkness thins, pales, and slowly sifts in through the windows to settle on the goodman's eyes. By degrees the darkness lifts from the closed lids; light sinks through to the pupil; gently, with never a jarring, it stirs the blood, warns the senses that rest must end. As yet the mind still sleeps. Nature is like a passionate but no rude lover. It spent nine months to prepare this man for his first light and now it moves in its complex way to rescue him from the shorter night. In the distance a rooster crows, a dog barks. There is an answer from the nearby barn. The turkeys lift their heads, stretch, and fly down from the tall pine. The chickens, the good layers, for the fat lazy hens are the last to leave the roosts, are down and scratching for the worm or corn that was missed the night before. The cows move about. The work stock shake themselves in their stalls. The hogs grunt, or the sows fall before the squealing pigs. The song birds chirp. The sky grows brighter, and the world is full of familiar noises. And these sounds, like the unfolding of a drama, penetrate the house and the ears of the sleepers. Suddenly like a gay fan snapping open, the heavens run with color to announce that the high lord of day approaches. The goodman, the master of a few acres, suddenly finds that his eyes are open. He yawns, and the saliva flows to tell him he may taste. He stretches, and his fingers tell him he may feel. He breathes deeply, and the fresh morning air, sweeping before the sun, shows how good it is to smell. His wife stirs beside him; gets up and dresses; calls the girls. Soon blue smoke from the kitchen stove rises over the house like a Byzantine column. The man is still in bed, enjoying the luxury of keen senses come alive and with no thought as to whether he may spend another five minutes without missing the car, being late for work, and possibly losing his job. He lies there, giving no thought to the tremendous ceremony that has gone into his morning levee. He is thinking of the day's work, for soon he must be up and with the boys feeding the stock, drawing water, and milking. Then he will have no time for planning. Like a good general, once he is dressed, his thoughts are of tactics not strategy.

As complicated as the beginning of this day is, it is only one day in a lifetime of years. There is continual variety. There are the seasonal changes, the time changes, the imperceptible lengthening and shortening of light hours, the variable weather. The richness of these phenomena defies the hardening of a rigid routine. It is a scene in nature's drama, a complete pattern in itself and a part of the larger pattern, the constant performance of death and renewal. Each morning the farmer wakes to some new action. There is the time for breaking the ground, the time for planting, the exciting moment when the crops begin to show themselves, palely green, upon the surface of the earth, the steady progress toward the ripe harvest, or it may be a barren harvest. He may wake, day after day, in a drought, when the sun is hateful. The terrific suspense, the sullen face of the world in a dry time when even the cattle in the fields catch the common fear, he must withstand. How often do the eyes seek the north, the flash of lightning, for the sign of rain. And the thanksgiving when in the sultry night a wind blows and the gentle rain falls on the hot shingles and down the crevices of the hard-cracked earth. The farmer, the farmer's wife, the children listen to know whether it will be a delusive shower or a real season. Then, when the patter becomes steady, restful sleep falls upon the house.

Next morning with what joy does the farmer breathe in the crisp
damp air. No perfume would possibly so exalt this one sense of
smell. And his eyes look upon the world and see it come to life; see
the brown ruin leave.

Or it may be there is too much rain, and the overhanging clouds
encompass a rotting world. Then what a sight it is when the sun
drives down the morning mist and sucks the fields dry. How busy is
everybody killing the grass and saving the moisture. But this work
must be done at the right time, for if the cultivator is hasty, is illy
disciplined, he may plow the ground too heavy and not only injure
the crops but do such damage to the soil as many seasons may fail to
heal. Without conscious knowledge of the part he is playing, the
farmer is dignified by this continual struggle with nature, with the
seed time, the growing season, the gathering time, the storing away,
and at the end the great dénouement with its relieving catharsis, for
if there is death, he has learned that always it makes for new life. It is
not possible to distinguish the needs of the flesh, the senses, and the
spirit, for when the farmer thinks of making a good living for his
family, this good living means physical, sensory, and spiritual welfare.

This is why the genuine farmer (and it takes a proper society to
make a genuine farmer) never loses his belief in God. And the
greatest flowering of formal religion will be found when society has
the right understanding of this natural drama. When religion
grows formless and weak, it is because man in his right rôle as the
protagonist in the great conflict is forgotten or disbelieved. He
becomes vainglorious and thinks he may conquer nature. This the
good farmer knows to be nonsense. He is faced constantly and
immediately with a mysterious and powerful presence, which he
may use but which he may never reduce entirely to his will and
desires. He knows of minor successes; he remembers defeats; but he
is so involved in the tremendously complex ritual of the seasonal
drama that he never thinks about idle or dangerous speculations.

In isolation such farming would be of no force in the common
life. There must be enough of such livelihood farms to restore a
conservative balance to the country community. Like the individual,
no farm can stand alone; but—and this is the important issue—it
must stand as a part of a healthy country life, not as a division of an
internal colonial province to be exploited according to the irrespon-

sible desires of commerce which, like a barn fire, increase the more they are fed. The livelihood farm is proof against exploitation. By giving security, it makes a self-respecting and stable citizen. It will have its influence, also, on the larger farms, of necessity having to do more with money crops. Seeing these semi-independent farm units about them, the large farmers will have a constant warning against the ruinous influence they have followed for over three quarters of a century, the ruthless and speculative demands of foreign trade, the sole interest in the money crop, and a bad system of tenantry—bad for the proprietor as well as for the worker, since he is the tenant to the credit system as the cropper is the casual worker of the land.

But even under a bad system, the livelihood farm will show virtues and make for stability. In hard times unrest and suffering will be reduced to the minimum, since these freeholds will always secure first the necessities of life. Depressions and public peril can only deprive them of comforts and some few luxuries. Good times can add only material comforts, vanities, and bought luxuries. And if the State is overturned in revolution, the freeholders are the last to be swept into chaos. Having something very definite to risk by change, such men will be slow to follow the demagogue, whereas, the tenant will be quick to follow him, since the tenant has been reduced to squeezing all he can from a system that gives him at best enough to eat and wear. In the seasonal drama which gives purpose and dignity to the small proprietor the tenant plays the part either of a churl or buffoon.

There are other negative virtues to a program of encouraging the livelihood farm. By taking much land out of the money crops and repopulating it with people instead of with wheat, cotton, and tobacco, with people who will consume most of its produce, the overproduction in the major crops will be naturally reduced, not artificially as the A.A.A. orders. At the same time the problem of distribution will be simplified. Food, housing, and to an extent clothing will not have to follow the wasteful process of being gathered into large centers and wastefully redistributed, for every hand that passes goods about must take its share. *Such commodities will be produced and consumed at the same place.* And without too great a disruption of the present trading set-up, for although the measure of each farm unit's produce for the general trade will be small, over and above its living consumption, its multiple will be large enough to maintain a healthy traffic between industry and agriculture, supporting the trade of the larger commercial farms, small merchants, the local professions, and the community of artisans.

It must be understood that everybody is not fit to follow the life of the livelihood farm. There will always be men incapable of responsibility and ownership of property, even on so small a scale, just as there will be other men whose wits and wills and imaginations demand larger possessions and the honor of command. Regional, climatic, or cultural differences would forbid that so large a territory as the United States should all be divided into yeoman farms. But if our country might boast even one fourth or one third of the population so situated, rural life and therefore the life of the nation would by present comparison become wonderfully stable. And the commercial farms, instead of a machine tenantry, held steady by such a leaven, could be served by that large body of people who are unfit for responsible ownership or who by ill-luck are reduced to the state of temporary dependence. On such a basis foreign and internal trade would find itself confined to a more constant and less variable rise and fall in prices. But the greatest good to result from such an economy will be its more natural living conditions. This should be the important end of polity, for only when families are fixed in their habits, sure of their property, hopeful for the security of their children, jealous of liberties which they cherish, can the State keep the middle course between impotence and tyranny.

# John Taylor of Caroline

## PART I

THE study of American history is a most disheartening occupation. If it is taken to be the record of those acts which have precipitated the sorry evils responsible for the chaos of modern society, there is only one conclusion to be drawn—it tells the triumph of senseless greed. No other explanation appears to account for the viciously rapid destruction of the physical treasures of a continent, treasures once so rich that, had they been intelligently husbanded, they might have kept a vast body of people in plenty for a thousand years. The waste of these resources is the dissipation of the physical basis for a healthy state of society. The destruction began seriously after the first American revolution; proceeded with devastating speed through the nineteenth century; and has now, in the first third of the twentieth, brought us to the prospect of a long period of economic and political servility.

The physical resources of this continent were bait thrown to jerk from their natural currents those social and political ideas intended to secure to the farmers living under the new Union the gatherings of their fields and to the townsmen the reward of craftsmanship. The early republican leaders of the Revolution had manoeuvred to make the Union a medium pliable but strong enough to generate such well-being. It was understood by these men that private property must be generally distributed throughout the body politic; otherwise the state is corrupted by its core and is destroyed by the very agency which, with better luck, would have given it life. They

failed—but not until after a long and bitter fight. Their failure is
our tragedy, for it has robbed posterity of its inheritance. Now there
is everywhere such general discontent, so much criticism of those
who have transferred to their aimless use the energies of millions of
people, that all earnestly look for a way out. In view of this it might
be profitable to take from the obscurity into which he has fallen, a
gentleman who exerted his talents and strength to oppose the trend
taken by American affairs: John Taylor of Caroline County, Virginia.

He was born in Orange County during the middle of the eighteenth century. His family and connections were gentle people,
belonging to that squirearchy which ruled Virginia and the United
States for so long. Left an orphan at the age of ten, he went to live
with his mother's brother, Edmund Pendleton, a gentleman of parts
in the Colony. He was prepared by tutors for William and Mary
College. After graduation he read law, entered politics, and helped
to destroy the political machine which had governed Virginia for
twenty years. He had attached himself to Patrick Henry and Richard Henry Lee in this matter and was to be found acting with them
throughout the Revolution and their campaign to keep Virginia out
of the new Union. When the fighting began, the Continental Congress elected him a major. He took part in the campaigns around
New York and Philadelphia; but when it became necessary to reor-
ganize the army at Valley Forge, he refused to serve as a private and
retired to Caroline County. From here he entered the House of
Delegates and worked for the retirement of Washington, whose
management of the army he disapproved. When danger threatened
from the South, however, he took to the field again and remained
under arms until the surrender at Yorktown. The war ruined him,
but he was granted five thousand acres of western land for his
services. He turned to account his knowledge of law and managed
to accumulate a considerable fortune during those fat years of
1781–1792. Then, following the inclination of his kind, he bought
Hazelwood, an estate near Port Royal, Virginia, and went there to
live the life of a country gentleman . . . in the fullest sense of that
phrase.

It is hard today for the understanding to grasp the place and
function of the country gentleman in Taylor's time. This is because
agriculture—not Southern alone—has been degraded since the

North-and-South war. It has been only a province to be annually denuded for the uses industrial-corporate finance might have for its treasure. But before his overthrow the country gentleman was the most powerful single influence in early American society. His decline and fall measures the decline and fall of American independence. When he ruled the Union, his political action came directly out of a complete philosophy of life. It had, naturally enough, its limitations; but since the gentleman's basic idea of the Union's polity was the preservation of private property, society had a stability it has never had since, under the rule of irresponsible financiers who have usurped the powers of government but have refused the responsibility of this power. This confusing condition did not attend the gentleman's rule. Because his wealth and power depended partly upon his personal relations with the governed, he assumed the moral responsibility for his action; and when the economic well-being of his society was threatened, he did not shirk his obligations. If he failed to maintain the independence and dignity of the agrarian concept of this society, it was not from any ignorance of the forces which threatened it or of the means to be used to preserve it. It was because the fortunes of war are unpredictable.

When Taylor set himself up at Hazelwood, agriculture was falling into desuetude. It was still the most honourable occupation for a gentleman, but there were two forces threatening its continued well-being. Externally, in the political world, the Federalists from the East challenged its supremacy; internally the farm economy had become inefficient and extravagant. The thin soils of the eastern shore had become exhausted by a reckless cultivation, and the farms were slow to recover from the neglect of eight years of warfare. Taylor, as a member of the feudal aristocracy, at once set to work to reform the economics of agriculture and overthrow the dangerous Federalists. He became one of Jefferson's best lieutenants and the publicist for the party in Virginia. In 1803 he published, under the title *Arator*, a collection of articles on farming. The thesis of the book is that agriculture and politics are the sources of wealth and liberty. Both contain internal good principles, but both are liable to practical deterioration. If one is vitiated in practice, poverty ensues; if the other, oppression. If the agriculture is good and the govern-

ment bad, we may have wealth and slavery. If the government is
good and agriculture bad, liberty and poverty. The third alternative
is implicit in his argument: a bad government and a bad culture of
the land. It has been left to this generation to know the terrifying
effects which follow from this state—servility with poverty.

To be able to establish in the Union the desired political economy
for agriculture it was first necessary to institute for the farms and
plantations a more intelligent agronomy. Towards this end Taylor
laid down certain generalizations which are as important today as
they were then. First, the land must sustain that fraction of the
population living on it; next, the farmer must have a surplus to
exchange for those products his land cannot bring forth economically and for which he feels the need. To make this possible the
strength of the soil which is withdrawn in the form of crops or
vanishes by way of erosion must be returned and added to. Care for
the soil is basic, but the buildings and fences are constantly falling
into disrepair and must be mended and made stout and trim.

In the prevailing plantation economy, when the fields fell exhausted, the planter turned them out to sage and cleared fresh
grounds to be mangled by the same irresponsible cycle. Cattle
wandered about the country and wasted their manure on the public
roads; and, if they escaped starvation over the winter, were driven
up when leather or meat, of poor quality always, was needed. There
was nothing permanent or profitable about this sort of farming,
and Taylor saw ruin ahead if it continued. It was making a western
nomad of the labourer, confining him to the hardships of pioneering and threatening the stability of the Union. For no state is secure
unless it has a sturdy agricultural body to rest upon, and the agriculture of a people is rarely secure unless the cultivators work
continuously the same acreage. This should be a primary axiom of
political economy. That nation which abuses its farmers is committing suicide, and when it becomes necessary for a government agent
to feed a landed tenant and dictate how much or how little his land
will produce, the condition of that nation is desperate.

The greatest single cause of soil impoverishment Taylor believed
to be that prime minister of plantation government, the overseer. It
was customary to pay his wages with a share of the crop. This meant,
in effect, that the master and his chief lieutenant connived together

to impoverish the land, since it was to the overseer's interest to make as large a crop as possible.

It is common [writes Taylor] for an industrious overseer, after a very few years, to quit a farm on account of the barrenness, occasioned by his own industry; and frequent changes of these itinerant managers of agriculture, each striving to extract the remnant of fertility left by his predecessor, combines with our agricultural ignorance, to form the completest system of impoverishment, of which any other country can boast.

Since overseers seemed essential, he suggests a regular wage as the cure. Planters, especially small ones in the middle South, were to find the solution by setting over their hands a responsible slave.

This vice is to be seen in the South today in the much more aggravated form of the share-cropper. Instead of one man it becomes the practice of every farm labourer to destroy the soil; and it is bound to be ruined with more efficiency and speed, since a number of men can do more damage than one. This system was fastened on the planting states during Reconstruction by Eastern and English capital which, in the post-war extremity, could be had to finance the money crops and only the money crops. The white and black cultivators who took the place of slavery were forbidden to grow anything but cotton and tobacco. Land spared for gardens was the exception, since gardens reduced the profits of the furnishing system. This introduced that abstract slavery feared and prophesied by Taylor and Calhoun. The planter no longer exercised the responsibility of the master; the relationship had become a business matter, that is, it was predatory. The tenant depended upon the planter for his food; the planter upon the local merchant or the bank when he acted as merchant; the local merchant upon the wholesale house; the wholesale house upon its bank; the provincial bank upon some New York or London house, those private rulers of the public credit which belonged to all as private citizens. There was the excuse of necessity for this bargain during Reconstruction. Now it is madness. And yet it is hard to find where to lay the blame. The inertia which is so salutary when society is strong becomes the greatest deterrent to the return of a healthful condition when its functions are congested. The tenant cannot afford to improve land which may be worked by somebody else the following spring, and the landlords are so hard-pressed by the system that they are unable to take any out of cultivation for its much-needed rest. A four-shift system is well-nigh impossible with itinerant cultivators.

The personal slavery of Taylor's day had the great virtue of fixing the worker to the soil and defining the relationship between master and man. The loss of this has done farming incalculable damage. If means were found to put people back on the land and bind them to it, the problems of agriculture would not solve themselves overnight—there are too many things sucking away at its vitality— but until this is done, there can be no cure for the soil's anaemic state. The English in better days discovered that even a twenty-one-year lease was too short a time for the land to receive careful culture. A long lease is only one method, and it concerns only that body of the population which requires the landlord-tenant status. Bulking large in any agrarian state, there must always be the small, independent farmer who believes that no man can do better than take his living from the ground by the sweat of his brow and the grip of his hands. His small estate must be cultivated like a garden; and, though it will be necessary for him to sell part of his surplus, this should concern him less than it concerns the large farmer. His aim should be not to make money but to make as good a living as his land allows; and that will be, taking into consideration the original strength of the soil, as good as his intelligent attention to the arts of farming will allow. The present administration's experiment in subsistence farming is a move towards the re-establishment of this class of men; but the implication, that it is a way to diminish unemployment and avoid the dole, is negative. It has all the earmarks of a temporary measure which is to be abandoned when the country swings back into the highway of prosperity. As such it will never lay the foundations of a sturdy yeomanry.

After dealing with those things which destroy fertility, Taylor next takes up the matter of restoration. There are three kinds of manure: mineral, vegetable, and atmospherical. He is inclined to link together vegetable and atmosphere as the same thing. Mineral manure is applied directly. Vegetable manure presents complications. It is destroyed by a bad system of grazing, especially summer grazing. The three-shift system was responsible for this: that is, corn one year; wheat the next; and the land turned out to grazing the third year. It is common knowledge, he says, that both corn and wheat exhaust the soil two out of the three years. The question to be answered is: Does a third year of grazing restore it? The ground is soft from recent tillage; the cattle tramp restlessly over its sparsely covered surface in search of nourishment. The pores of the earth are closed and beaten to death. The sun bakes it and the winds crack it. The repetition of this soon finds the cattle starving to death on land that has been abused. The three-shift system has only one merit. It promises to kill the lands: in practice it fulfils this promise.

As an escape from this Taylor suggests inclosing and the four-shift system. As a first principle he separates land to be grazed from land to be cultivated. With clear logic he argues that grazing and cultivation are always at cross-purposes. He might have said they represent two ages of society, pastoral and agrarian. The cultivator works to kill the grasses which are the life of grazing, whereas the pasture to give nourishment must abound in the cover which is so detrimental to the hoe and plow. In his four-shift system one-fourth of the farm is put down in a permanent pasture. This would be made up principally of the wet lands. Of the land to be cultivated, one-third will be rested in clovers every third year; of the land left so much will be put in corn and so much in wheat, according to the needs of the farm. The cattle will be penned and manure made by their droppings and a litter of corn stalks and leaves. This will, in rotation, be spread over and plowed as quickly as possible into the lands under cultivation. According to results from experiments over a period of fifteen years he found that one-fourth of a farm will produce as much as the entire place did under the three-shift system. To strengthen this economy he insists on rock or live-tree fences built on a rise. Besides the labour wasted in the repair of dead-wood fences, they have still a greater drawback: they do not protect the soil from washing. A farm bound by rock or green cedar fences, properly drained by open and closed ditches, about whose details he is very specific, cultivated on the four-shift plan, will reward the farmer and his labourers for their industry.

As to the labour which cultivates the land, it must be well-housed, well-fed, and well-clothed. Taylor warns his readers that a strict discipline, stern authority, and complete subordination must be combined to attain any success at all. The free Negro he declares a nuisance to society. He has freedom without position or property. This renders him open to any mischievous influence and increases pilfering. He interferes with the accepted form of labour and makes it dissatisfied with its lot. Taylor advocated removal by colonization or by more desperate measures. The fact that labour took the form of personal slavery in Taylor's time does not completely invalidate his directions on this matter. The Negro is free, if you like; but he is still a Negro. This fact means that the fundamental relationship between the races is unchanged. His position now is subordinate whereas formerly it was servile, but it is questionable whether he has gained by the change. He owns property, but he has no political power to insure this ownership. A great body of his race works on the farms of the dominant race. Any outside influence which stirs up trouble makes him inefficient as a labourer, and makes successful farming doubtful. The Communist Party and all such factions who aim to upset the *status quo* stand in the shoes of the Abolitionists and free Negroes of the days of the old Union. They cannot be disciplined because they stand without the jurisdiction of Southern governments; but their agents in the South can and should be dealt with, with the greatest severity. The Southern governments have failed in this, and they are suffering from their impotency. They fail to act because they fear outside opinion. The relative positions of the races is tacitly accepted; it should be openly stated. The increase in lynchings stems indirectly from this. It is a sign that governments are refusing to function on a matter vital to the states—not because they fail to apprehend and punish the lynchers but because they have countenanced mischievous opinions which have raised false hopes among certain members of the subordinate race. Mobs in a civilized state are the more responsible citizens resuming delegated functions of government because their agents failed to exercise these functions. Mass action of this sort is always an act of self-preservation. It indicates that race integrity must not be tampered with. The liberal attitude of Southern cities shows how far they have isolated themselves from the countryside and how far they have become the exploiting agency of industrialism. The South is being shaken by this, but in a crisis it is always clear on fundamental issues. The real wealth and voting power belongs to the country; and if the issue becomes acute enough, the cities may again be reduced to their proper positions, places of exchange for the country's produce.

This discussion at first may appear irrelevant; but it is one purpose of this essay to show that Southern interests, customs, economics, and problems have been, still are, and will be, fundamentally the same. The character of its people, its soil and climate, its geography, its history, and its relations to the other sections have determined this. To ignore it is to beckon disaster with both hands; and disaster does not always fall below the Mason and Dixon Line, as the rest of this continent has learned.

After everything else is considered, there is one general principle underlying all successful farming—liberality. It is, according to Taylor, the solitary human occupation to which the adage, "the more we give the more we shall receive," can be justly applied. A pinching miserly system may very well keep a farmer alive, but it will never make his living bountiful. Great profits depend upon great improvements of the soil, and great improvements can never be made by penurious efforts. The discrimination between useful and productive and useless and barren expenses contain the agricultural secret for acquiring plenty and happiness. A good farmer will sow the first with an open hand, but he will eradicate every seed of the other. Diminutions of comforts, necessaries, and expense are too often mistaken for the means of producing the ends they obstruct.

> The cottagers [writes Taylor] who inflict upon themselves and their families the discomforts of cold houses, bad bedding, and insufficient clothing to acquire wealth destroy the vigour both of mind and body necessary for obtaining the contemplated end at which, of course, they never arrive. The farmer who starves his slaves, is a still greater sufferer. He loses the profits produced by health, strength, and alacrity; and suffers the losses caused by disease, short life, weakness, and dejection.

Liberality to the earth in culture and manure makes a bountiful harvest. Liberality to slaves and work stock is the strength which gathers it. Liberality in warm houses produces health, strength, and comfort; preserves the lives of thousands of domestic animals; causes all animals to thrive on less food; and secures from damage all kinds of crops. And the liberality in the utensils of culture saves a great deal of work.

Liberality, however, is impossible without foresight. Foresight consists in preparing work for all weather and doing all work in the right weather. Many a crop is lost by impatience. Plowing too wet can ruin the ground and make the plants perish. Planting out of season is equally injurious. Perhaps the most exciting moments in a farmer's life are those when he must decide which crops will be worked after a week's rain. Impatience to catch up will often mean the doing of the same thing twice. This is to be avoided. It is vicious, expensive, and keeps the hands on the run—in circles. Under such an economy the hands will be constantly occupied, but there will be little to show for their labour; and the planter driven always by makeshift plans will be denied that leisurely activity and peace of mind always reflected upon the brow of the man who is vassal but not slave to nature.

And this is the end the goodman and master should seek, for then each knows the joys of agriculture. And they are the fullest and most satisfying the intellect and sensibility can know. Under a free government nature continually throws out from its secret places inexhaustible sources of human pleasure. It fits ideas to substances and substances to ideas in a constant rotation of hope and fruition. With a passion for proper living somehow lost to this century Taylor's words break away from the usual constraint of his prose:

> The novelty, frequency, and exactness of accommodations between our ideas and operations, constitutes the most exquisite source of mental pleasure. Agriculture feeds it with endless supplies in the natures of soils, plants, climates, manures, instruments of culture, and domestic animals. Their combinations are inexhaustible, and an unsatiated interest receives gratifications in quick succession. . . . Poetry, in allowing more virtue to agriculture, than to any other profession, has abandoned her privilege of fiction and yielded to the natural moral effect of the absence of temptation. The same fact is commemorated by religion, upon an occasion the most solemn, within the scope of the human imagination. At the awful day of judgment, the discrimination of the good from the wicked, is not

made by the criterion of sects or dogmas, but by one which consti-
tutes the daily employment and the great end of agriculture. The
judge upon this occasion has by anticipation pronounced, that to
feed the hungry, clothe the naked, and give drink to the thirsty, are
the passports to future happiness; and the divine intelligence which
selected an agricultural state as a Paradise for its favourites, has here
again prescribed the agricultural virtues as the means for the admission of their posterity into heaven.

Genuine agronomy is also the best patriot. A conqueror may
double a nation's territory; but a nation's farmers can double the
territory by making it twice as fertile, and without the expenditure
of blood and treasure attendant upon foreign conquest, or the
threat to the state always lurking in the ranks of a victorious army.
Not one agricultural virtue does Taylor neglect to extol. He reduces
them all to a comprehensive phrase—agriculture is the architect of
the complete man. The American continent is the suitable back-
ground for his habitation. It has a climate and soil where good
culture never fails to beget plenty and where bad cannot produce
famine; it is favoured by accident with the power of self-
government; the risk of invasion is less than in other countries. In
the face of such odds agriculture can only lose its happiness by the
folly or fraud of statesmen, or by its own ignorance. Taylor's thorough experiments in plantation economy had gone far towards the
substitution of knowledge for ignorance. If they did not prove equal
to all soils and all conditions of farm life, certainly his agrarian
principles must always be the principles which will be the universal
underpinning to a stable agriculture.

But without political protection a good country life is impossible.
Indeed a proper agrarian economy cannot function without its
counterpart, an agrarian polity. The security of the agricultural
states is dependent upon the political acumen of those first citizens
who rule. All the improvements man can add to the arts of farming
and the crafts of the town do not make for his prosperity if he has
lost his political freedom through the folly or fraud of statesmen.
The more he builds up his soil, and the more he produces upon it,
by that much more does he enrich some special interest which is
using the government for its private ends. The end of the eighteenth
century saw two conflicting political moralities. The triumph of one

meant the defeat of Taylor's way of life. This state of conflict turned Taylor from the economics of the farm to politics for farmers—which brings us to the second part of his political economy.

## PART II

No farm's well-being can be assured by an efficient internal economy alone. The farm's internal economy and its external relations to society are the two poles of a very special world. This fact, so obvious to an agrarian, bears restatement, since it has fallen out of common knowledge even among the agricultural states of the Union. The farm as a cultural unit—and again it is necessary to be explicit: the land, the people who live on it, its peculiar history, its myth, all that goes to make it a living organism (today a farm's definition is generally limited to a statistical appraisal of its fluctuating cash value)—the farm, to resume, is either the physical and spiritual support of our state or the creature of an irresponsible oligarchy which in its reach for power has destroyed those special qualities that give a state strength and life. This analysis is the root of Taylor's political economy.

In the early stages of the American Union it was of supreme importance that the state governments should fall into the hands of men who would watch after agriculture with jealous care. This was of more immediate importance then than now, for the colonies so suddenly metamorphosed into states had a population chiefly agricultural or related directly to the land. And since a government's attitude towards the land, especially in our temperate zone, is the key to a nation's private and public life, the wrong attitude could easily make abortive the winning of political independence.

There had been general discontent in both worlds with the loss of feudal independence in Europe. The greater body of those who emigrated to this continent were motivated by this discontent; but unfortunately there was no real escape, principally because those who fled were confused as to the causes of their distress. They realized they were living badly and that their surroundings were not what an Englishman had a right to expect; but as is always the case, it was difficult to find why this was so. Life in the new world was used as a lure to send the disaffected into other countries as the servants of the masters of Europe, just as a yeoman will turn stock into fresh pastures after one pasture has been eaten dry. When the same pressure was felt in the new world, an accident brought about a political severance and the possibility for changed conditions.

These changed conditions were expressed in the terms of liberty and independence and freedom. The amount of freedom to be expected in this world is extremely limited. About this there is little to be done, just as there is little to be done about the time and place of birth, marriage, or death. But it was the American's assumption that the individual acting with other individuals can predetermine the form of a common set of limitations. The important consideration for those who pretend to better their condition is that they take care to define the exact nature of their limitations. Two sets of opinions, among many, showed themselves in the new political field to be the dominant rivals. Under the outward calm of Washington's administration these antagonistic opinions gradually shifted into party organizations. As will be seen, neither party was pure; but the most active elements in both have a definable political activity and historical meaning. One party wanted to continue the same exploitative rule which had usurped the power of the monarchies of Europe. Those of this opinion were miscalled monarchists at first; and later Federalists, another misnomer. In Europe such a group of interests had usurped the credit power from a monarchy shaken in its principles, and, letting the monarchs take the blame for the conditions thus brought about, consolidated their power under an irresponsible financial system disclaiming responsibility to any control on the earth or in Heaven. In England this power had rendered the people tractable by removing them from the land where their self-dependence had in the past saved them from slavery, bringing them into large cities where they must depend upon another's bread and another's tools. And even those who continued at farming found conditions so changed, due to the inclosure of the commons and the dishonourable surrender of the nobility, that their plight was little better.

In opposition to the Federalists the Republicans under Jefferson espoused liberty of speech, freedom of the press, freedom of conscience, as little government as possible, no entailment of land, no foreign wars, and a state where most of the population owned land.

This was Jefferson's answer to the evil practices of the recent past.
As publicist and strategist for the party John Taylor rested his
defense finally upon this liberalism which he had caught in his
youth as one might catch the pox. If this were all that might be
claimed for him, there would be little reason to disturb his dusty
bones. But he has much greater title to distinction in the quality of a
strategy which, if the tacticians had but known how to construe it,
might have changed the course of American history. All the noble
abstractions that drifted like miasmal vapours through the political
atmosphere, where so many lost their way groping with out-
stretched hands and had their pockets picked, failed to dim his
sharp eyes or throw him off his path. He was like a swordsman
whose skill had laid his enemies low only to find, when he turned,
that his back had not been against his bridge and keep as he had
thought but before a precipice, in front of which he has been
carrying on a masterful but useless fight, separate from his
companions-in-arms who had allowed the bridge to be carried. The
dead that lay about him only mocked his skill, when the noise of the
enemy breaking open the chests in the donjon struck his ears.

Taylor's predicament was common to most of the early Republicans: conservative instincts and desires coupled with liberal intellectual principles. Because of the conservatism natural to all
land-living people, at the close of the Revolutionary War there was a
better chance for the survival of the European tradition on the
American continent than in England. This was so, in spite of the
many decades of exploitation by Crown, Crown companies, and
Scotch merchants who had only been able to eat away a small rim of
top-soil near the coast. But that view imbued with the philosophy of
materialism, which had undone England, quickly manifested itself
in its destruction of the Confederation which had prosecuted the
war. The Confederation promised care for tradition by allowing no
vicious interference from the outside with the forms of the American commonwealths. Hamilton, the leading disciple of materialism,
made plans for a strong central government. He acted with consum-
mate tactical skill. The instructions to the delegates who were to
consider revision of the existing Confederation, and no more, were
explicit: they were to make a more perfect union. What went on
behind the closed doors in Philadelphia has been revealed only in

the most fragmentary detail, but it is clear that three schools of opinion struggled for supremacy: the monarchist headed by Hamilton; the nationalist; and a third gathering about those who insisted on following the states' instructions. The monarchists, according to Taylor, failed and threw in their strength with the nationalists; compromised with the third party; and the Constitution was the result. This is known as the Revolution of 1789.

It is common history how difficult it was to get the states to agree to this revolution. Taylor opposed Virginia's ratification. He understood that the new Union was a move towards consolidation; at best it was a postponement of the struggle with every odd in favour of the monarchist-nationalists. A real monarchy might have been the best form of Union—consider the peace it brought to Austria-Hungary after 1848—but the monarchy proposed by Hamilton was no real monarchy. It was to have had upon its throne a king who would rule for special interests, one of those capitalists' kings relatively new to the world. A national republic would for all practical purposes serve the same ends, as Hamilton was shrewd enough to realize, except that instead of one man, the Congress, a more numerous body, would have to be subjected. The American conservatives failed to realize that the English kings had lost their power, and at George's door were laid their troubles; while he, in turn, was set at odds with his rebellious American subjects when they were only rebelling against a Parliament of Whig nobles and merchants who would, through the king's person, end the struggle between monarch and representatives of the money power. After George no English king would forget his place. Perhaps the reason for this misinterpretation may be found in the landed gentleman's inherited jealousy of the king's power and property.

At any rate the compromise to which the Confederation group finally agreed is the basis of the great experiment in "free government." A free government should have been recognized by these logicians for what it was, a contradiction in terms. It may seem pedantic to insist upon it, but the loose use of certain words by the early fathers made their position needlessly difficult. The new Constitution authorized a very complicated form of government. The states, the sovereigns to the contract, delegated certain powers to a central government, notably those powers which would be neces-

sary for protection against foreign dangers. Their internal life was
to be directed by their varied polities. This, it seems, is the essence
of the early American principles of government. The arrangement
was to be perpetual . . . a negative government with a division of
powers among the separate departments, with the constitution a
sort of holding company telling the rules which would prevent
various spheres from encroaching on one another.

Assuming that all government is an evil, the Republicans sought
to preserve this system of checks, believing that the continuous
friction and jealousy among the varied spheres would lessen the
opportunity for tyranny. Their experience had taught them that
government, especially strong government, means exploitation. In
the Federal sphere the divisions—the Executive, the Congress, and
the Judiciary—had powers not only of a certain kind but powers
which were weakened by further subdivision. It is not the purpose
here to go into a Constitutional discussion, but to emphasize the
great stress which the framers, following Republican interpretation,
laid upon a negative form of government; the evidence of their
concern for the wide ownership of and non-interference with private property, upon which they grounded their stand for order in a
world falling into chaos.

Just how desperate this stand was may be observed by any student
of our subsequent history, for the Confederation had been supplanted by a union which might become anything. A confederation
is formed between sovereign bodies. Its powers are temporary, and
they relate strictly to foreign affairs. Its duties are carried out by
ambassadors. But this new union had raised up a form of central
government which would *permanently* decide on foreign policies as
well as on certain relations between the participating states. The
states had now signed away important functions of sovereignty to it,
and *forever*; and no matter how much the strict constructionists
might declare that it could perform certain acts, clearly nominated,
its recognition as a fixed part of the government with a heart, a
mind, and a liver, gave it a mechanism by which it might usurp
complete sovereignty. The rub lay in the nature of foreign affairs
which, by the crises arising out of world conditions, are able to
subvert the best constitutions and reduce the ordering of the internal affairs of a union to the support of a foreign policy which may
bring distress, suffering, and revolution. It was not long before New

England was asked, on account of foreign policy, to acquiesce patriotically to laws dealing injuries and ruin.

It was clear from the start how dangerous were the powers assigned to the Federal sphere of influence, for obviously no tyranny lurked among the rights withheld by the states. The direction of internal affairs could injure very little, even when this direction was at its worst, other member states. A state might nullify certain actions which threatened to do it harm, but the advantages of the union were so obvious that it would hesitate to do this unless injustice was marked. In the two historic instances of threatened nullification, the Hartford Convention and South Carolina, the final results might well have been to strengthen the Union and add to the general prosperity if each had acted upon its threat. Both arose from severe grievances, and the cure, pursued in the name of a central policy, was worse than the disease. What were a few sailors worth, or what the loss of a part of the shipping, against the ruin of the whole? And what has the ultimate gain been to ruin the South, that last conservative balance to a Union which had lost its course? Practice found the central department acting very positively and beyond its power under Jefferson as well as Adams, not from a despotic purpose but where its foreign policy pushed it. The Louisiana Purchase is a striking case, though not as important as the embargoes and the War of 1812.

It was this state of affairs which brought the Quids together: Taylor, the political theorist; Randolph and Macon, parliamentarians. They offered opposition within the party itself; they were the pure Republicans, the strict constructionists; and it is tragic that they were unable to discipline Jefferson. Of these purists and their allies, Taylor principally concerns us here. His weight was felt in Congress, but his personality did not seize like Randolph's, whose brilliant and destructive and slightly mad mind terrorized so many mediocrities. But Taylor's principles and his analysis of the evil forces working like false yeast in the wine of American life became the complete guides for future conservative action. Those who came after added little to his original argument. The later additions, with one marked exception, were confined to new tactics. They all owe, directly or indirectly, their position and arguments to him. His influence on the mature Calhoun is clear. This does not detract from Calhoun's greatness; indeed he is the greater man. He does not so much derive from as fulfill Taylor. Calhoun's dialectic was the expression of a culture just becoming conscious of its fateful rôle. Taylor was the political prophet who ignored the Wilderness; Calhoun the Messiah who should not have had to consider it.

Taylor's chief contribution may be found in his several books on the unsatisfactory state of political affairs; that is to say, on the state of affairs, for life was pretty much regarded at this time through a political eye. He turned to this writing and to a behind-the-scenes activity when he recognized the futility of openly opposing Jefferson. He became what Dodd calls the Peacemaker of the Virginia Dynasty, and the olive branch in his hands turned into the executive crown on Monroe's head. Monroe was the hope of the Quids. But Taylor never placed too much faith in one individual. He relied more on showing what blessings the proper construction of the Constitution would bring to the people of the Union and, above all, the dangers which threatened it.

In 1814 he published his *Enquiry*,* and this was to be followed by other books, amplifying his thesis or exposing the changing positions of the enemy. The *Enquiry* was ostensibly an answer to John Adams' interpretation; but he used Adams and the Federalists as convenient blinds for his real purpose, the preservation of the balances and the exposure of those evil moral agents which would upset them. And though the Constitution had given rules for keeping the balances, the government of the United States, morally considered, was both good and bad. The happiness of the Union depended upon the predominance of a good morality. Adams argued for a balance between different orders and the necessity for an aristocracy. Taylor replies, in effect, that Adams is dealing in anachronisms. There can be no danger from fixed orders in society, for they no longer exist; or where they do exist, they no longer have any meaning and consequently no power. But by setting them up and discussing their relative merits and demerits as if conduct were actually influenced by them, the real destructive forces were enabled to work without opposition. This evil moral force he called the Aristocracy of Paper and Patronage. It hoped to subvert the Consti-

---

* The full title is *An Enquiry into the Principles and Policy of the United States Government.*

tution and thereby gain the property of the Union by destroying the liberties of its people.

Taylor's chief claim to resurrection rests just here. In spite of the contradictions which Republican liberalism subjected him to, he detected and never lost sight of this inherited materialistic philosophy as the central force which threatened a miscarriage of the independence won from England. As faithfully, he laid bare the weak defences where it might enter in and establish itself. Taylor fears the growth of the executive because of the excessive power given him, his secret treaties through which he may involve the country in war and further entrench himself in power. This same power appoints the judges who will be dependent upon it. Judicial power relates to municipal, not to political law. Its functions have to do with individuals, not nations. When it allies itself to an individual or to a party it may usurp for that individual or for that party. Judges can only be impeached. Taylor believes they should be removed for incompetency as well. Their proper responsibility is to the sovereignty, not to one branch of government. The executive may also corrupt the legislative branch by offering patronage. In moments of crisis the executive power overbalances everything else; therefore Taylor is suspicious of a large standing army. He relies on an effective militia which the President may use in times of common danger, and which the individual state may rely upon for its own protection when its sovereignty is threatened. It was for this reason that the Constitution provides against executive invasion of a state. The state in trouble calls upon the militia of the rest of the Union— not the executive at Washington. Both Andrew Jackson's threat and Lincoln's invasion therefore were revolutionary. Through such perversions can come the evils which corrupt men into usurping power and stealing the liberties of sovereign bodies, to be guaranteed by division of power, responsibility, and legislative purity.

This Paper-and-Patronage Aristocracy was already well entrenched by the time Taylor's books appeared as political warnings. He takes up in order of time the various interests composing this aristocracy as they manoeuvre for position. Funding and banking are the most dangerous interests to receive the legislative patronage. The funding of a depreciated continental currency and the assumption of the state debts by the central government created the means

by which a banking interest came into being. (Jefferson's administration inherited an eighty-million-dollar debt.) The funding of the
currency put into the hands of a small group of speculators the
paper by which so much property would be automatically transferred from the hands of the producers and the taxed into the
hands of the unproductive and taxing interests. That is, a branch of
the government deliberately misappropriated collective property.
As one evil begets another, funding, a temporary confiscation, established banking, a permanent instrument by which the common
wealth would be transferred to a special group. "Our mistake," he
writes, "in estimating titled nobility and paper stock is exactly that
of the mouse, terrified with the cock and charmed with the cat," for
into the hands of such an irresponsible business house the government turned over the public credit. The moment this was done the
sovereign bodies lost their most precious safeguard, and their governments abdicated in fact if not in title. The people's trustee had
given away the most important function delegated to it, for whoever
controls the public credit controls the Union; just as, to quote Taylor
again, he who receives the income from property is its actual owner.
His comment upon the specious reasoning of this aristocracy that
the increase of its wealth was an indication of a general increase is:
"Genuine public credit is enthroned not upon gold gathered by law
into a bank, but upon property distributed by industry." This is
true, but it is a half-truth, and as a half-truth it failed to redress the
grievance. Law is the means by which any rulers enforce their rule.
There will always be rulers; even Taylor's representatives and not the
people themselves were the actual rulers. The problem of government is how to get responsible rulers who, at the same time, for the
perils and labours of their functions do not charge the ruled too
dearly; who will rule, be well rewarded, but will not deprive the
subject of too great a share of the fruits of labour. To say the people
rule themselves is to beg the question. Taylor speaks of the distribution of property by industry, not law. Industry does not distribute (at
least not in his sense); it produces. A good law reserves to the
industrious the product of industry; a bad one takes it away.

Following up this strain of reasoning, he defines money: it has a
double nature; it is both good and evil. Its good moral quality
derives from its usefulness in exchanging the produce of the world.
Its evil nature arises from its facilitation of this illegitimate transfer

which he has defined as the real danger. It is the government's duty to protect the public credit by sustaining the good moral quality of money and reducing its evil nature to the minimum. He asks, if the people must be taxed by paper, why does the government itself not use paper to pay its expenses rather than turn it over, gratis, to a vicious, anti-social economic influence? It would then have, as excuse for being, the performance of a necessary act.

The Aristocracy of Paper and Patronage, having captured the public credit, was ready to begin the conquest of a continent. There were many obstacles in the way, the resources to be reduced were vast and the population which would serve their purposes was as yet small. But this aristocracy had gained the first advantage, and it was well organized. It moved at first openly and directly towards its object: the corruption of legislatures, one of Taylor's evil principles. The Yazoo Frauds consigned lands equal in area to Alabama and Mississippi to land companies who bought up the entire Georgia legislature, barring one man. But this created so much opposition that the Paper Aristocracy was driven to another method. It was not long in discovering its cue—it must move by indirection.

## PART III

To put into effect the new policy of indirection that had been forced upon it, the Aristocracy of Paper and Patronage created a magical phrase, the implied powers of the Constitution, which would, to compress Taylor's comparison, transform a modest republican wife bound by a marriage contract into a gay, painted fancy woman promising all things to those who would keep her in chalk and silk. With logical irony he compared the pretenses of implication to the strict meaning of the compact: *Powers are divided between the Federal and state departments to restrain ambitious men in both*—therefore they may be accumulated in the hands of ambitious men in one. *Confederation is Union*—so is consolidation. *Each state has a right to make its own constitution*—that is, Congress has the right to make state constitutions. *Election is the best security against unconstitutional laws for usurping powers withheld either from the Federal or state governments*—the Supreme Court is better. *A mutual right of self-preservation, both in the state and Federal departments, is the next best*—such a right in one is indispensable, in the other pernicious. *The protection of property is an end of government*—that is, it has the right to take away the property of all men and give it to one or a few. *Taxes are to be imposed for national use*—over-rich corporations and exclusive interests are part of a nation; therefore taxes must be raised to enrich them further. *The Federal department cannot constitutionally invade state rights*—it may do so at pleasure. *Congress may establish post roads*—it may make all roads. *It may make war*—that is, it may make canals. *It may dispose of public lands*—it may give them away. *It was instituted for common defense, general welfare, and to preserve the blessings of liberty*—this means, when properly construed, that it was instituted to establish monopolies, exclusive privileges, bounties, sinecures, pensions, lotteries, and to give away the public monies. *It may not tax exports*—but it may invest a capitalist interest with a power to tax them very highly and very partially for its own benefit by means of commercial restrictions which diminish their exchangeable value and foster a monopoly enhancing the prices of those necessaries which the raisers of these exports may consume. *Finally, it has the power to govern ten square miles*—that is, it may govern all the states internally, with the concurrence of the Supreme Court.

Such were the underground avenues which transferred wealth and liberty from a union of states to a small group of irresponsible self-seekers—the Paper-and-Patronage Aristocrats. The tariffs levied for fostering infant manufactures became the most sinister subterfuges invented by the materialists. They promised independence from Europe; but in fact they threw the major industry, agriculture, upon the mercy of a few hundred men. They set at odds the mechanical and agricultural labourers, without allowing the mechanics to benefit by the revenue raised, all of which was divided among the master-capitalists. And by depressing agriculture they were able to draw off workers from a living that was reasonably sure and independent to throw them into the factory where they were not even assured of subsistence. A continual drain upon agriculture must eventually destroy the mechanic, since he lives by exchanging the products of his labour for the products of farm labour.

> If a combination of a small band of land speculators [wrote Taylor] united in one interest by a small capital, might shake the Union, what

may be done by the mighty combination of banking and manufacturing capitalists, stronger in number, in influence, and united by an enormous annual income? And if a policy which must have vanished, when the uncultivated lands were exhausted, was yet an object of apprehension, ought not the same policy, which may last as long as land is cultivated and labour is exerted, to suggest some degree of foresight?

With the opening of the cotton lands and the West generally, the anxiety of the settlers to enrich themselves as quickly as possible played this section into these Eastern hands. The West believed that quick wealth would arrive by a speedy programme of internal improvements, which the East promised in return for support of the tariff. But as the West, certainly the Southwest, became more settled, it gradually came to realize that it had betrayed its lasting interest, agriculture; for the canals, improved roads, and railroads were only more speedy avenues over which its wealth flowed eastward. But the wilderness was so rich that its settlers were slow to observe into what pockets clinked the real profits of internal improvements. By the time of the Southern war for independence the Southwest had definitely allied itself with its true ally, the Southeast; the border states were confused; and the Northwest, although suspicious of the East, was tricked into a war waged to reduce its people to servitude.

The laws of nature make, according to Taylor, the most lasting unions. They are based upon geography, climate, traditional inheritance, the weather, desires, passions, interests, and numerous unknown and unknowable causes. It is upon these unpredictable phenomena that international trade is based, a trade whose laws are as mysterious as nature itself and which will eventually break down all artificial interference as well as destroy those agents who have introduced this interference in political spheres. Man may for a time violate the laws of nature, but he does so at his peril.

The symbol for commercial exchanges, the point of contact between all such unions, is free trade, the non-interference with the ebb and flow of the world's goods. In a country primarily agricultural there are three mediums responsible for its well-being: first, agriculture, the producer of certain crops which the world needs and which it can produce more economically than other countries; next, commerce, which will carry its goods in exchange for those things it desires and which it is unable to produce or must produce at great expense; thirdly, there is the merchant, the intermediary between commerce and agriculture. Supplementing these mediums, there is local manufacture (household and plantation) which is able, through the crafts of spinning and weaving, to make crude garments that will serve a basic need and act as a threat to the highly organized manufacturing nations. This is the only true independence for a nation; it is also the only realistic basis for wealth, since wealth is the enjoyment of the abundance of the earth's goods, and the more Europe imports American farm-stuffs the more of her manufactured goods must be returned in exchange; and if the manufacturing nations attempt to demand too much (an agreement between them is purely theoretical) for their wares, the agricultural nation need have no fear. It holds the strategic position from which it cannot be driven. It is the manufacturing nation grown up at the expense of its agriculture that has manoeuvred itself into a perpetual state of expediency. England is the perfect example. Its countryside has been ruined; its farmers have been driven into the cities to serve the Paper-and-Patronage Aristocracy. All of its labour goes to increase the power of this interest, an interest dependent upon the British navy, for without the navy its goods could not be impressed upon its colonies and the more primitive societies of the distant continents. The American Revolution was fought to escape from this sort of bondage, and now a deluded political philosophy is trying to fasten upon the new Union the very masters it fought to escape from. Is a tyrant more pleasing in republican clothing, Taylor asks? "Had they [the revolutionary fathers] been told that they were fighting to destroy the militia and to make agriculture food for charter and paper capital they would have discerned no reason for making themselves food for powder."

Taylor answers the loose constructionists with definition, a thing that Jefferson and his followers should have done the moment they took oath and power. Then a definition might have cut like a broadaxe; when Taylor agitated, the blade was flicked and dull. Nevertheless, he turned the stone—Congress is a precise word used to designate a congregation of deputies from independent states. If the phrase "Congress of the United States" had conveyed implied powers, it would have been useless to grant special legislative powers. Congress, through representatives, cannot exceed their delegated powers. It is upon this principle that the Congress cannot alter the terms of the Union. The word "federal" means a league between sovereign nations. The word "state" means a political community. Therefore the consolidating school takes refuge under the word "people," that word which, without limiting terms, may mean anything. If a minority of counties in a state dissent from a constitution, it is obligatory on all, because no county comprises a people politically independent. But the Constitution of the United States was only obligatory on those ratifying states because each state comprised a sovereign people; and no people existed invested with a sovereignty over the thirteen states. This brings Taylor to his conclusion: if the art of construction shall include the power of dispensing with the meaning of words and also with the most conclusive current of facts by which these words have been interpreted, it will be able, like the dispensing power of kings, to subvert any principles, however necessary to secure human happiness, and to break every ligament for tying down power to its good behaviour.

The art of construction nullifies the full connotation of representation: legislation for internal affairs must be made locally; legislators will live under the laws they make, and for this reason their legislation will conform to the true interests of the community. There was one strong safeguard against the abuse of this principle of government; it was the traditional safeguard which had for so many centuries preserved the meaning of liberty to Englishmen and which Englishmen had brought with them to the new world and which their progeny were to neglect: the militia. This militia had somehow brought the rebellion against the mother country to a successful end; it would be well used against the Indian and at New Orleans under Jackson; but its neglect in favour of a national army finally rendered representation a farce. If South Carolina had maintained its militia in a state of efficiency, that state's representatives might not have backed down before this same Jackson who had ridden to power on its back. In the last extremity a people which pretends to govern itself must base its pretensions upon a

self-discipline, for only that can make a militia efficient. One wonders if Taylor was familiar with John Dryden's Civic Guards of
Rhodes:

> *The country rings around with loud alarms,*
> *And raw in fields the rude militia swarms;*
> *Mouth without hands; maintained at vast expense,*
> *In peace a charge, in war a weak defense;*
> *Stout once a month they march, a blust'ring band,*
> *And ever, but in times of need, at hand:*
> *This was the morn, when issuing on the guard,*
> *Drawn up in rank and file they stood prepared*
> *Of seeming arms to make a short essay,*
> *Then hasten to be drunk, the order of the day.*

These lines might have been written about any county muster in the
Union. It was such a condition that caused Taylor to be concerned
for constitutional government, but not to despair. He believed that
errors might be remedied; that principles had not wandered too far
astray but that they might be returned to the pens and folds of
checks and balances. And who will say that the first quarter of the
nineteenth century was too late?

His argument, heavy with the passion only logic can confine, did
make its impression in Virginia. There his books were read as
chapters of a political bible. But outside of the state they were little
known; and only later would they influence more widely, through
indirect channels, those politicians who had inherited the failure of
the Virginia Dynasty. His prophetic warnings sounded in the sweaty
halls of democracy like the cries of Priam's oldest daughter; and like
Priam's daughter when Troy fell down, agriculture was carried into
the enemy's house as a slave. The excessive taxation—direct and,
above all, indirect—of agriculture left its farmers and planters little
or no capital to maintain the fertility of wasting fields or keep up the
necessary repairs of farming establishments. This condition has
forced landed people to live off the top-soil without allowing them
to restore to their ground its vanishing fertility. Consequently the
farmer has been brought to the condition a banker would find
intolerable, that of living off capital without replenishing it by
usury. And so the farmer since the Revolution has been driven to
hunt new grounds; exhaust them; take up others. Each westward

move (Go west, young man, go west; be a slave, young man, be a slave!) has made his debasement more complete, while the paper financiers have been enriched beyond sensible comprehension. They have held in their hands the symbols of the accumulation of a hundred years' exploitation out of a rich continent. Instead of using it as other conquerors have done, to establish their authority upon a secure basis, or expending it in great shows of pomp and luxurious revels, curious sins and evil practices, their atrophied imaginations confined them to a repetition of their practices in foreign fields. But Europe had played the game much longer, and that branch of the paper aristocracy filched in a decade the loot of a century and a half. The mathematical abstractions of this school of finance inevitably drove them to dupe themselves. They had ignored natural laws, which leads to confusion and madness. When, oblivious to reality, with hardened sensibilities, they turned to replenish the gambling purse, they found exhausted fields, exhausted moral character, hungry mobs, and banks stacked full of paper. The real wealth gone, this paper is seen in its true light, in the character given it by old Taylor a hundred-and-twenty-five years ago: a medium for transferring wealth. Since the wealth has been transferred beyond American political jurisdiction, the paper is useless and will remain idle. There are still isolated pools of riches which this paper, by its spongy nature, may absorb; but the ocean bed, for the most part, is drying sand. It will take a long time to fill up again such an immense reservoir; and it may never be filled until the paper lords, whether as the old unofficial plutocracy or as occupants of the seats of political power, have emptied the Union of its people in wars of senseless fury, hungering after the dope of abstract power to satisfy a mania so strong that only complete ruin may end it. The world is too disillusioned to believe that this interest would await the long process of nature, the long process of rebuilding a leached soil, and the longer one of restoring dignity to shattered morals by putting the citizen in possession of property which has the ancient meaning and the ancient regenerating power.

In such a triumph of the Paper Aristocracy's invisible finance may be read the defeat of Taylor and his school; but the triumph of materialism is not due altogether to its organization, nor to its skill. To understand it we must look to the principles and programmes of the Virginia Dynasty as well; and especially to Taylor, the most consistent and clearminded among them. There are three stages to his dialectic and to his political action. In all of these there are apparent contradictions which disappear under an analysis that shows the contradictions to be a change of strategy forced upon him by events and by the Virginia Dynasty. First, it has been seen that he opposed Virginia's ratification of the new Constitution, on the grounds that it meant the subversion of his state's independence by a consolidated central government. He is next seen as the defender of the Constitution whose balances would preserve to the states, and hence to Virginia, local self-government and the life he loved, leaving to Washington the management of foreign affairs. The contrariety between his early and middle opinions may be explained on the grounds of making the best of a bad bargain; and since his party had come to power, it was possible for him in good faith to hope that a strict construction might preserve, in the hands of that party, those qualities he deemed necessary to the Union. But when Jefferson, after being elected to overthrow Federalism, made but the feeblest effort to reduce the judiciary, behind which the Federalists retired as into a stronghold, Taylor allied himself to the Quids. When the Quids failed to bring the party back to principles, there was nothing left to do but, along with the others, to follow Jefferson. Half a loaf, Taylor must have argued, was better than a handful of mouldy wheat. From this time on he worked behind the scenes for Monroe, the man he expected to fulfil the principles of the Revolution, while publicly he turned out books full of argument. His last stage was that of pessimistic defiance with a threat of secession. The Missouri Compromise brought forth this alarm, as he saw the goods he had laboured for caught in a current leading directly to war. He contemptuously dismissed the slavery argument as a ruse which his old opponents were using to throw the sections for their own private ends into hostile attitudes. This party reliance on a balance of power between the sections, he announced, was nothing more than an abandonment of the Constitution and the reliance on a struggle for power which had always been and was still a tacit conflict and a prelude to real war:

I see a nation dissected into pecuniary and political corporations; legislation dabbling in the frauds it fosters, and sharing in the spoils it bestows; representation converted into personal motives, incapable of detection; legislatures sinking into exchequer spendthrifts; hordes of speculators gambling with legislative judicial patronage; for private and public property the recommendations of frugality as indispensable to the continuance of our free form of government, so often recommended, and so steadily practised by two of the wisest and most virtuous patriots [Washington and Jefferson] derided; in short, I see a picture bespangled with noxious meteors, gliding before our eyes and the admired system of government, under which we have enjoyed so much happiness.

How bitterly he must have regarded the drying ink which recorded these words in his old age, for these words admitted his failure. It has been left to this generation to discover the reasons for this defeat, a defeat which his successors have had to bear. If it were necessary to say what America needed at the end of the war with England, it should be said that America needed leaders of a counter-revolution. The revolt against tradition had been going on in England for a long time; and whereas the Americans revolted against the revolters against tradition in attempting to redress the plight to which these revolters had brought them, like the leeches of the time they let blood instead of taking off the sucker. The difference between the Federalists and the Republicans was superficial; they both were concerned with the income of industry. The Federalists believed that the talented, the strong, but above all the shrewd should receive the greatest part, making all others render up a part of their goods to this class of individuals whom Taylor named the Paper-and-Patronage Aristocracy. The Republicans, under Jefferson, believed that, with most of the population living on the land, men should be left as much of their earnings as possible. What they did with these earnings, or rather what they did with the property on which these earnings were made, seemed not to concern them; and yet this was the crux of the situation. In this way the English revolution was to be repeated on American soil, the Republicans with their agrarian doctrines representing the earlier, therefore the more stable stage of revolution against mediaevalism, the Paper-and-Patronage school the urbanized and more chaotic stage. Because the Republicans represented this earlier stage of revolt, it contained much more that was traditional, formal, and stable. But Jefferson and Taylor went much farther than the Whig nobles who began by conniving with the Tudors for the Church lands—with the result that their sons and grandsons were able to wrest the power of kingship from the Stuarts. Jefferson wrote some mighty pretty words: life, liberty, and the pursuit of happiness; and in their name he destroyed the Church and primogeniture, the high tower and strong rock of traditional society. The concern of the leaders of America's revolution should have been, what kind of life? what basis for liberty?—and then there would have been no further need for a pursuit of happiness.

Traditional elements existed in both parties. It must not be forgotten that Washington and General Lee's father, great landowners both, were Federalists. It might be argued that the beginning of the conflict had the following setup: the Republicans, traditionally speaking, were composed of the yeomen, the intimates of the soil; the Federalists, of the rich landowners whose duty it is to protect the soil and keep it in good state, culturally and politically. Therefore each party contained a large body of opinion which was strictly conservative. But each had disintegrating alloys; the Republicans with the propertyless democracy of the cities, the tools of a plutocracy, as allies; the Federalists, the new capitalist financier whose concept of property had less in common with the land-owning branch of the party than these land-owners had with men like Taylor, Randolph, and Jefferson. The great landowners, furthermore, were to let their conservative sense of the land's meaning be confused by the financier's; and the Republican conservative let his principles be compromised by liberal abstractions.

These impure principles forced John Taylor, a large planter and owner of slaves, a thorough aristocrat in tastes and discipline, into calling himself the economic familiar of the artisan and clerk of the city. It deluded him into his support of the attack on primogeniture, which would make it impossible for his descendants to continue his way of life, just as the separation of state and church would render them agnostics, humanitarians, or brothers in the Y.M.C.A. The appearance of Andrew Jackson, the land speculator, as the leader of this rootless democracy both of country and city, clarified the issue in the next quarter of the century. He came forward as the defender of the plain man, the little man everywhere in the Union; but his defence was that the little man might have an opportunity to grow rich, to exploit the riches of the wilderness as well as the Eastern financier. Although in the South and West there was a social democracy behind him, he must bear his share of blame for reducing this democracy to the state of landless tenants and helpless workers in mill and office.

It was at this time that true conservatism manifested itself in the Carolina school of statesmen. Hammond, Harper, Dew, Fitzhugh, Rhett, and Calhoun denied the early liberalism and attempted to bring about a union of all conservative elements towards the establishment of a complete society. They failed, partly because they rested their defence, in crises, upon the sovereignty of states. Affairs had so clarified themselves by the 1830's that the true strategy was in the regional concept. Using the analogy of military tactics, they loosed the offensive by brigades instead of by corps. Even after secession, as Dr. Frank Owsley's *State Rights and the Confederacy* so clearly shows, the antiquated states' rights destroyed the very things its apologists sought to set up.

At a crucial moment the over-developed political instincts of Taylor and other leaders misled them into believing and acting upon the belief that the Constitution, a political contract, could take the place of all those traditional institutions which make for an abundant and complete life; and when the next generations tried to correct this eccentricity, their failure was already foretold. The doctrine of union spread; then broke under the strain of the religious, patriotic, and conflicting cultural functions with which it was loaded and which it could never, because of its limited form, assimilate or carry. But while this belief lasted, it gave some form to a common life. It localized the trouble and made it possible to be dealt with. Now the disease of a "higher law" is scattered through the whole body politic, and the protection of what is good and permanent in American life is left to the disconnected efforts of noble individuals of humanistic education on the right hand and the left-handed action of humanitarianism, of which the latest example is "planning," raised to some dignity by its inclusion in the heterodox policies of the present Administration. The degeneration has proceeded apace. Taylor, a farmer, did not weaken his position by limiting his defence to agriculture. He defended those principles necessary for the happiness of the whole state, for only in such a state could agriculture prosper. If in the end this defence failed, it was because it did not try to re-establish those different estates and permanent institutions which make for a spiritual unity. It is such guards and only such that tradition must set up against natural chaos always a-pounding upon the doors of society.

# The Backwoods Progression

THE American backwoods is unique in history. It is the one feature, along with pioneering, that is common to the different sections of this no longer commonly-minded country. It is, in fact, the only common ancestor, for pioneering and settling are the successive stages of one movement. This is especially true of the early period in the great Southwest when the pioneer would settle, pull up his stakes, and settle again. And for Americans today, on those rare moments when they consider the past, the backwoods citizen, partly nomadic, partly agricultural, alone has any real meaning. His qualities of sheer physical strength, self-possession, and courage have been abstracted into a state of mind which gives directly to the big business man his ruthless drive, to the gangster a cruel realism, and to the walkers of asphalt a vicarious feeling of power which readily makes them tools of those who possess power. And his reported self-confidence and will to liberty have injected into the nation's foreign policy a strange combination of arrogance, naïveté, and greed—a combination which has regularly made our foreign office the dupe of astute European politicians. Because of this backwoods-pioneering figure's singular importance to us, he will probably epitomize North American civilization for world history as the crusader epitomizes Christian Feudalism. Such habits of mind and body were noble qualities for the backwoodsman; without them he would have perished; but as our only inheritance from the past, this backwoods spirit in its modern manifestation denotes a diseased body politic, a case of arrested growth in the public mind which forbids the establishment of any economic, political, or social stability.

It seems proper, at this time, when those mediums by which our common life was held together have broken down almost entirely, to examine into the historical implications of this legacy. When everybody lived in the woods, the term backwoods defined a peculiar sort of isolation, almost a half-savage autonomy. It was a fringe of near-anarchy to the agrarian society of Colonial times. Its contemporaneous meaning for the ruling gentry was a sort of lubberland. While running the line between Virginia and North Carolina, that English gentleman, William Byrd, commented that those backwoodsmen made

> their wives to rise out of their beds early in the Morning, at the same time that they lye and Snore, till the sun has run one third of his course, and disperst all the unwholesome Damps. Then, after Stretching and Yawning for half an Hour, they light their Pipes, and, under the Protection of a cloud of Smoak, venture out into the open air; tho' if it happens to be never so little cold, they quickly return Shivering into the Chimney corner. When the weather is mild, they stand leaning with both their arms upon cornfield fences, and gravely consider whether they had best go and take a Small Heat at the hough; but generally find reasons to put off til another time. Thus they loiter away their Lives, like Solomon's Sluggard, with their arms across, and at the Winding up of the Year Scarcely have Bread to Eat. To speak the Truth, tis a thorough Aversion to Labor that makes People file off to N. Carolina, where Plenty and a Warm Sun confirm them in their Disposition to Laziness for their whole Lives.

Undoubtedly a great part of this first American backwoods was made up of such men: escaped indentured servants, men who were tired of living on poor lands, criminals, hunters, the nondescript. But this universal fear of falling under Virginian rule cannot be set down to congenital lassitude. "A thorough Aversion to Labor" is too glib a definition to fit the case. The backwoodsman's fears of aristocratic Virginia has a more profound significance. When so many appear lazy, the matter is not with the individual but with society; and the matter with Colonial society was the Tory gentleman's rule. Byrd voices the contempt held always by the oppressor for the oppressed. Change the antique spelling and it will at once become evident how closely his remarks resemble the current criticisms made by the city man about the farmer. The ploughman's bankruptcy, economic and spiritual, is laid to shiftlessness and ignorance, cardinal sins in the aggressive man's eye, to be punished by a most thorough exploitation.

The Colonial backwoods was the extension of an advanced stage of a European revolution; and the Colonial gentleman, like his English counterpart, was the agent of these disrupting forces which had been at work since the sixteenth century. The gradual disintegration of Feudalism, hastened by Henry VIII's lust, broke down by degrees the forms of the estates, reducing the Kingdom's subjects to the unrestrained mercy of the ruling will or wills, since power quickly slipped from mitre and sceptre. In feudal England the sovereignty had rested in Heaven; the King was God's overseer. But as the influence of the Church declined, he ceased to be the suzerain; dropped upon the defensive; and attempted to retain his position by absorbing in his private character the powers of sovereignty. This change progressed very rapidly through the Tudors, until rule by Divine Right took on with the Stuarts a very personal meaning. This house acted as if God had made it a present of the three kingdoms. Such a psychological change in the nature of the kingship would not have been understood before the Wars of the Roses. But certain sixteenth-century noble houses and most of the seventeenth-century commoners were quick to learn. The successful demands by these houses for a share in the church property confiscated by Henry VIII made their position in the State so strong that they were able to challenge the King's power. In the past the Church had seen to it that ambitious barons did not upset the social equilibrium; but there was no check now from distant Rome, and since the Church in England was responsible no longer to God but to the Government, those who might dictate its policies owned the British Isles as a cotton-planter owned his bale of cotton. This struggle with the Tudors and Stuarts, culminating in the Stuarts' overthrow, was the struggle with the king as a powerful individual over the new meaning of money. By the time of the Whig revolution of 1688 the idea of the State had completely changed in the English world.

The vanity of the Squirearchy and the upper yeomanry proved as great as that of the nobles and princes, until every beef-eating Englishman was saying, in imitation of Louis XIV, "I, too, am the State!"; and the Presbyterian and Puritan ethical societies made the logical transference of God's beneficence to their lay concerns. To say that the State exists for private property is to say that it exists for the private will. It then follows that any individual who is cunning enough, or powerful enough, or lucky enough, may make of the State, of a group of States, or even of the world, a possession answerable to the commands of his desire. This is the old war against the gods. Out of it came the moral revolution that changed the mediaeval concept of the economic commodity from the thing-to-be-used to the thing-to-be-sold: the revolution at the bottom of the anarchy of the modern world.

The enclosure of the lands common to landlord and peasant took away the basis for the peasant's economic freedom; and when the North American continent was discovered (the world was now a thing-to-be-sold), it served as a refuge for the disaffected and a new field to conquer for men already masters of the technique of conquest. It was against this exploitation that the backwoods in the new world, where the land to the West was plentiful, grew darkly on the fringe of Colonial society, for the Colonial backwoodsman was not one of the conquerors. He was fleeing from them—from the same sort of domestic conqueror he had encountered in the old world. For a land to be invaded as the Normans invaded Britain may result in a cultural metamorphosis. But the backwoods is evidence of decay.

At the same time, the Colonies themselves were large blocks of the English backwoods; and out of this condition of private exploitation came the American Revolution. The English Parliament, serving certain interests, did not have the imagination to visualize the temper of a people whose spirit of self-dependence had not been broken and could not be broken so long as there was plenty of unoccupied land. Because of this tremendous economic fact the exploiting gentry in the old world and their Tory allies in the new lost a continent. Liquors carry in their dregs the concentrated flavor of the drink; and the dregs of revolutionary society meant to share in the distribution of the continent. Their dissatisfaction with the Tory rule, shown explicitly in their fear of the Order of the Cincinnati, now took form in new theories of government springing from the natural-rights school. These theories crystallized around a new party, the early Republicans. Those who sought to continue the system of exploitation quickly formed a party, the Federalists, in opposition to the so-called Mob demands.

It was apparent that wise leaders could put this discontent with the old rule to noble uses. Jefferson came forward, and for one precious moment he and his supporters had it in their power to correct the mistakes of the Whig revolt of 1688. But Jefferson's political philosophy turned out to be inadequate to the changed set of circumstances; his strategy worse, although tactically he often displayed brilliance. His line of attack was an abstraction, the right to life, liberty, and the pursuit of happiness. The Federalists opposed to this a concrete, well-organized array of property rights. The weak point in Jefferson's defense was his own belief in a distorted conception of property, albeit a specific kind, landed property and the kind of life it supported. This meant that his political activity concerned itself fundamentally with the same thing the Federalists espoused: the principle that the chief duty of the State is the protection of the property of individuals and aggregates of individuals. This is certainly one duty of government, but only as a means of guaranteeing the security and self-perpetuation of the family. Prohibiting kings, then allowing private citizens to own the State is certainly hopping from a very slow pan to a very hot fire. Instead of laying the broad foundations a State needs to rest upon— and these foundations are best laid upon the dogma of one religion—he raised the question as to which will, the middle-class or the agrarian, would own the continent.

He did not intend this. He hoped to produce a stable farming society, predominantly yeoman, in which the head of every family might be assured of an independent living for his dependents and the promise of security for his posterity. Much of Jefferson's special legislation—especially the abandonment of primogeniture and the separation of Church and State—contradicted his general idea and obstructed the establishment of the agrarian State. He placed his faith in a central government which would be the trustee for a league of free commonwealths, a trustee which would interfere as little as possible with the private wills, the yeoman Olympuses, scattered throughout the sovereign States. He managed to destroy the Federalist Party but incorporated, because of this faulty strategy, its most dangerous elements into the Republican ranks. And so the balance between the State governments and the central government, within the central government itself, was never definitely secured. By placing this security in the hands of delegates who had only their political acumen to protect them from the more concerted middle-class designs, he postponed settlement to the future. Before his death he was to see the enemy dressing in the garment of free government to overcome more easily its principles. Like all eighteenth-century liberals he and his chief lieutenants were confused. The temporal policies of a Church which had been thrown down had perplexed their minds on religion and its corruption. It is difficult to know how far an individual is responsible for the times and the times are responsible for the individual. The scriptural admonition makes a partial answer: "For it must needs be that offenses come; but woe to that man by whom the offense cometh."

But with revolutionary grants in their pockets, confident in their new power, great bodies of Jefferson's followers marched upon the Western wilderness. The words "life, liberty, and the pursuit of happiness" rang through the legislative halls at Philadelphia; but life, property, and the pursuit of wealth gleamed in the eyes of these adventurers. This was the beginning of the great period of pioneering. The movement grew to tremendous proportions, re-enforced by Scotch-Irish and German immigrants and by Easternshore planters whose lands had become exhausted by an extravagant cultivation. There were numerous hazards: the Indians, the French and Spanish intrigues, drought, hunger, and the crouching panther. But most formidable of all, was the hazard which they did not visualize—that postponed issue: where would the power ultimately lie, in the Eastern cities or on the Western and Southern farms?

The lower Mississippi basin and the region north of the Ohio now became the West. In a remarkably short time farms and plantations appeared in the wilderness, and the new ground stumps remained to tell of the conquest. Two backwoods grew up: the local backwoods, and the West as the backwoods of the nation. The first was made up of those men who had lost out in the scramble for the best land. These men, in the main, were thrust into the mountains and upon barren soils—although the "Barrens" were later shown to have adequate fertility for a good living. Because of frontier conditions, there was at this early time little difference in the way of life between these and the more fortunate land-grabbers. Everybody was on the make, and no man questioned his destiny. This first group would become conscious of a backwoods status as the pioneering ways were polished away and the planter stood out to define the form of polity growing from frontier chaos. But it is the West as backwoods, as an agrarian state of mind, opposed to the middle-class state of mind, that is the concern of this essay. On account of Republican failure, from now until the War between the North and South, the West would struggle to hold its conquests against the rising power of the new capitalism.

As this struggle over the nature of American society increased with a population pushing back the Colonial boundaries, the two opposing schools began to head up in sections. The South and West became predominantly agricultural. The East, because of its sea-port cities, and later its industrial towns, became the base for capitalist operations. At an early stage it became evident that the South, with its intelligent planting class, would furnish the leadership for an agrarian school. The West, still in a transitional stage, divided, according to the interest of the moment, its allegiance. But since it was primarily a farming section, ultimately its proper course would be to ally itself with the South, unless by shortsightedness it should make an Eastern alliance, an alliance which would begin with the appearance of a partnership but would inevitably end by making of the West a creature of the bankers and capitalists. At the turn of the century the field was set. The first six decades marked the periods of this, the most critical phase of the struggle.

The settlers, as they passed by large bodies of fertile Western land owned by speculators in the older states, were faced at the outset with the tactics of the enemy. The Yazoo fraud, an attempt to steal the states of Alabama and Mississippi from Georgia, showed how little the delegated authority of the people might be trusted. But it also showed the backwoods what kind of leadership it might rely upon. John Randolph of Roanoke, the aristocratic planter, not Jefferson the political theorist, rose up as the defender of the faith. He understood that the success of this fraud would imperil those institutions which offered security to the farming life, for the fraud meant traffic in the public domain at the expense of the people for the aggrandizement of the few. This was no Federalist ghost he was raising from the grave. Without his strenuous and sustained attack upon these speculators in millions of acres they would undoubtedly have succeeded in their designs, for they brought to bear upon the

Government the strongest pressure. Jefferson had hamstrung himself with the all-Federalist-all-Republican doctrine. He undoubtedly meant that all were to be Republicans; but the fraud, spreading even to his cabinet, told another meaning. At the time, Randolph was spokesman for Jefferson in the House. This meant that he had to buck his own Party, a Party as completely at the call of the executive as it is now under Roosevelt. His rigid defense of principle was at the expense of his career; and later, when he tried to uphold the dignity of the legislative branch and curtail the growing power of the executive—to preserve the fine state of balances in the Constitution—he practically prepared for his political suicide. He could not be read out of the Party, because his principles were ostensibly those of the Republicans; but from this time on he was gradually thrown upon his own. He remained powerful for the next ten years, and he was feared. Never did those measures which tended to sacrifice principle to expediency go unchallenged by him: the embargoes, standing armies, war, speculation, and the tariffs. He had seen, from the beginning, "the poison under the wing" of the American eagle. His long, withering finger struck terror to the hearts of many men; but it fell limp and helpless before that dangerous Federalist, John Marshall, seated on the Chief Justice's bench. Randolph overthrew the Yazoo men; but in overthrowing them, he divided a strength needed later to preserve the idea of the Union as a partnership between sovereign states.

In trying to keep the Ship of State afloat during squalls from foreign parts, Jefferson and Madison neglected domestic principles, until dissension spread into mutiny. The embargoes and later the War of 1812 ruined New England's shipping and turned her capital towards manufacturing. At the conclusion of hostilities the factories demanded protection. The depleted currency and the debt contracted to prosecute the war made the richest ground for patronage, a National Bank, and the sectional taxation of the Southern planter and farmer. Randolph had foretold these conditions with Cassandra-like prophecies. The metamorphosis of prophecy into reality took place before the eyes of the backwoods wing with magical speed. The task which would absorb the energies of the Constitutional defenders for the next forty years lost its opacity, and the added difficulties became apparent by degrees. The crib door had been left open and its lock broken. It would require heroic exertions to fasten it again, after the stock had found where the corn was stored and rats had slipped in to nest and breed. Randolph found an ally in the person of John Taylor of Caroline County, Virginia. They became the two most powerful figures in the backwoods camp for the first twenty years of the new century. Calhoun, a young man just entering political life, should have stood beside the conservatives. Instead he and Clay became the lights of the Administration and the foremost instigators for war. Randolph said one day to a friend, "They have entered this House with their eye on the Presidency, and mark my words, sir, we shall have war before the end of the session!"

Taylor redefined the conflict and put the issues where they belonged, between the agronomy of the Union and the incipient industrialism of the East. In answer to John Adams, who had proposed a balance between aristocracy, monarchy, and the Third Estate as the means of giving security to the State, he replied that such a balance no longer applied. The only real danger now was from what Taylor termed the aristocracy of the third age: a rule of paper and patronage. In his *Inquiry into the Principles and Policy of the Government of the United States* he posited the "confession" of this aristocracy:

> Our purpose is to settle wealth and power upon a minority. It will be accomplished by a national debt, paper corporations, and offices, civil and military. These will condense king, lords, and commons, a monied faction, and an armed faction, in one interest. This interest must subsist upon another, or perish. The other interest is national, to govern and pilfer, which is our object; and its accomplishment consists in getting the utmost a nation can pay. Such a state of success can only be maintained by armies, to be paid by the nation and commanded by this minority, by corrupting talents and courage; by terrifying timidity, by inflicting penalties on the weak and friendless, and by distracting the majority with deceitful professions. That with which our project commences, is invariably a promise to get a nation out of debt; but the invariable effect of it is, to plunge it irretrievably into debt.

This precise summation of the exploiting-capitalistic policy was to need no new terms for a hundred years. It will serve today as the basic premises which inform this interest's action.

This "confession" was published in 1814. Another treatise, *Tyranny Exposed,* points out in detail the fallacy of the manufacturers' report calling for more manufacturing and higher protection. In these volumes and others Taylor states the exact grounds of conflict between the two theories of society, dismissing irrelevant and confusing arguments. He makes the philosophical defense of agrarianism; but it is because it is a philosophical defense that it fails. His truth, that good government cannot come from bad moral principles and that the American centralizing principle is bad (as it certainly was at that time) cannot be denied; but like Jefferson, he fails to offer a medium by which the bad may be destroyed and the good set up and maintained. He can only appeal to the intelligence of the voter for the remedy. Liberalism inevitably used the terms good and bad. It needed, as a fighting cry, virtue triumphing over evil. Cromwell's leadership was shrewder. He did not concentrate on discussions of the morality of the Stuarts. He threw his Ironsides against the devil's agents.

Although philosophy proved a handicap to Jefferson, Taylor, and men of their class, the form of the plantocracy, given a tremendous impetus by the rise of cotton and the spread of negro slavery into the West, shaped Southern and Southwestern society into a feudalism, greatly different from European feudalism, but preserving the inertia and fixing the form so that the European tradition could be preserved. The planter ceased to be the small farmer's oppressor as in Colonial days. The conditions had changed. He had now an alien race to serve him. His interest was identical with that of the small farmer and the plain man generally, since they all were the objects of capitalistic exploitation. And the plain men, or dog-run class—a name taken from the form of dwelling universally used by this class—furnished vigorous recruits to the plantocracy. The vocabulary of the gentleman gradually changed from that of liberalism to a speech more proper to his social rôle, the rôle of the First Estate. The planter stood in place of the feudal lord; the general movement in the place of the suzerain; and the Jeffersonian farmer in the place of the yeoman. These lines had become so generally fixed by 1830 as to be officially announced through the Pro-Slavery arguments of Dew, Harper, Hammond, and others. So, in spite of the fact that liberalism made the effort to found a State on capitalistic private property, a Southern nation began slowly to grow up in the changing Union.

But this growth into a social and spiritual unity continued, until the South's destruction, to be retarded by the handicaps which have been discussed. Its blind devotion to the Union would lead Northern politicians to say that it could not be kicked out. It was thrown on the defensive from the beginning, and its only hope of survival was an intelligently directed offence. Its churches were brought together on the matter of slavery, but its politicians never could agree upon any common action. While tariffs and the criticisms of its institutions tended to emphasize for the West its bond with the South, under Clay's advice the West was so eager to develop that it gave heavy support to the centralizing interests in return for subsidies and internal improvements. When the South-West eventually found out that these gifts from a consolidated government were intended, like the corn thrown out to the hogs, to make the killing more profitable, it was too late to do more than reflect upon its own stupidity. The two most persistent and effective attacks against the backwoods were made by means of the tariffs and abolition, the one economic, the other moral. Protection was first in time, although the abolition agitation was soon coupled with it when it became apparent that the tariffs alone would not destroy the South. South Carolina, under the prompting of such men as Rhett and Hammond, made such active opposition that the great leader of the state, Calhoun, abandoned his nationalistic stand and proposed his Nullification theory of redress. Andrew Jackson's romantic idea of the Union and his dislike of Calhoun joined together in his stubborn mind to play him into the hands of the enemy. Although he had destroyed the National Bank, he threatened to send troops into Carolina to make tariff collections. For a moment war seemed inevitable; but Henry Clay came forward with a compromise. Calhoun accepted it. The Congress voted favourably on Jackson's force bill, and voted to reduce the tariff. Two great blows to State rights were struck at once. The South got temporary relief, and for this relief agreed to a sacrifice of principle. There can be no compromise between two antithetical ways of life. What appears a compromise is a postponement of the issue. The South, by accepting this postponement, doomed itself to ruin. The high prejudices of his heart and a limited political vision led Jackson to squander the great strategic moment by which his backwoods could have established its rule. Like a good backwoodsman, he took "the responsibility" and

Calhoun refused it; but the South, not Calhoun or Jackson, suffered the consequences.

There was after this only one avenue left open to the South—secession. Calhoun still hoped to concentrate Southern leadership and make the fight within the Union. But his plans of effecting his ends by controlling the Democratic Party failed. With desperation he took up a last position, secession through the common action of all the Southern States. But Clay's American plan—an extension of capitalism—and his compromises, the god of all opportunists, had done their work. In this crisis Calhoun's chief lieutenant, Robert Barnwell Rhett, proposed a policy of coercion. He contended that if one State acted separately, the other States, all believing in their own sovereignty, would follow the lead. He supported his contention by reminding his political peers that the revolt against England did not take place until the tea had been thrown into Boston Harbour. When common action did take place, it came about by South Carolina's single-handed withdrawal; but it came ten years too late and brought Appomattox, not independence.

The fall of the Confederacy removed the last great check to the imperialism of Big Business. The Northwest, having been induced to aid in the overthrow of its natural ally, was to pay for this action by its servility to Eastern capital. The Northern Democrats, who had been naïve enough to think they had been fighting for the Union, began to renew their connections with the Southern branch of the Party. This reunion would have turned the government over to the Democratic will. The Radical Republicans saw at once the "fruits of victory" about to vanish into air; so they set to work again the reliable abolition propaganda and spread the news that the planter was reenslaving the Negro. This brought popular support to the radical reconstruction programme and allowed Stevens to disfranchise the white South and enfranchise the Negro. The Negro was told his freedom would last as long as he voted the Republican ticket. In this way the South became a pocket borough for the capitalist party; and the Northern Democrats discovered for whom they had been fighting the War. But the white South was not to be reduced so easily. Out of economic, political, and social chaos, under the sting of defeat, in the face of a victorious enemy, and with troops quartered in the land, it recaptured the machinery of government through the Ku Klux Klan and re-established its control. It was the last and the most remarkable display of political genius its planting feudalism would show.

But victory was only temporary. The capitalist interest, with its railroads through the Far West and its growing industrial enterprises, was able to consolidate its gains and begin that conquest of the North American continent which had been so long delayed. Its tactics were simple and effective. They were relearned from Clay who had absorbed them from the Biddles of his day: hold out a lure of wealth; allow a few to gain it; and the rest, with this will-o'-the-wisp before their eyes, will be satisfied with the system and lend it support with their labours and talents. Not for one moment did the real power slip from the hands of those who intended to keep it.

Such was the policy the capitalists carried into the war-exhausted South and, having failed in supplanting the whites, they began to corrupt them. A New South, repudiating the beliefs and economy of the Old, was expounded from the platforms which had once heard the call of States Rights and Secession. Southern men like Henry Grady, Lanier, Watterson, and the young men who listened to them, counselled the South to get on the bandwagon. The Democratic Party abandoned its original principles and played the underdog at the rich man's table, grabbing what crumbs it could. It was reduced to making gestures against the exploitation which it was unable to curb: power is the twin brother of wealth, and wealth no longer belonged to agrarian descendants. Cities grew, industrial not cultural cities; farming population diminished. Henry George, in an effort to check the business, aroused a momentary flare of rebellion with his concept of land as common property; but he was too late to do more than cry the ruin of the experiment in liberty. The Populist Party, grounding itself on too scant a foundation, quickly subsided into defeat. Both efforts were the laboured, violent gasps of death. The mortal injury had been done in 1865.

The full significance of what had happened and what was happening was not understood at the time. There was still plenty of empty land into which the dispossessed might go. But in the meantime the shores of the Pacific have been reached. It is no longer possible for a general migration to get under way in an effort to escape the dominant factor in American civilization. Nevertheless, the backwoods still rises up, although the trees are little in evidence. It is not trees which define the backwoods. They were the physical

properties, along with the Indians, the wild animals, and the treach-
erous rivers, which once formed the setting. Today it is different.
There is, indeed, no setting. The backwoods of a full-fledged industrial society is without location. The long hunter's shadow has
ceased to glide upon the bending prairie grass but his spiritual heir,
the tramp, on wheels, on foot, is always in motion, driven without
direction because there is no longer any place to go.

But the tramp is only the symbol for the outcasts created by the
paper system. All those who have been discarded, who have been
supplanted by the increase of machines, who consciously rebel
against the slavery of technology; the unemployed of factory, mill,
and farm; and, in a small degree, the hangers-on in the moun-
tainous districts—all Ishmaels thrown upon the constantly changing scene, driven by a vague nostalgia to wander upon the face of a
continent—it is these who make up the mass of this century's backwoodsmen. As their numbers increase, their rulers become more
baffled. Their frame of mind is dangerously close to that of the
Tory gentleman's.

And a situation similar to that which destroyed the Tory gentleman is generating itself again. The middle-class concept of property has triumphed in a far grander way than Hamilton ever
dreamed it would. But the increasing confusion which follows its
swelling up indicates inevitable failure. The State, through which a
people expresses its destiny, cannot stand on such a basis. Property
no more makes a State than a bed makes a marriage. Man begins to
think he is a god, but he has only unshackled his will. A curious,
modern Prometheus, he has stolen no living but an abstract fire;
and all the energy of his filched knowledge must go to replenish a
liver, food for the insatiable appetite of Time the Vulture, drawn to
the jailrock by the odour of the crime. Like the successful pick-
pocket the modern industrialist lives by his wits. He dreams and
boasts of riding the four million horses of power. If he were not
blinded by this delusion, he would see that he had seated himself
upon the back of the communal flying jennet, whose wooden tail
and mane are given to an abstract breeze. Others of like mind he
sees to his front, seated safely in a chariot or gleefully on a pig that
does not squeal. Around and around they go, until the machine
stops.

The common admiration for the ambitious man and the contempt for the unambitious come to us as direct results. The ideal of progress promises so much that he who refuses to enter the race is only a craven, puny being who must be thrust quickly into the ranks, where he can be used. One must use, or be used. The myth of the backwoodsman rises from the past and hovers near, an inspiration to encourage the modern American when the fight grows hard. This ancestral giant reduced the strongholds of nature, the endless woods of gloomy oak and impenetrable cane; he rode upon the surface of wilderness rivers; he crushed the Indians; he cleared away forests and planted seedbeds around the slow rotting stumps. If he did these things, might not his descendants crush obstacles just as great, riding the backs of the proletariat and the farmer?

The ancient capitalist policy of "corrupting talents and courage . . . terrifying timidity . . . inflicting penalties on the weak and friendless . . . distracting the majority with deceitful professions" has finally reduced the Southern scene to a unit of the general scene—but with a difference. Historically it is still the seat of opposition. It has become the fashion to forget this; but fashions change; tradition lodges in the blood. That is to say, tradition holds to the great body of people who live according to custom and not in chameleon style. It is no more possible for Southern people to remove this element of their tradition than it would be for certain of their old and distinguished families to open their arteries and let out the tainted African blood which for generations has commingled democratically and darkly with the purer strains. The words of its local industrial leaders which deny this tradition are empty words. They can never extract it from Southern consciousness. Leader is not the term to apply to these modern strong men and their literary and scholarly sycophants. They are the modern scalawags who have cut themselves off from the country-side and withdrawn into the cities, where they openly acknowledge their servile dependence upon New York. For a small share of the booty, comparable to the share of the cotton crop formerly allowed to the overseer by the planter, they have either consciously or unconsciously become the sucking mouths of those industrial octopuses whose long arms wrap about the "provinces."

Whatever they have done to this section economically, they have not succeeded in emasculating it spiritually. As long as the great body of people, still living chiefly in the country, feel that there is something about the South which no other section can claim; as long as its people go, though stumblingly, in the ways of their fathers; in different language, as long as tradition, sullen and inarticulate, continues to flow through their cultural expression, it remains possible that at some future date circumstance may produce genuine leadership which will express this feeling of separate destiny. And then such leaders may not fail as Jefferson, as Randolph, as Taylor, as Calhoun, as Jefferson Davis, failed. The recent fall of its hereditary enemy, the Republican party, may mean much or nothing. Mr. Roosevelt's attempt to give security to the economic life of this country has not, as yet, had time to show its effect. But unless he succeeds in destroying the great moneyed interests and reestablishing the farming classes in their former dignity and independence, his concentration of power in the executive branch will only facilitate the establishment of a servile state.

But if the ascendency of the middle class has not destroyed the agrarian South, it has done it great damage. The share-cropping relation between landlord and tenant was an effort, after the war, to bind together what seemed a disintegrating world. Industrialism has made it the worst sort of tyranny, for unfortunately emancipation did not free the Negro. It merely rendered the landlord impotent, enslaving both classes by substituting the money economy for the planting agronomy—economic foundations of great difference in meaning for society, in spite of the fact that the planter grew to power from the factory demand for cotton. What set him apart from the industrial mechanism was his feudal organism which could produce for consumption even while producing for exchange. If it had not been disrupted by war, it would have stood without strikes, or unemployment, even if the demand for cotton had failed.

But the share-cropping system is not feudal. In spite of its barter element it is fundamentally industrial. It is built almost entirely around the money crop. The only thing in common between the different participants is money, which means that there are several elaborate medias of mutual exploitation. The planter is able through the furnishing system to make it impossible for the tenant to do more than make a bare living. On the other hand the tenant, to protect himself, has learned a most intricate method of theft. And no family will attempt to take care of land some other family may farm next season. But it goes further than this. The landlord soon finds himself in the hands of the local banker, who is dependent upon a larger banker, who, in turn, is dependent upon the New York clearing house. This is the final commentary upon the early effort to establish a State upon private wills. But even so, the relation between the man who owns the land and the man who rents it has much of the old-time goodwill. And when an injustice is protested or a trade is made the two parties have the great advantage of being able to see each other and discuss such subjects in person.

Another important economic and social loss has occurred. Before the war the sturdy Jeffersonian yeomanry furnished its best men to enlarge the planting class. Now the best are drawn away from the country, going either to the Northern or to the Southern city, the one being about as bad as the other. Those of this class who are left on the land have largely lost their independent position by moving in as tenants on the modern plantations. The small farmer has by no means disappeared, however. There are many of them scattered over the South who still work for themselves. Although they have become implicated in the system, they manage to live with a reasonable amount of security. They have their money crops, but in times of depression they naturally tend to spend more hours on making a living and less on the more hazardous production of these crops. So long as they can feed, warm, house, and clothe their families, they practice a partial freedom. At least they may expect more security than any other branch of the industrial army. However, their position in the State is always hazardous, for they exercise so little control over the machinery of government that the defeat of the internationally-minded bankers would carry them along in the common ruin.

The prevailing concept of private property prohibits the middle-class moneyed princes from becoming rulers in any sense except in the possession of an irresponsible power. Their economics are bad; their morals worse; and their common sense has long been dead. The recent depression has shown how puny are their hands when the four million wild horses get out of control. The nearest that they come to social usefulness is an eccentric philanthropy, and this philanthropy must inevitably remain unsocial because of its private and whimsical nature. It is not a power which resides in the body of the people, delegated to the rulers for the common good; nor a power handed down from a society resting in the Godhead of some religion. It is a power transferred from the people to individuals, until the state has become not a protector of private property everywhere but a protector of a few men who have monopolized an impersonalized wealth. Having once become "mastered," this wealth becomes a monster apart from its owners, though driving them. There is never any rest, for the greater it becomes the greater grows the number of those who would change places with those who nominally control it. The man is nothing. The thing is everything. In this lies its inevitable destruction, and in this lies the germ of the universal condition of servitude that logically follows the breakdown of the capitalist state. For this reason the Socialist or Communist state is not at all "radical" but a rationalization of the drift of the present system, though in this country there are indications that we may skip a communistic or socialistic polity and be metamorphosed into the Caesarian condition of servility.

The New England elders, the patroons, and the Tory gentlemen of the South had an outward fringe of people for their backwoods. This aristocracy of paper has a section, the South, for its backwoods. It is as confused, as inchoate, as apparently degraded as those inhabitants of William Byrd's lubberland; but though it may "lye and Snore," it is still potentially powerful. It represents the only group of states in this country with enough form left to shake off their lethargy when the walls of steel and concrete tumble down upon our heads; when the electric webs break loose from their poles to dart and sting like scorpions.

# PART II

# STEADY WORK

# R. E. Lee

MANY years must pass before the general history of the great war of the sixties is written, before ultimate judgment may assess the relative value of the leading performers; even before the meaning of victory and defeat can be taken. Already much work has been done on the campaigns in the east, but this present biography[1] of the Confederacy's first general will stand for a long while as the last word on his military performance. And this word has a larger implication than the narrative of other army commanders. The definitive lives of Lee and Jackson, but especially of Lee, mark the final record of Southern defense in the east. And because of the great strength of his name and his genius for victory, in the darkest hours of the last months, Lee defined Confederate resistance for the Southern nation. This consideration gives Freeman's biography special importance and justifies its length. He has spent nineteen years in gathering material and putting it together. Factually it is complete. Other material will undoubtedly be uncovered; but one cannot believe that it will question the finality of Freeman's selection. The four volumes of over two thousand pages have been beautifully and expensively presented. Illustrations are liberally inserted; and for the first time there are sufficient maps, intelligently placed, which make it easy to visualize the army's movements in campaign and battle.

Any life of Lee which proposes to be definitive must of necessity lay great and special demands upon the author's critical imagina-

[1] *R. E. Lee*, by Douglas Southall Freeman.

tion. From the length of this narrative and the time taken in its preparation, one may safely assume that the author has set himself to his task with such a design in view. He begins by going very fully into Lee's early life, showing racial traits, social inheritances, his mother's training, the tragic end to his father's career. These sections are conventionally done; and although they assemble fresh incidents of his youth and early manhood, the incidents do not expose much additional knowledge of his character. He is a Christian gentleman with great energy and capacity, thrifty, practiced in self-denial, dependent upon family life, and suffering at times from frustration due to the slow promotion of army life. A great deal is said about his ancestry and the distinguished station occupied by his contemporary connections. This does much to place him in the mind of the reader; but, in the light of this society's destruction, it could have been more imaginatively handled. When times were stricter, as in the eighteenth century, it was not necessary for the biographer of a great soldier to explain the society from which he had sprung or his particular place in it, because the reader, being a part of that society, intuitively understood its nature, its divisions and institutions. In that time, when a political quarrel was settled by war, nothing was changed fundamentally. But with Lee it was different. He was called on to defend the society itself which produced him and the life he loved, a thing which he seems never to have understood. He conducted his campaigns largely in the eighteenth century fashion as he had seen war conducted in Mexico. This fact gives to the tragedy of his life a flavor of irony which the author has singularly missed.

But the moment the biography becomes military narrative the tone of the writing and the interpretation become sure and skillful. The style takes a direction which only the most superior knowledge and understanding of the arts of war can give. No matter how difficult the maneuver or how confusing the tactical dispositions, there is always the greatest clarity of exposition, from the conclusions reached by the commander from the intelligence reports to the final shock of brigades on the field. Freeman understands the dramatic power of restraint, and the high quality of the prose testifies to his effective use of understatement. Throughout, he combines in the most adroit manner exciting description with the analysis of elements which have brought about the particular military conclusion, so that the reader's judgment is assisted in the most useful way. His chief and most dramatic device is what he terms the "fog of war." The method proposes to show only what was in Lee's mind at a given moment; how he reasoned in this fog and came to his conclusions. This allows for a truer judgment of his ability as a commander, and disputes in the most telling way critics who, in the knowledge of after events, have blamed him for decisions he was forced to make while laboring in the "fog." The one valid criticism to the exclusive use of this method is the limited information it gives to the reader. To get the full effect the reader needs to know the strength and dispositions of the opposing army, what was going on in Lee's army which Lee did not know, and something of those influences which led the enemy into miscalculations and blunders. Often Freeman, in the summation at the end of chapters or in footnotes, gives this additional information; but at times he so orders it that the reader finds himself wandering in a fog of his own which borders on obscurity.

But the method is a valuable and permanent contribution to military biography, a contribution which must greatly improve it. It is most successful in Scott's march on Mexico City, for here Lee is not a commander but an officer of the staff, operating for the most part on detached reconnaissance duty. The approach, therefore, to any situation is concrete and personal: Lee performing in dangerous positions, making hazardous scouts; or sustaining terrific hardships, such as crossing the *pedregal* in foul weather, on a black night, to carry information that would help assure victory. During this entire campaign he proved the perfect subordinate, and the thorough way in which his part is displayed serves as a fine introduction to him in the familiar role as commander of the Army of Northern Virginia.

Freeman keeps in mind this very fact, and while the description of the advance on Mexico City is one of the best things in the book, remaining with the reader as the equal to the best which follows, he is not allowed to forget that Mexico was the laboratory where Lee learned the rules of combat. For there he studied and was later to adopt Scott's theory of high command. The commanding general's function, according to Scott, is to plan the general operation, acquaint the corps commanders with the plan, and see that their troops are brought to the proper places at the proper time. Here his duties cease. After a battle is joined, it is not the commander's function to fight it in detail. Since the too rigid practice of this theory has been considered as Lee's greatest fault as a general, the Mexican War was destined to have a profound influence upon the American concept of society.

But his military education did not end with this. It was advanced by six other lessons: (1) audacity; (2) the value of working with a trained staff; (3) the relation of careful reconnaissance to sound strategy; (4) the advantage of flanking movements; (5) the relation of communications to strategy—how an army, as Scott's did, may abandon its line of supply and live off the country; (6) the value of fortification, an art very little developed at that time in open warfare. In addition to these things, he saw the necessity for the commander to remain on good terms with his lieutenants. Scott's quarrels with his division heads, after the entry into Mexico City, almost wrecked the army. This example became such a warning to Lee that he went to the other extreme, often to the detriment of the cause. To sum up—at the close of hostilities Lee had observed an army under all conditions but that of retreat. A practical knowledge of cavalry and tactics was also missing from his military education. These lessons had to wait for more desperate days.

It has been the common belief that his genius was constant from beginning to end; that his powers were at times intuitive, if not actually metaphysical. The memoirs of one of his staff officers state as much. But another school, arguing from doctrinaire rules of war, misunderstanding the special nature of the American issue, has accused him of rashness. The peculiar value of Freeman's narrative lies in its demonstration of Lee's growth as a soldier, in its insight into, and instruction with regard to, the obstacles and limitations imposed upon his decisions at every vital moment of maneuver and battle, from the time he is charged with the mobilization of the Virginia forces to the bitter resolution to surrender his army. Always he was forced to take the second-best way of doing things, either because of the failure of the commissary, when a well-fed and well-equipped army might have made victories decisive; or because of the lack of forage for his animals; or because of the sloth and incapacity of his officers, even their insubordination (Longstreet at Gettysburg; Field in the wilderness); or because of more general situations having to do with the nature of the general defense.

We watch through the four years of war his great mind work: the cohesion of intellect, character, and physical endurance, united by a sensibility which gives to every thought and action a common genesis. We watch it analyzing intelligence reports until the purpose of the enemy seems clear. And once he has made up his mind the decision for action is quick and irrevocable. If it is to maneuver, the orders he gives for marching are clear and specific. This quality of his orders and not the speed of the march moved his brigades to the proper place at the proper time, just as the order to engage rested upon a confident synthesis of all the elements which denied any alternative. It was this functioning of a complete man of great power which justified the confidence of his army and turned it into a fighting machine; which warranted a boldness that in lesser men would have been mere rashness; which turned the blunders or inadequacies of his subordinates into Confederate victories; and which helps, finally, explain the ultimate defeat of the man and the cause he defended so well—for the flaw in the character of a person of such near-perfection must be commensurate with his virtues.

In reading military history it is very hard to find a writer who understands how campaigning, losses in battle, and other causes are continually operating to change the nature of an army. But in this quality of narrative Freeman excels. The variable temper of the Army of Northern Virginia, influencing Lee and influenced by him, is handled in the most thorough way, until its special character before every battle helps define the outcome. For example, during the Seven Days the army was a loose agglomeration of regiments, at best six semi-independent commands, ordered upon faulty maps, and under the control of a leader who had taken charge after the campaign was under way. These particular movements of troops are the most difficult of the war to clarify and bring alive; yet it is here that the author's technique proves most successful. In the narrative proper, in footnotes and appendices, he sets forth step by step why Lee failed to crush McClellan, although he was able to bring relief to Richmond. Never once was his grand strategy realized tactically. Always each battle was fought by a part of the army with excessive loss because the turning movements never reached the desired point at the desired time. Freeman sets forth the probable reasons in a clear argument, and he is always careful to withhold a positive judgment when the nature of the evidence is conflicting.

After this campaign Lee welded the divisions into effective combat units. The men had already shown their superior fighting abilities; but for the most part the general officers, with certain exceptions, displayed serious shortcomings. With a fine union of decision and tact—he had already won the confidence of all arms— Lee quickly undertook its reorganization. Very quietly he shelved the incompetent generals and, so gradually that it was not noticed, shifted troops from those officers who had not distinguished themselves to more skillful commanders. Building up the staff, he combined the divisions into two corps, making the army's efficiency depend upon three men: Longstreet, Jackson, and Stuart. This was the reorganization which would make both Lee and his army famous—Jackson, the combat wing; Longstreet, the support; and Stuart, the intelligence.

Having once taken their measure, he would plan his marches and battles upon his knowledge of their joint capacity; and the soundness of his judgment was always borne out by their actions. Stuart never brought him a piece of false information; Longstreet, until circumstances called upon him to play a part for which he was unfitted, once he got into action, slow though he was, showed superb tactical sense. It was not by accident that Lee pitched his tent near this general's headquarters. And Jackson, the spearhead of the army, was the perfect instrument to carry out his chief's daring resolutions. From the beginning there was a perfect understanding between the two men. Lee's orders to Jackson were terse and professional. He knew there was no need for the diplomatic approach which he used with certain of his citizen generals. Jackson often disagreed about plans; but if he was overruled, he would make Lee's plan his own and carry it out as he alone could do it. He is reported as saying after the Seven Days that he would follow Lee blindfolded, which has a curious corollary, for Lee at that time seems to have doubted Jackson's willingness to serve under another. Lee, daring in conception; Jackson, daring and deadly in execution . . . from such a marriage of genius sprang the triumphs of Second Manassas, Sharpsburg, Fredericksburg, and the supreme trial of their spiritual union, Chancellorsville. The most stirring scene in the four long books is their last conference together, when Lee decides to divide his small army (Longstreet's corps is absent) and send Jackson with a force around Hooker's flank. It is the only way by which the Confederates may retain the offensive. "What do you propose to make this movement with?" asked Lee. "With my whole corps," answered Jackson. This was Jackson's own conception, writes Freeman; his major contribution to the campaign. He would not attempt a simple turning movement that would leave an opening for a general assault. Lee had not expected this, for it would leave him only two divisions to face an enemy who might easily have 50,000 men in his front. Boldness matched boldness. He replied calmly, "Go on." "Such an executive officer," said Lee some days after he had watched Jackson disappear into the forest for the last time, "the sun never shone on. I have but to show him my design, and I know that if it can be done, it will be done. No need for me to send or watch him. Straight as the needle to the pole he advanced to the execution of my purpose."

The time from the Seven Days through Chancellorsville marks the great period of Lee's generalship and the army's highest performance; and it was Jackson who was the qualifying element. After his death the nature of the army changed and Lee's generalship was modified. Before, when the army had to undergo reorganization, the refitting and substitutions took place according to the structure assumed after the Seven Days. And the test of this structure was Sharpsburg. On that field the army showed it could stand on the defensive, and Lee showed he could handle troops in actual combat. In the stress of the battle there he was forced to direct the tactical dispositions, and they were done so well that every movement was exactly timed to meet the emergency, just as, strategically, the divisions reunited on the field in time to prevent disaster. The one criticism Freeman makes of Lee is of his failure to estimate the fatigue of the army after Second Manassas. Straggling on the way to Maryland had sadly reduced its strength. But Lee had come a long way from his first battle. He no longer attempted grand movements. He satisfied himself with simple flank attacks and quick marches to the rear; and he had become a master at patching up the combat units after the battle's damage. At no time until the end of the war was the morale of the army so low as after Sharpsburg; yet by careful rebuilding, rest, food, and refitting, it was brought to the high efficiency of Fredericksburg, the Confederacy's high noon, and Chancellorsville, the beginning of the decline.

When Lee heard of Jackson's fall, his calm face was overcast with anguish; and his voice choked with emotion as he dictated a reply to that soldier's message, telling him the victory was his. When it was learned that the doctor had given up hope, Lee knelt in prayer and, as Freeman says, "went down spiritually to the brook of Jabbok and, like Jacob, wrestled with the angel." He would not believe that Jackson would die, and who can say that his refusal to accept the inevitable was not a dread of ultimate defeat as well as personal grief, for no one knew better than Lee that Jackson's place would not be filled. Freeman closes the second book with the following paragraph. It is worth quoting, as its splendid prose brings to an end his brilliant handling of the army's first phase—"There was a stir outside the tent, a moment of hesitation, and then some one brought in a bit of folded paper. It contained the brief and dreadful news. In the little cottage at Guiney's, Jackson had roused from his restless sleep and had struggled to speak. His mind had been wandering far—who knows how far?—but with an effort, in his even, low voice, he had said: 'Let us pass over the river, and rest under the shade of the trees.' And then, as so often on marches into the unknown, he had led the way." As Lee read the note, in his distress he too must have asked that same question—who now would lead the way?

He answered it by dividing the Second Corps into two segments, placing Ewell over the reduced Second, and Hill over a new Third Corps. The entire reorganization of the army was the most drastic ever undertaken; and although Lee did the best he could in the exigencies of the war (Confederate fortunes in the west were desperate), Freeman states that the army was back where it had been before the Seven Days. What it could do without Jackson was unknown. But the Pennsylvania campaign must be undertaken with the least delay to relieve the pressure on Vicksburg, before the officers and men would be able to accustom themselves to their new relationships. There were two untried corps commanders, the character of one of these, Ewell, being unknown to Lee; a third of the divisions under new leaders; one corps with two new divisions; seven freshly promoted brigadiers; six infantry brigades commanded by senior colonels; a third of the cavalry directed by officers who had not previously served with the army; and the most experienced corps commander, Longstreet, inflated with self-importance and believing he controlled his commander's mind. There was, to offset these disadvantages, the high morale of the troops; and there was Lee. But even Lee without Jackson was an unknown quantity. It was the fate of the Confederacy that such conditions prevailed in the Army of Northern Virginia on the eve of its most critical battle. The reorganization after Chancellorsville, states Freeman, explains Gettysburg.

Gettysburg was a Confederate reverse because Lee failed, as at the Seven Days, to get any coordination in his attacks. On the first day Ewell failed to rise to his new responsibility. The discretion Lee always gave his corps commanders confused Ewell, who had been accustomed to Jackson's explicit orders. But equally, Lee failed to adjust his habits to get the best out of Ewell; therefore, the success on the first day was only partial. When it became apparent that Ewell would do no more, Lee's military sense told him his line ought to be shortened by drawing in on Seminary ridge; but when Ewell protested, he surrendered his judgment and acquiesced in the fish-hook formation. Freeman condones this decision, but Lee violated his own theory of the commander's function. It is the general's duty to make the plan, the subordinate's to carry it out. On the second day things drifted badly. Lee gave only one positive order, and that was to Longstreet to attack at eleven o'clock. He did not stay to see it executed, although he was fully aware of his most capable lieutenant's sullen behavior, his passive resistance to the offensive, which was Lee's announced plan of action. Freeman goes so far as to say that the army was without a commander on the second day. On the third day it was the same thing, except that Longstreet became openly insubordinate. Stuart's absence partly exonerates Lee for his lack of control, for he was in the dark as to the enemy's strength and position; and under such circumstances his action could not have the drive which accurate information would have given it; but it does not completely excuse him, and he did not ask to be excused for his failure, once he had settled on a plan, to have it executed. Freeman lays the principal blame upon Longstreet;[2] but finally, Lee cannot be absolved. There is a difference between leaving the tacti-

[2] Recent opinion presents Longstreet in a better light. However, the most recent word is not necessarily the last word.

cal management to the corps commander when he is obedient and when he is insubordinate. It was Lee's plain duty to force Longstreet to obey him, or to turn the corps over to somebody who would. Freeman concludes that Lee had to put up with his subordinate's behaviour, because he was his most skilled commander; but, as it turned out, Longstreet did no actual commanding. He merely stood in the way to block whatever chance there was of success for Pickett's thrust. The author further explains Lee's action on the grounds of his overconfidence in the butternut ranks. This may partly interpret the reasons, but it does not excuse his violation on those three days of his conception of the commander's business: he failed to get the troops into position at the proper time; he allowed his subordinates to interfere with his plan of battle; and he failed to see that the battle was joined when ordered.

Afterwards, in the Wilderness, in the shifts to the right at Cold Harbor, and finally, in the trenches at Petersburg, Lee showed that he had found out what a change Jackson's death had wrought in the army. More and more he assumed direct responsibility. It took the battle of Gettysburg to make him aware of what he must expect of himself under the new conditions. It was the South's misfortune that it had to be that particular battle, for afterwards his power was seen at its fullest. And Freeman's treatment retains its convincing analysis of the army's defensive operations. He dismisses Longstreet's contention that, saving his wound, he would have pushed his advantage in the Wilderness flank attack to victory, by demonstrating that the enemy had been pushed as far as circumstances allowed when the bullet struck. When Grant finally slipped to the south of the James, the author defends Lee's surprise by showing in detail how little exact information Beauregard furnished, and how Lee's care and prudence did not allow him to move until he was sure of the enemy's intentions.

In the preface and in the short summation at the end the author states that there is nothing in Lee's life to interpret. We are told that he was a simple Christian gentleman. That he was a Christian gentleman of the old school, the most disputatious would not deny; but that he was a simple man seems far from the truth. An action may be simple and direct but have the most complex implications. Lee's code was strict. It extended into all his relationships, his duty to himself, to his family, to the army, to the Confederacy and its civil authority. It was complete as no code can be today. But this completeness does not prohibit the necessity for interpretation. Indeed, every author, whether he recognizes it or not, interprets his protagonist by writing about him. The arrangement of his material, his constant selection and analysis, form opinion as assuredly by implication as by statement. The failure to recognize this is to make a specific interpretation often masquerade as something else.

This, perhaps, has led the author to ignore the full relationship between two phases of Lee's conduct: his dealings with the civil authority and his attitude after Appomattox. The first is important because it bound Lee's army to a fixed object, Richmond. The defense of Richmond should have been a secondary object. The aim of the war was to bring about Southern independence. Lee is excused on the ground of his belief in the subordination of the military to the civil government. In a recognized nation this is a sound attitude; but, actually, since the Confederacy assumed the role of revolution, there was no civil authority until it had been established by the armies in the field. Lee's relationship, therefore, could not be to the civil authorities of a revolutionary government what it had been to the old United States. Did Lee recognize this changed relation? If he did not, was he not unfit for the fullest performance of the greatest military leader of a revolution? The consideration of this matter cannot be dismissed in the definitive life of the gentleman. To state, as the author does, that Lee felt the military must subordinate itself to the civil, in the light of the situation, begs the question. His model, Washington, certainly did not view the question in the same light.

Most of the last book is taken up with the final, what some may consider the significant, phase in this great man's life. But the treatment here does not match the skill with which the war period has been handled. It is diffuse and uncertain. It accumulates fresh incidents; it goes into great detail about the management of Washington College; it treats extensively the changing curriculum and the growing endowment of the college; it takes Lee to the springs, on visits to his kin and admirers. Lee in all this activity has been interpreted as the guide to Southern salvation. This salvation is to be achieved by building up the character of Southern youth; by accepting the decision of battle through the faithful adherence to the terms of surrender with the hope that, by the mercy of God,

things will come all right in the end. This is a valid interpretation—
it has been the common one—but it is inadequate. The mercy of
God did not bring independence. Nor was the war over. One phase
of it was done, but the old wounds were kept open by the Reconstruction policy and the worst form of guerilla warfare. The avowed
purpose of this policy, which broke the terms at Appomattox and
Goldsboro, was the destruction of Southern civilization. Did Lee not
see that the training of a few thousand students at Washington
College was a futile thing, if their civilization was to be wrecked?
And what was submission but the worst form of slavery? Fortunately
the leadership changed to the middle South, to those who led the
Ku Klux Klan, that society which made survival possible. If Lee
did not understand the implications of the policy of the Northern
radicals, who were the government, his nobility conceals a serious flaw.

It is just this attitude of Lee during the days of peace that needs
interpretation, and it is the lack of interpretation in the present
biography that fails to explain his acceptance of personal defeat. It
is hard to believe, as Freeman would have us, that this acceptance
was passive. His "I had rather face a thousand deaths than meet
General Grant"; the furious pacing under the apple tree after surrender; the partial withdrawal from life; the refusal to discuss the
battles; his distrust of politicians; the coldness his old officers noticed on occasion; his simple statement to Captain White on one of
their rides, *apropos* of nothing, that if Jackson had been at Gettysburg, he would have won the battle; his rapid transition from
maturity to old age—do not all these things point to a terrific
struggle to maintain his mask? Do they not show that resignation
was not in his heart? All the time he must have been fighting again
the battles and questioning his actions. And must he not have tried
to find the answer to his failure in a comparison of his career with
that of his father—careers so different but both ending in defeat?
Must he not have asked himself how virtue can fail or did he know
how the noble man may be pursued by Fate and overthrown? Or did
the flaw lie deeper, somewhere behind that irreproachable mask, in
the refusal to demean his personal code to save the cause?

These questions are not proposed in this work; but they must be
considered before the biography of Lee can be said, in all respects,
to be definitive.

# John C. Calhoun

VERY few men who have helped determine the direction of society are remembered in their true character. They too often have attached to their names some felicitous phrase or symbol descriptive of a given moment in history which is never more than a half truth at best, but is generally a distortion of everything the once sentient man represented. This is due to the myth-making instincts of the people. People will make myths, or have them made for them, suitable to the cultural images they want to hold in their minds. Of all the great names in American history Calhoun's has fared the worst. The defeat of everything he cherished by its political opposite allowed the victors (angry and vicious enough even in their triumph to order the desecration of his tomb) to misconstrue for posterity the nature of his genius. His name evokes a narrow, vindictive sectionalism. It should call forth another metaphor, the liberality of federal compromise. He was accused of doing more than any one man to bring about disunion; yet his Union sentiments were constitutionally pure and never changed. Secession has been laid to his politics; yet his constant effort was to show how it might be avoided. Believed to be cold and ambitious, three times in his career he deliberately sacrificed his prospects for the presidency, an office he desired above all others, for a principle that was more American than Southern. Branded even during his life as a mere theorist, a "metaphysician," no mind performed with more realistic logic—not one of his contemporaries foretelling as accurately as he what conclusions might be expected from the trend of political action. Vilified as the defender of slavery, his concept of liberty was sounder than Jefferson's. Above all, though he was accused of possessing a narrow sectionalism, and though he did define in his life and action the best that was Southern, he was American to the roots of his hair. This is the man Mr. Styron has chosen for his subject, and for the first time Calhoun is presented with some critical justice.[1]

*The Cast Iron Man* is not, however, in the strictest sense a biography. It is, rather, a critical introduction to American history; or, to be more specific, it examines, while it introduces, those causes which bear upon the failure of the American Union. Today, when political knowledge and intuition are at their lowest, there exists the greatest confusion in the popular mind over the nature of the Union. But this disorder has, with certain exceptions, always endured. The only difference has been in the degree of misunderstanding. It is the confusion between the Union, a political experiment, and the geographical union, or, as Calhoun defined it, the *land* of the Union. Indeed, this confusion was one cause for the substitution of the rule by party for government by constitutional principles. It might almost be said that the Union failed over a definition of terms. In the first quarter of the nineteenth century John Taylor of Caroline complained that the Constitution was being destroyed through a perversion of its terms. At any rate, it is now a clearly evident, if not understood, fact that the political union was destroyed in its name. The United States of America in 1937 is with its strongly national government a contradiction in terms. There has been no *United States* since 1865. There has been, as there always will be, the land which fell within the geographical confines of the various colonial sovereignties composing the American states.

There was not one of those eighteenth-century gentlemen who met in convention in 1787 to make a better Union who did not know that any polity must be measured by the degree of security and liberty it gives to the individual citizen. It is significant that there was then no talk of plans. Rule by planning and rule by principle are antithetical. The wide disparity between the political genius of those days and the present may be seen in this difference. Planning is a regulation of special masses for special and temporary purposes, leaving the delusion that the particular plans, necessarily conflicting because of their particularity, have general and perma-

---

[1] *The Cast Iron Man: John C. Calhoun and American Democracy* by Arthur Styron.

nent application. They subordinate the individual to the mass acting in relation to other masses, just as they continually change the
limits in time at which the mechanistic perfectibility will be reached.
The Constitutional Convention debated in terms of principles
which would have universal application, acting upon each individual as an individual, be he great or small, in his social, economic,
political, and religious relationships. Planning either comes from or
prepares for the servile state, whereas political principles stand back
of the traditional society. From principles to planning—this, with all
that it implies, might be the subtitle to the conclusions one inevitably
draws from Mr. Styron's thesis, for the author looks at his material to
judge it. American history is no dead subject to him. The events,
clash of ideas, the pure and impure ambitions of leading protago-
nists filling the period of his study he regards as directly antecedent
to the present state of the nation.

It is this quality which gives the book much of its value. Treating,
as it does, chiefly of ideas, it has the strength and weakness peculiar
to its bias—strength as a philosophical commentary on political
concepts and action during the first half of the nineteenth century,
weakness as a biography. As a biography it is not circumstantial
enough. Calhoun is still a controversial figure, and the risk of judgment which Mr. Styron so admirably assumes requires more support than he has been able to gather into the present work. It may
also be objected that in a book of such length he should have limited
himself more to the American scene and restricted his comparison
with European ideas and political movements. In a short study such
as this, the space devoted to them is out of proportion to their actual
influence upon American conditions. Nevertheless, the book is a
brilliant piece of work.

Any study of Calhoun is a study in failure, for no public man has
failed more thoroughly. Historians, however, should never tire of
disclosing the causes behind it, for Calhoun's political defeat cannot
be separated from those acts and policies which undid the Federal
Union and destroyed a civilization. Every great statesman must
necessarily fail. Only the politician succeeds. The very material of
great statecraft precludes success. It is creative. Its ideologies propose for society ideal patterns of conduct. The stubborn imperfec-
tibility of man foretells the failure, but without these patterns there
would be no civilization. The individual's inability to realize fully

the ideas in his conduct merely emphasizes the cultural retrogression their lack must bring about.

The very few great men who stumble into public life find their statecraft blocked in every direction. If they were not men of high moral tone, of a will to deny the world when necessary, and of a character enriched and made useful by this denial, they could not surmount the difficulties which work to turn them aside from their purpose. Usually they are endowed with personable qualities that attract and hold others to their service. But this does not always follow. Parnell was a cold man and a stern disciplinarian. Nobody was ever intimate with Calhoun. If he had had some of Henry Clay's warmth and magnetism, the course of American history would undoubtedly have been changed. But Calhoun would not then have been Calhoun, nor Clay, Clay, nor the Devil, the Devil.

The politician, if he is an honest man, serves his faction, at best the material interests of his constituency. If he is an opportunist, he serves himself. Unlike the great men of history he senses, if he does not understand, the irrefrangible social law that it is the inferior who survives. The noble and the great govern by principle, but, unless they can determine the rules, more often than not end by dying for it.

If there was one thing the majority of the Revolutionary leaders agreed upon, it was that this country must cut off from Europe, start anew, and somehow build a better world. Jefferson was able to put this desire into popular language, although there was no clear understanding of what the new world had revolted against. The ex-colonists were inclined to repudiate the whole European tradition when, had they been able to distinguish more sharply, they could have seen that their sufferings had sprung from corruptions of that tradition rather than from that tradition in itself.

English pragmatic materialism with its economic expression, industrialism, and its political expression, plutocracy, threatened the American experiment at the very outset. Hamilton maneuvered with great skill to have the proposed Constitution set up finance's rule in the new world. But the Federalist Party was composed of two groups with opposing interests. The great landowners of the South and the Middle states must eventually have discovered that the rule of the rich and well born would end, if they followed Hamilton all the way, in the rule of the rich. It was this branch of the Federalist

Party that made any compromise possible, for their concern was a happy and workable union.

Their natural alliance was with Jefferson. Very likely what frightened gentlemen like Washington, the Lees, and the Pinckneys was the false identity of Jefferson's theories about the common man with the violent stages of the French Revolution. Jefferson meant an entirely different thing. He promised a better life to the common man, but he meant to upset the old order only to the extent of making it possible for the propertyless to get property out of the vast resources at hand. It was not Jefferson but Hamilton who threatened the kind of property Washington possessed. Jefferson was looking to a stable society, and if he meant for every man to vote, he meant for his vote to be responsible. He meant for every man to hold some property which, by giving the individual a stake in society, would produce the responsibility necessary to preserve it.

The issues would be slow in clarifying themselves, but it was soon known that the fight for leadership must rest at last between New England and the South. New England represented the more recent European tradition, the South the older humanism of Christendom with, of course, definite modifications. The South alone promised a Renascence of traditional society—the cultural inheritance of Europe modified by the fresh energies of the wilderness. The seventeenth-century colonials had been too timid, too preoccupied with survival to tamper overmuch with the material resources around them. Their weakness confined them to the narrow seaboard strip of land. This condition preserved the conservative instincts of the traditional mind so that later, when the wilderness tempted, there would be a pattern of social life strong enough to transform its chaos into social order. The dynamics of the frontier, the inertia of formal institutions—out of this opposition came the promise of a civilization strong enough to balance a world given over to trade and business.

The more recent European tradition, which New England represented, differed sharply from the older tradition represented by the South. The New England tradition, by the doctrine of Election, denied man's spiritual equality.

This was the reverse of the Southern libertarian position. In spite of Jefferson's announcement that all men are born free and equal, even in Jefferson's time the Southern aristocracy never experimented much with such a dangerous doctrine. To their realistic minds social and intellectual equality were absurdities, but the greatest landed nabob among them would never have denied the spiritual equality between his humblest slave and himself. He might defend any number of antisocial theories with friends before his fireside, but the danger to the established order went with the smoke up the chimney. Later, in the 1830's, with the pro-slavery arguments the Southern position swung away from Jefferson in theory as well. Calhoun replied that men were not only not born free; men were not born. Children were born and, far from being free, they were born in a state of complete dependence. In the "Disquisition on Government," as elsewhere, he further argued that people must have only so much liberty as their situation, morals, and advanced intelligence entitled them to. Furthermore it was a vicious error to assume that liberty cannot be perfect without perfect equality. To make equality of condition essential to liberty would destroy both liberty and progress. When Calhoun says progress, he does not mean the increase of physical goods as the end of society.

With societies so opposite in their cultural aims, if they were to unite in perpetual union, it was seen by all that there must be an explicit bond between them. The old Confederation had failed in war and peace, and the cause for this failure was the same in both cases. It was first a mere league between revolting colonies and later became a league between sovereign states. It carried the weakness of all such arrangements between principals who undertake a common venture: there was no final authority to decide upon action in emergencies. There was great opposition to a better union, but it became very clear that the preservation of independence depended upon a government strong enough to resist the ambitions of the European chancelleries. It was no less necessary for the states to agree on a suitable domestic policy. The nature of the former association had, therefore, to be radically changed and a government established which could command the recognition and support of the states. The difficulties were great—jealousy and fear of a change of masters.

Happily the even balance of power between the dominant sections allayed jealousy, and the difficulties were disposed of in the new Constitution. There are two things to remember in this connection. First, the Constitution introduced practically a new form of political association; second, because of its newness, there was no doubt in the minds of the leaders that the Constitution was highly experimental. The old Confederacy had been like all confederacies which the world had previously known, that is, a *union of the governments* of sovereigns; but the Federal Union was a *union of the sovereigns themselves*, the Constitution being the compact defining the terms of agreement. This difference Calhoun stressed as being of the utmost importance.

This being the novelty, it was also the danger. Would those agents who exercised the power of sovereigns usurp the actual sovereignty? The very complexity of the system, with its numerous checks and balances, emphasized the chances for failure, because those who administer affairs are all too likely to identify themselves with this power and forget their trusteeship. Here was a group of governments and departments within governments, all holding divided powers, one government with national powers without actually representing a national state, others local powers without being entirely local. There would be in each state officers of the general and local governments, some officers with general and some with local powers, to whom the individual owed obedience, but to whom the people of the state could owe no allegiance, since it is an anomaly for the principle to owe anything but support to its agent and that only so long as the agent abides by the limitations of his agency. The general and state governments were merely different expressions of the sovereign wills, the composite people of each of the thirteen states.

It was natural that conflicting interpretations would result from such an arrangement. The conflict in the Convention was carried over into the Federal government. Hamilton and the Federalists tried to bring about by indirection what they had failed to effect directly. Jefferson answered with the Bill of Rights; and when Adams assumed sovereign powers, the Virginia and Kentucky resolutions made way for the advent of Jefferson and his Republicans to office. But just at the moment when the Constitution seemed to have the conditions for a fair trial, the struggle between Napoleon and England forced Jefferson through his foreign policy to precipitate a sectional strife.

The War of 1812 had brought to an end the colonial era. There was a return of harmony, but underneath, great changes had come about in the economy of New England which would ultimately be a greater threat to the common peace than danger from abroad. This was the shift from an agrarian-commercial economy to a commercial-manufacturing economy. But at the moment this danger seemed remote. There was a general desire to avoid the weakness which had threatened the trial of union. Calhoun had been one of the younger men in the House to support the war, and he was now one of the harmonizers of the Era of Good Feeling. He supported a modest tariff, internal improvements, and various measures which tended to strengthen the central government. His action has brought the charge that he began his career full of nationalistic purpose and ended it in the spirit of narrow sectionalism. But to believe this is to misunderstand Calhoun's entire career.

Mr. Styron makes this answer to the charge: Calhoun, he writes, was a man whose intellect was touched with genius which is always independent of time and place, his nationalism a broad Unionism which died with the War Between the States, his support of Madison's war an answer to England's arrogance and demanded by his constituency; and lastly, he did not speak for the slave-holding interests because the make-up of his constituency was an up-country people.

This defense is not quite up to the author's later brilliant interpretation of Calhoun's action. It is true that Calhoun's constituency was not slave-holding, but it is equally true that he was connected by marriage with the seaboard aristocracy. There is a better reason for his failure to speak for slavery at this time. Slavery had not yet become a sectional controversy. The South looked upon it as a burden and even towards eventual abolition. There would be no defense of slavery until the extravagant and bitter attack had been launched by the militant abolitionists of the thirties. Then Calhoun met attack with counterattack, for he recognized the dangerous political uses to which abolitionism must inevitably be turned. Finally, to say that any genius is independent of time and place begs the question. Mr. Styron would have done better to relate the Era of Good Feeling to the decades which followed as better ground for interpreting the earlier and later phases of Calhoun's career.

The great question always in Calhoun's mind was the preservation of the Union, the peace and harmony between its sections. He was never anything at heart but a Union man, but his kind of unionism was not inconsistent with his Southern position. He did not emphasize strict construction at this time because there was occasion to fear more the weakness than the strength of the central government; and since it is the nature of democratic society to live by compromise, he was willing, for the sake of harmony, to make concessions to the new manufacturing communities in justice to their complaints over the burdens of the embargo period. Nor did he see why the western portions should not have the improvements necessary to their growth and a closer connection with the seaboard states—especially with the Southern half. In all this he saw the fulfillment of and the justification for the new experiment in government and union. He was merely supporting the general policy of the Virginia Dynasty to foster the good of the whole, so long as this did not interfere with the internal affairs of the states. It is true that under Jefferson and Madison the embargo had brought distress to New England, but if New England's ships rotted at their wharves, so did Virginia's tobacco and wheat and Carolina's rice rot on the farms. It was the action of Europe, not Republican government, which had been responsible for this condition. But the interesting thing to consider is the reaction of the two sections. In the South the planters were willing to take a temporary loss for an ultimate triumph of principle, whereas in New England the merchants rebelled at any restriction put upon the rich profits of the carrying trade in time of war, holding the Republican government responsible for sectional oppression.

The South, when it finally looked to its sectional integrity, did so only through force; and its reluctance to think of itself in sectional terms—the North would one day complain that the South couldn't be kicked out of the Union—led finally to its undoing. It was the purpose of South Carolina, soon to become the first Southern state, to rule the Union through a Southwestern alliance, within the limits of the Constitution. Such an alliance would have done much to restrain the machinery of exploitation developed by Northeastern finance. That such must be the result of this alliance was so well understood and feared by the ex-leaders of the extinct Federalist Party that they deliberately set about to introduce discord between the two staple-producing regions. No political strategy has ever achieved so great a success in so short a time. With the Missouri Compromise the sectional rivalry was given formal recognition. The passage of this act held for Jefferson, now an old man and not much longer for the world, the terror of a firebell at night. Old Taylor, on the brink of the grave, uttered a solemn prophecy of ruin. These Revolutionary leaders saw with doleful clarity that for the first time in American public life a political principle had been attached to a geographical line, that this must engender strife over balance of power, and that such strife must end in violence.

From this time on, the history of the country is the record of the struggle between the North and South for the support of the West. The major conflicting interests and social theories were from the beginning sectional, but the sections had no constitutional status. They could act politically only through their units, the states. This condition aided the strategy of the Northeast, whose purpose it was to disguise the sectional color of its interests, which it could well do through the nature of its defensive-offensive tactics. The South, on the other hand, actually on the defensive, was made to appear to have assumed the offensive. If the South could have acted as one political unit, the Union might possibly have been saved; but never during Calhoun's life did all the Southern states agree on any common strategy.

Apart from the tactical limitations, there is another reason, as fundamental and more important, which obstructed concerted action on the part of the Southern states. The very nature of Western aims played into the hands of Northern leaders. The only appeal to the West was an appeal to its interests, whatever they happened to be at the moment. Its earliest interests had been relief from the Indians, the acquisition of land, the right to trade in furs (which the British hindered), and assurance of an outlet to the sea. The recognition of these demands by the Virginia Dynasty continued it in power, made the War of 1812, and called forth from New England the threat of secession. But the success of the alliance destroyed it. In the Era of Good Feeling settlement of the Wilderness moved apace. With the spread of cotton culture in the Southwest and grains and stock in the Northwest the interests of this section became bound up with internal improvements, such as making waterways navigable, establishing post roads and canals, and all means of getting their money crops to the markets of the world. There was no way to sidetrack Western demands for these improvements, nor for the Indian lands.

The North, by now well identified with the financial and manufacturing groups, offered the West governmental subsidy to be raised through tariffs. This meant that the internal improvements would be paid for by a tax on the export of staples, that is, by the South and West. The West would pay a fraction of this tax, but its part would be far outweighed by the increased value to its lands. But such an arrangement could only put a severe restriction on Southern property and labor. The Old South must suffer a great hardship and its trading practices serious disarrangements. Its lands were worn; it was losing citizens and wealth to the new territories, and it was finding it impossible to replace them by immigration. The tariff to this older section seemed to spell ruin.

But the North had nothing to lose and everything to gain by the tax. The tariff, by raising artificially the price of manufactures, would increase the wealth of the industrial leaders. The government subsidies, swelling the Western markets, would bring to Northern finance fresh territory to be drained of its wealth through finance's control of the banking and credit systems of the country. The North had put itself into the enviable strategic position by which it might transfer each year more and more of the property of the South and the succeeding "wests" into its hands. With each fresh accession of wealth would come a fresh accumulation of power, economic and political. Money attracts population, poverty makes it flee; so whereas both the North and South lost people to the West, the North was able to replace its loss by immigrants from Europe who would fill, at starvation wages and long hours, its factories and counting houses.

Some of the wealth which this policy transferred to the growing financial centers of the Northeast filtered down to the general population, but the greater part of it and always its power—witness Biddle—remained in the hands of the bankers and manufacturers. Factory laborers who were being sweated after the fashion of the English were told, when they demanded better wages, that they could expect no increase since they were competing with slave labor. This evasion was made to hand for the factory master and shows how far a decadent puritanism had spread throughout the Eastern states. Agricultural labor and industrial labor do not compete. In a free-trading world the actual competitor to American labor must have been the industrial classes of Europe; but the tariff had practically done away with any form of competition. In all justice the increased price of manufactured goods ought to have increased the pay of Northern workers, but it was labor's master, not the Negro slave, who kept labor's standard of living so low. In this way finance would increase its profits on the industry of two sets of slaves, besides taking what fees it could from the free agricultural labor, North, South, East, and West.

The South, as an alternative to governmental subsidy, could offer only the slower and less effective internal improvement by the action of each state within its own boundaries. This the West was in no position to listen to. The upper Northwest was settled by New Englanders, and although the Southwest under the influence of the plantation economy would find its interests eventually identified with the South, at the beginning of this sectional struggle for power both Wests were too close to the frontier to value the forms of traditional society for which the South was fighting. The North appealed to a temporary interest which would finally lead to a colonial dependency of the worst sort, the South to a true but remote interest that would lead to the promise of a long-time well-being and independence—or rather, the promise of independence, because each generation must win and keep its own.

It is in these terms that the sectional struggle may best be explained, because only by subverting the Constitution and establishing a strong federal government as the final authority would the financial interests be able to carry out their antisocial purposes. I do not mean that those men who were so largely responsible for the bitter and unhappy direction given to American society always knew what they were doing, or saw in their actions more than some immediate profit or the advancement of some personal ambition. There is so much accident always in human affairs that it is folly to hope to discover the ultimate causes for social change. But there can be nothing more false than the concept that some Manifest Destiny, beyond the inscrutable mystery of the Godhead whose secret no worldly wisdom may probe, controls the actions of men, for such a destiny manifested in such a fashion is only an appeal to the "higher law," or a justification for an impending breach of faith.

With the passage of the tariff of abominations in 1828 the sectional struggle entered on a course from which there could be no turning back. The South took this act for what it was, the exploitation of its labor by a sectional majority, acting through the general government. In spite of the disadvantages inherent in the Southern position it showed exceptional strength in one respect—its public men. Upon their strategy would depend the independence of the staple-producing states, the unification of their various cultural strains in a unique social pattern, and the perpetuation of the Union. The general sources of the political opposition which Southern strategy had to meet is described by Mr. Styron in the division of the democracies: Popular Democracy, or the Revolution of 1828; National Democracy, or the Revolution of 1840; and finally, Industrial Democracy, or the Revolution of 1861. It may make the meaning clearer to say that Popular Democracy is more exactly a social impulse, National Democracy its political expression, while Industrial Democracy, if there is any such thing, designates the economic control of the national state for special and private ends. These divisions serve very well as the expression of what was taking place in the different stages of contention, although there was much overlapping. They renewed under changed conditions the early question—an absolute government commanding a servile people, or a Constitutional government protecting a people's liberty.

South Carolina stepped into the leadership of the defense almost overnight. Its prestige had been great during the Era of Good Feeling, that period of calm between the first and second trials of union; but now, with the complete identity between the people and their leaders, South Carolina named the political strategy for the South and forced its reluctant sister states to acknowledge its leadership. It could not command obedience, only persuasion. But this was not the only reason for a lack of early concerted action. It lay partly in the state's divided councils. It was just here that I missed especially in Mr. Styron's book the chronological detail so necessary for an interpretation of the results of political action.

For the first and last time after Calhoun had reached political maturity he would follow, not lead his state. He was aware of the gravity of the tariff situation, but he expected it to be settled in favor of the South with the election of the ticket which Jackson and he headed. So the leaders were forced to suppress discussion, allay the excitement existing among the state's representatives in Congress, and muzzle the press. The tariff of abominations passed almost without comment in South Carolina. For three weeks there was silence.

Then "the abstract, isolated principle of liberty" was hurled down in defiance by an obscure young representative from St. Bartholomew's Parish. What the accepted leaders of the state had failed to do, Robert Barnwell Rhett and the people of the Colleton district might and did do. They addressed the governor and asked only that the voice of the people be heard. "They were not," writes Miss Laura White in her biography of Rhett, "concerned about constitutional theories. For years the state had talked and protested. Now the time had come to act, and action must consist in open resistance to the laws of the Union. They did not desire disunion; rather they would preserve the Union by forcing the Constitution back to its original principles." More than once in later years people would recall that Rhett had said, "the day of open opposition to the pretended powers of the Constitution cannot be far off; and it is that it may not go down in blood that we now call upon you to resist." A communication to the *Mercury*, which seems to have been Rhett's, marked out his program, a program containing little constitutional argument and much appeal to action. The Union must be preserved and reformed by presenting the threat of disunion as an actual alternative; this threat to be delivered through a state ultimatum. The state should welcome support but, if it must, it would act alone. These ideas for which Rhett was to become chief advocate, secession, state ultimatum, separate state action, represent one school of Southern strategy—the separate state actionists.

At Rhett's revolt Calhoun rushed home, saw the gravity of the situation, secretly wrote the South Carolina Exposition (secretly because of the approaching election) propounding the doctrine of nullification. There was no doubt of his choice, but he determined to resist within the Union and on Constitutional terms. The state was brought under control and Rhett into the sphere of Calhoun's influence. But things did not go as Calhoun had hoped. The result of the nullification agitation is well known. Jackson came into power, and with a soldier's belief in absolute obedience violated the principles of the Constitution and laid the precedent for a strong national state. The issue came to a head in the Force Bill which Congress passed coincidentally with a reduction of the tariff: Clay's compromise.

The two authors of the events leading to this compromise came from the West. Their characters personified in the crisis the confused sympathies of their section, Jackson representing an agrarian imperialism, Clay the dependency of his section upon the economic imperialism of the East. Jackson, an honest but vain gentleman, with a passionate loyalty to his friends, most of them second-rate politicians who returned his loyalty with the intrigues of ambitious subalterns, had few generalizing qualities of mind and so failed to deduce from the political confusion an intelligent program which would advance his section's lasting well-being. He destroyed Biddle's bank, but he never understood the full implications of its power; nor did he reason that by substituting his absolute will for constitutional government he had set a precedent for the control of the state by other absolute wills, which the North must produce in time, hydra-headed and blood brothers to the bank. Like all frontier men, Jackson valued a friend who would fight on call and discuss the reasons later. But it would then be too late for discussion, as Calhoun might have informed him. The historic quarrel between the two men was politically ominous, and nobody better than Calhoun understood why.

And yet despite this antithesis Jackson and Calhoun were closer together in their social sympathies than Clay and Calhoun. They were all three country gentlemen, but Clay was not one at heart. With the comfortable facility of all who have their being upon the surface of life he blithely set about betraying his country without actually understanding what he was doing. The very nature of his character, which was ambition, did not allow him to concern himself with any reason for his action beyond his desires. Nor did he feel it necessary to look more deeply into any matter than the immediate occasion demanded. That is why he seemed the perfect compromiser. The West not being unsympathetic to the tariff for the reasons already given, Clay readily saw the means to political preferment in the conjunction of protection and internal improvements, a strong central government, and a national bank. It is no accident that it was Clay and not Webster who formulated the American system, just as it had been Hamilton, the bastard emigré, who grasped and interpreted the extreme materialism of that element of an old society which did not make explicit the ends towards which it was moving. Corruption working from within advances so gradually that the odor of decay is more quickly sensed by the ambition of the unscrupulous or rootless foreigner, who, for his own purposes, seizes upon the weak features of any given order as a courtier upon the vices of princes.

Clay's compromises, which are supposed to have saved the Union at dangerous moments, were in no sense genuine; and they did not save the Union. With his uncanny facility for judging the weakness of an opponent's position, he would make the conditions for a declaration of a truce, a truce to give his system another chance, for it was impossible ever for his policies to stand up to a direct trial of strength. When they finally prevailed, it was through a disguise and by indirection.

Once the issue was joined, and it was well joined in the nullification controversy, Calhoun turned his erudite mind upon a thorough study of the Constitution, examining every subsequent legislative proposal in its light. From this time on he was more and more two men: an actor trying to resolve the issues and reach a workable agreement among all parties; and the commentator, taking part in debate and strategy, but aloof, withdrawn by his wisdom from acrimonious dispute, the melancholy prophet foretelling the ruin of a civilization. In his speeches and public documents, and especially in his last work on government, there is the careful argument of a man who foresees his failure and the destruction of everything he loves and, seeing this, leaves for posterity an account of the genius peculiar to the American form of constitutional government with a complete defense of his part in the drama.

But never for one moment did Calhoun forget the end of all political action. Every compromise of principle made by his school of thought drove the South to rest its defense upon expediencies. No contemporary of his knew so clearly as he that this meant ruin. Expediency was the enemy's instrument, to be opposed only by principle, the South's one sure defense. After the rejection of the principles clarified in the nullification controversy he ordered— Calhoun's wishes were so considered—the State's Rights men to hold aloof from either party, using both to strengthen the Southern position and block hostile legislation. Finally his efforts were turned towards an attempted control of the Democratic party by the South. This party, informed by constitutional principles, would govern the country and settle the sectional quarrels which had diverted the Union's peaceful progress towards a unique fulfillment.

But his efforts were continually thwarted in this as in his other major strategy. At every crisis in public affairs the South, although it got a restatement of its principles, was forced to agree to some action which meant an eventual sacrifice of its position. Calhoun was not for a moment deluded, but he refused to abandon his policy. This was his one great blunder, or his one great weakness, according to the way his career is construed. He could not bring himself to admit that Southern control of the Democratic party could fail. To accept this failure as inevitable left him and his colleagues but one other course of action—secession. And he would not face, until the very end, this alternative. When he remembered the happy days after the second English war, the image of a working Union was too strong in his mind, it confined too much of his life and efforts, for him to abandon it so long as there was the remotest possibility that it might be saved.

But younger men, like Rhett, did not remember the Golden Age so well. They were more familiar with sectional oppression and a progressive loss of power and prestige. Rhett had followed Calhoun's tactics with intelligence and zeal until the handwriting on the wall, he thought, had become so clear that even the blind might see it. Then he asserted his independence, the only man in South Carolina to survive such boldness, and returned to his earlier position of separate state action and, if necessary, secession. The Union was not so sweet to him as Southern independence. With a realistic, objective mind he faced the ultimate consequences of his position with a courage and will equal to the risk. "Smaller states," he said, "have before us struggled successfully for their independence and freedom against far greater odds . . . To meet death a little sooner or a little later, can be of consequence to very few of us; whilst duty performed, may remain in its consequence to many generations, and a fair name, live forever, looking to that undying reputation which has ever followed every people who have dared all to preserve their liberties." Having learned from experience that the Southern states would not cooperate, he urged the separate action of South Carolina, again for nullification and later for secession. Turning to history, he reminded the Southern people that the American Revolution was made possible by the single action of Massachusetts, throwing the tea into Boston Harbor. If South Carolina acted, either within the Union or without it, the other Southern states must perforce cooperate and follow her lead.

But the other school, the cooperationists (that is, those who believed in acting only when all might agree on method), prevailed until 1861; and Calhoun is largely responsible for the postponement of Rhett's tactics. If he had thrown his great weight and dialectical powers behind the younger man, the South might very likely have seceded in 1850 when both the physical and spiritual odds would have been in favor of a Southern Confederacy. But Calhoun, under the most favorable circumstances, would have been reluctant to countenance any action leading to a dismemberment of the Union. It could not be expected that he would be shown the way by an insubordinate lieutenant. There was no open break between the two men, and Calhoun made no effort to discipline him, evidence in itself of the widespread sympathy for Rhett's theories; but this schism in the ranks of the State's Rights school would extend far beyond suppression of Rhett's revolt. Calhoun's rule of his native state had been so strict that after his death the local leaders, obedient but always restive under his restraining hand, were in no mood to render the same homage to one of themselves. Calhoun's mantle should have fallen on Rhett; but whereas the political leaders were agreed on principles, they could never agree with one another. In addition, no small measure of this disagreement was due to jealousy of Rhett for the courage he had shown in breaking with the great man. But the difference between the separate state actionists and the cooperationists, who distorted Calhoun's doctrine, became entrenched in Southern affairs, finally doing a fatal damage. Calhoun was no doctrinaire, but it is the irony of his life that his political heirs, fascinated by his teachings, became doctrinaire in their politics and even after secession, as a party in the Confederacy, made state's rights rather than independence the end to be followed, thus subverting the entire meaning of the master's political philosophy.

How could the South remain the South and stay in the Union? Or, as Calhoun was to present the question squarely to the Senate in his last speech, how can the Union be preserved? This was his only and constant theme. In one sense, because of the terrible logic of his mind, his position may be reduced to the simplest and clearest syllogism. This is the hazard anyone runs who tries to understand, either for presentation or a private pleasure and discipline, the complexities of his character. With the repeated failure of his practical politics he was constantly driven to a refinement of his theory, until there were times when the old charge of "metaphysician" seems justified. At the last, beyond the calling of the Nashville Convention, he was reduced to a plea of mercy for the South. To ask for justice from a hostile majority, whose workings he so thoroughly understood, showed the depth of his despair. It was admission of complete and final defeat. His fight had always been equality for the South within the Union. Secession, the alternative, meant equally the ruin of his hopes. But confronted by that spectre of defeat which all men must know, he was relieved of further decision. "The South, the poor South," he would say over like a dirge the last months of his life, "I don't know what's to become of her." Who can deny that this lament did not disclose regrets for his action at the time of Rhett's revolt and that in his anguish he did not feel the South's dark future lying heavily upon his conscience because of the refusal to face squarely the warning of his logic?

Men fail, but ideas withstand both success and defeat. Calhoun's practical politics miscarried, as have those of other men; yet his reputation is secure. It rests primarily upon a lucid statement of an idea which seems, in retrospect, the proper resolution of the difficulties of union. The particular problem of states is to prevent government from becoming the instrument either of majority or minority rule. The American Constitution, as interpreted by Calhoun, answered this problem by an emphasis upon a central feature, the concurring majority, which operated through two sets of powers, those reserved to the states, those delegated to the federal government. Powers are not delegated to a state government. In purely local affairs the sovereign acts directly. Without the concurring majority, the divided powers are meaningless. This, in its simplest terms, discloses the genius of American polity.

Where sovereigns form in union, there are certain principles on which government must be set up to resist, by its own interior structure, the tendency to abuse of power. Since power can only be resisted by power, suffrage is not enough to assure justice, for it allows only for the responsibility of the rulers to the ruled. Representation at best merely restrains the representatives. This kind of suffrage considers the entire community as a unit with but one common interest for all sections, a manifest oversimplification. The community, therefore, will divide itself into a major and minor party, the one trying to retain power, the other to get it. Under this system those who make laws would be, in reality, merely the majority's agents, holding the minority at their mercy. Such a government Calhoun calls the government of the numerical, or absolute, majority.

It is his thesis that the Union recognizes a great diversity of interests. These interests are balanced, the one against the other, by the concurring, or constitutional, majority, a method of compromise which takes the sense of each interest through its organic majority, and *the united sense of all* as the final sense of the community. The great and broad distinction between governments, therefore, is not that of the one, the few, and the many; but of the absolute and the constitutional. Force is supplanted by compromise. The mutual negative among the various interests invests each with the power of protecting itself, placing the rights and safety of each, only where they can be placed, under its own guardianship. It is this power of arresting the action of government—be it called interposition, nullification, check or balance—which makes the Constitution.

Outside South Carolina nullification had little popularity even in its own day and has found no apologist since; yet the theory is the ultimate measure of a workable union between sovereigns. Where secession acts to dismember the union, nullification acts to make it just and strong. There is no connection between the two acts except the sovereignty of the principals. If the state may not prevent an unconstitutional action by the Federal government, it has denied its sovereignty and the union of states comes to an end in some form of absolutism.

The contemporary criticism of this doctrine was that one state might obstruct the united will of all. To this Calhoun replied that since the reserved powers are negative, they cannot usurp the active powers of delegation. If, however, a state violated the bond by attempting to include in its reservation a delegated power, the debated right might be settled forever by the amending clause. But the inertia of the reserved power was so great that, in actuality, he considered the danger to be nonexistent. Even granting such an obstruction, it was the lesser of two evils, for the usurpation by the general government must end in some form of absolutism. There was no logical answer to Calhoun's logic.

There was, nevertheless, an answer. Eleven years after this argument had been put into final form, a ball of iron hurtled over the waters in the harbor outside Charleston. Its report rattled the panes in the city and brought the people to their feet. The hour was dawn, but it was not the beginning of a new day. It was a prophecy about to be fulfilled.

# A Hero and the Doctrinaires
# of Defeat

IN the study of history the scholar always finds himself involved with the old problem: how far the individual is responsible for any given action; how far that individual is representative of the general cultural movements, those mysterious forces which we can trace only after they have become apparent. There are various interpreters who try to foretell from the palm of history the future, to find its general laws; and there are the determinists who show the greatest folly in these matters. Yet their attitude still carries great weight, for theirs is the philosophy of the middle class. Not until the nineteenth century did these words which brought death into the world achieve such purity of belief: *sicut eritis dii,* the first half-truth to sound like truth, so spoken as to suppress the *sicut* until *you will be as the gods* sounded upon the corruptible ear, *you will be gods.* Historians are to be blamed no more than the rest of us, but the best historians are more modest. They approach the material as an artist might, for history is never a science, although in sifting and examining the materials it must use the methods of a science, as indeed any craft or art does. A science predicts from identical conditions identical results. It produces the formula, which is its triumph. But a formula for an art is death. For history it is an impossibility. The cultural structure and beliefs of a given society at a given moment must be understood (this can never be completely so) before the actors can be understood and interpreted. Yet in any given action there is always a common quality recurrent in differing ages, whatever the form which constrains it and makes its appearance unique. Kingship, for example, bears a universal denotation. How different in concept, however, is the connotation of the title, the King of the French from that of the King of France.

Under the king of the French the bourgeoisie, as a class, had its well defined place. Under the kings of France it finally usurped and distorted all the estates and older divisions of Christian culture, reducing their forms to a meaningless formalism, for once the material thing becomes the end in itself, it obliterates the multiple appearances of matter, those substantial forms through which the divinity multiplies itself. Such a monstrous indignity to mankind could not altogether be practiced; but gradually it became the end and aim in theory of the former states of Christendom. Nor should the colonies and later the states of America be denied their places in a Christian society. The states of the South were particularly congenial to the continuance of the fullest pattern of its cultural forebears. The South, though not entirely, was predominantly an agrarian country; and farmers know, whether they be great or small, that the material thing is subject to mysterious and supernatural forces beyond itself. There are the seasons, always the same and yet never predictable. Yet its political and economic leaders did not always sustain this fuller knowledge of experience. Especially was its theology unequal to its knowledge. This led to confusion of counsel and was one of the major causes of its defeat.

Those who believe in the inevitable superiority of wealth and numbers have assumed that the Confederacy's defeat was foredoomed. It has led certain historians, as well as common opinion, to argue from an anachronism, that an agrarian culture is no match for the might of industrial power. This is an *ex post facto* argument, for the industrial state as we know it came to power only after the defeat of the Confederacy and the change in the construction of the Constitution following this defeat. Furthermore, Mr. Frank Owsley, the most eminent Southern historian until his recent death, has clearly shown in *King Cotton Diplomacy* and other research that it was England's industrial arsenal which largely furnished arms and munitions, as well as supplies, to both sides, certainly in the first two years of the war.

I am going to belabor this point, for to assume that pure numbers and weight of material is that which of necessity brings victory is a dangerous half-truth, which the most casual examination of historic circumstance refutes. Too much armor presents its own disabilities; it need not, but it can lead to over-reliance on the tool, which is never better than the man who uses it. Napoleon's axiom that God is on the side of the heaviest artillery received its rebuke at Moscow, as it later did in the Wilderness campaign when Lee lured Grant into a kind of terrain where his artillery, which outmatched the Confederate, could not be used to effect. As a matter of observation, Napoleon's re-introduction of a modified total war, which Europe had not seen since the Thirty Years War in Germany, had far more to do with his victories than his heavy artillery did. The man or nation who fights by the rules is generally at the mercy of the one who fights with no holds barred. A general whom Napoleon had defeated in Italy remarked: "It is incredible how this fellow Bonaparte ignores the most elementary rules of war!"

The American Civil War is a fine example of these two assumptions: one, that it is not numbers and materiel, but the use or misuse of such, that counts in winning a war; and two, after the initial phase, that the strategy of the North changed from the eighteenth century tactics of restricted war to that of what we now call total war, war on the entire population, with the immediate aim of destroying the enemy's means of conducting hostilities and the final aim not of conquest but the murder of the defeated nation. There are many other factors, of course, and not the least of these is luck, or if you will, accident. Nathan Bedford Forrest's career is the most illuminating instance of the misuse of talent. But it is more than this, as you will see.

Since this must relate to the general policy and vision of those in power, and the common attitude of the body politic, it will be necessary to say a little about these things first. The original constitution, based upon a division of powers between the federal and the state governments, had come to an end the moment war was declared. It had come to an end temporarily; it might become restored if the Confederacy won. The South, thrust into the position of defending state sovereignty, tended to ignore the more federal implications of the American form of government. This was general, among the leaders and people. In political debate the South had for so long defended states' rights that when the war came, this partial concept inhibited the federal branch of the Confederate government, first at Montgomery, later at Richmond, in the central control of military affairs. Again Mr. Owsley was the first to establish the extent of this in his revolutionary book, *State Rights and the Confederacy*. This is not the place to take the matter up in detail; but to presume it. I merely want to assert that the doctrinaire belief in states' rights bemused those in authority into a misconduct of the war. Once war was declared, there would be no Confederacy until it had in fact been established by victory in the field, or by some agreement growing out of a stalemate. It was the moment to neglect local rights and concentrate on the common, or federal, branch of the government. Until the very end the authority of Richmond was impaired, flouted, denied, and even rebelled against.

There is another major miscalculation in policy: the foreign affairs. English economists and writers had convinced the South that England's manufactories so depended upon cotton that this empire must of necessity enter the war on the side of the South. This proved to be a delusion, and a costly one to the Confederacy. There was a moment when Richmond could have bought ships for a navy. Rhett saw the need for this, but his counsel was ignored; indeed, this politician, the most astute of the lot, was banished from any participation in affairs. He better than any saw the true nature of the war and how to prosecute it. As well, this belief in outside aid had much to do with Davis' defensive position: to repel invasion but not to invade. Circumstances forced him to abandon this, but such an attitude lost to the Confederacy the initiative both in the east and in the western theatres.

After the first Bull Run, the first Confederate victory not to be followed up, the next move shifted to the west, specifically to Kentucky, which thought it could remain neutral. Lincoln saw the strategic importance of this state, saw that the side which could hold it, everything else being equal, would win the war. Davis, thinking in defensive terms and the doctrinaire attitude towards states' rights, refused to invade that state when he had the power to take and hold it, but not the power to defend, as Albert Johnston tried to do, a three hundred mile line. Kentucky fell by default to the Northern side, opened the way by means of the rivers into the heart of the Confederacy, threatening the interior lines of communication and finally allowing the enemy to isolate the Trans-Mississippi Department and later carve up the lower South into fragments. To allow

this was the crucial blunder in strategy, since the war might be won
in Virginia, but it could never be won if the middle and lower South
fell and remained in enemy hands.

Neither Davis nor the Congress clearly understood this; but
Grant and Sherman did. After the fall of Fort Donelson, Kentucky
and Tennessee were lost to the Confederacy. But after Shiloh and
the retreat into Mississippi, the feckless policy of Halleck gave the
Confederates another chance. Halleck at Washington, like Davis at
Richmond, looked largely to the occupation of territory as the aim
of policy, not the defeat of armies. But no territory can be garri-
soned for sure, so long as a mobile enemy army is in the field. Bragg
undertook to use his interior lines and recover what had been lost
by an invasion of Kentucky. This was made possible by the scattering of the Northern forces. If Bragg could get to Kentucky before
the enemy could concentrate there, he would draw the enemy after
him and, getting between him and his base, offer battle which, if
successful, would change the look of things.

Bragg won his race for Kentucky; he won it because of the entrance upon the scene of the one man who was to use in all its
possibilities the branch of the Southern army which, almost to the
end, was to remain superior to the enemy: the cavalry. It is the
saddest irony that, also almost to the end, Forrest, whom the people
called the Wizard of the Saddle, was seen by the War Department
only as such another raider as Morgan. Forrest was a raider too, but
his raids always had a strategic purpose, except when he was frivo-
lously misused. Which is to say that they were not raids proper but
were undertaken in direct relationship to the movement of the main
army, or to obstruct some larger movement of the enemy force. It
was his raid into Middle Tennessee which so delayed Buell and
interrupted his line of supply, by destruction of stores and the
railroad between Nashville and Chattanooga, as well as forcing the
capitulation of Crittenden's brigade at Murfreesboro, that allowed
Bragg time enough to use the interior lines and win his race into
Kentucky. In this movement Forrest joined the Army of Tennessee,
served as the army's eyes, depriving the enemy cavalry of performing this purpose, so that Bragg got squarely across Buell's line of
retreat. But Bragg lost his courage and withdrew and allowed
Buell to reach Louisville in safety. Time and again the cavalry
would place the enemy at a disadvantage, which the incompetent,

what we would today call the psychotic, commander would throw away.

After Bragg's failure in Kentucky he returned to Murfreesboro and took up a position guarding Middle Tennessee, with the enemy's headquarters at Nashville. Here the opposing armies faced each other in a stalemate. It was the cavalry which insured this, keeping Rosecrans, who now commanded in place of Buell, without forage or information. The cavalry is the eyes of the army, and it was Confederate eyes which saw. In the meanwhile Grant was making slow progress overland towards Vicksburg. The Mississippi was as yet open between this town and Port Hudson. Forrest made his second raid, this time into West Tennessee, and so destroyed the railroad which Grant got his supplies on that it was abandoned during the rest of the war. A raid by Van Dorn on Grant's depot at Oxford, combined with Forrest's raid, forced Grant to replan and take to the river.

Davis' dispersive strategy of trying to hold ground instead of defeating armies lost to the Confederacy a hundred thousand men, one-sixth of its total force, by shutting them up in forts and towns along the rivers—the Cumberland, the Tennessee, and the Mississippi. Forrest proposed a swiftly-moving mounted artillery, which could keep northwestern trade from using the rivers, as well as, of course, interrupting the enemy's supply line. Later, again too late, at Johnsonville, he showed how this could be done, even capturing and operating for a while a gunboat with cavalrymen.

This was the situation, all in favor of the Confederates who had the interior lines and were close to their supplies, particularly after Sherman's costly repulse at Vicksburg. But the Confederates lacked the initiative to use their lines with imagination. In the meanwhile Rosecrans sent a strong force under a good officer, Colonel Streight, to the rear of Bragg, with the purpose of blowing up the tunnel between Chattanooga and Atlanta to interrupt Bragg's supply line, as well as to destroy the arsenal at Rome, Georgia. Forrest was sent to discover the enemy purpose. After making the most careful disposition against a flank attack upon the main army, he made up his mind what the true purpose of the enemy was. With a much reduced force, outnumbered, and with a tired command he followed Streight over the mountains, overtook him, and bluffed him into surrender, although the enemy had twice as many men as he on the field of battle. But he had driven Streight so hard that this officer had gotten his powder wet and his men lay asleep in line of battle. The particular skill of this operation was the subtle way in which Forrest transferred the element of fatigue from his own men to those of the enemy. It was one of the most brilliant operations of the war in the west. To show the extent of the strain, most of his horses died after the race was won. As at Murfreesboro Forrest's name and the hope of victory went all over the middle South. Although in a subordinate position, his name carried that hope and belief in what was necessary and only necessary for the South to free its homes of the invader. Forrest had rightly judged the nature of the war: murder and rapine. He used a more telling demand for surrender, not unconditional, but to "save the further effusion of blood"; or, "I'll put every man to the sword." It was what Stonewall Jackson wanted to do after Fredericksburg, tie medical bands to the arms of his soldiers, because it was night, and drive the confused enemy into the river. Lee, the eighteenth century gentleman, refused. In the end Lee's restricted and humane warfare cost more lives than Jackson's brutal proposal.

The military stalemate in Tennessee was broken after Grant, with inferior forces (at first) defeated Pemberton in Mississippi in detail. Then Pemberton, disobeying his superior Johnston, who had ordered him to fall back upon Jackson, went into Vicksburg and let himself be shut up there. Then instead of utilizing the interior lines for a bold offensive against Rosecrans and afterwards turning upon Grant at Vicksburg, Bragg, lulled into a false sense of security by the long stalemate, agreed to detach Stevenson and reinforce Johnston in Mississippi. The old business of trying to hold territory instead of taking the necessary risk of defeating armies lost both Vicksburg and Middle Tennessee. Stevenson's force was not enough to relieve Vicksburg, but it reduced Bragg's army sufficiently to allow Rosecrans to maneuver him out of the middle basin, over the mountains, into terrain around and behind Chattanooga. Rosecrans was so elated that he widely separated his divisions within the mountain passes, on the false assumption that Bragg was in disordered flight towards Atlanta. Bragg was concentrated and in a position to destroy the enemy. He had sufficient information, but he would not believe it. He was so demoralized and had even done the impossible thing of asking of his generals a vote of confidence.

After sufficient blunderings he delivered battle at Chickamauga, for the enemy, once understanding his peril, concentrated there. Longstreet had been sent from Lee's army in Virginia to reinforce Bragg. This helped defeat the enemy on the field, and Rosecrans fell back towards Chattanooga in disorder. Forrest was in pursuit, saw the situation, that the enemy with a river at its back had no easy way of escape. He tried to convince Bragg, who did not know he had won the battle (Longstreet said afterwards he did not think it necessary to tell the army commander this fact) and refused to pursue. Forrest, who had so often seen victory thrown away by this very commander, could not contain himself. He confronted Bragg, who cowered in his tent, called him a son-of-a-bitch and told him he'd kill him if he ever again got in his way. Naturally he was relieved of command.

This was a low moment for the Confederacy. Vicksburg had already fallen and Lee repulsed at Gettysburg. Chickamauga, if it had been properly followed up, could have counteracted the severity of the other losses and raised morale, which never entirely recovered. But confidence in Forrest remained high. His reputation for victory was well-known among the people and was pretty well-known in government circles; certainly the soldiers knew. It was known everywhere except in the place for it to count, with Davis and his advisors. Even after Davis and Forrest met to agree on allowing the general to go into West Tennessee and North Mississippi to raise another force, Davis, face to face with the man who could yet save the situation, failed to interpret the signs. Davis made few mistakes in choice of generals, fewer than Lincoln; but those mistakes were crucial: his failure to understand the nature of Forrest's generalship and his fatal support of Bragg. Too cautious in the early days of the war, when there was less need, he would now begin to lose his sense of the actual state of affairs. As Confederate fortunes fell, he grew optimistic. The result of this state of fantasy was to raise Bragg, the one man who had failed decisively, to the head of his military family. Bragg was brought to Richmond, to work in close consort with Davis. From that moment the Confederacy, short of a miracle, was doomed.

Forrest on his own at last, with little more than his escort, went into West Tennessee, through ten thousand Yankee soldiers, stayed there over a month, brought out a small army and many supplies,

including a drove of cattle and hogs, back through the same ten
thousand by a bold use of feint and surprise. These he armed and
organized into a small army, although even now he was put under
the command of another man, who had sense enough, however,
generally to let him alone. The war was soon to enter its final phase.
The proper use or misuse of Forrest would go far to determine its
outcome.

Sherman was still in Mississippi. He began to make in earnest his
total war upon the population. This would serve a double purpose:
limit and disorganize the means by which the Confederacy could
carry on the war; reduce the efficiency of the Confederate armies by
desertion. Sherman had never been a very successful field commander. At Shiloh his division was knocked to pieces and thrown
back in disorder upon the river. He never forgot or forgave this.
Grant's army was saved only by Beauregard's failure to follow up on
the first day and by Buell's arrival on the second. Sherman had also
failed at great cost in his assault on Vicksburg. But Sherman was a
man who learned. He knew at last who the enemy was: the women
and children, the corn bins and smokehouses; and he knew the
weapons: fire and rapine. If he could only burn and destroy enough
houses and smokehouses and turn the women and children onto the
roads to starve on dust and weeds, the war could be won. He would
have to maneuver against the armies for a while; but he surmised
that if enough hungry and starving children would cry loud
enough, the armies would be so reduced in numbers that he could
deliver battle with the odds he needed to win. For a man can't stand,
"Daddy, I'm hongry." Sherman probably did not tell himself this.
He raised the cry, "War is hell and every Southern woman to the
washboard." If he could say this hard enough and long enough, he
wouldn't have to hear the children whimper or remember the rebel
cry at Shiloh, rising like demons out of the earth and sweeping him
back to the deep waters of the Tennessee River.

He began this kind of campaign in Mississippi, setting out with
four divisions towards Meridian. His cavalry, the eyes, were to meet
him at Jackson. It was a good body, some seven thousand strong.
With inferior forces Forrest met it and drove it back to Memphis
with considerable loss. Sherman called off his campaign, to put it
into effect later in Georgia. Shortly after, Grant, now in charge of all
the Northern forces, moved to the east to confront Lee. He put

Sherman in command in the west. Together, over the entire theatre, they would begin a general movement, concerted towards the end of defeating the two main armies of the Confederacy, Lee's in Virginia and the Army of Tennessee now under an efficient commander, Joe Johnston. Sherman took command of the western army in person.

Of the two main armies of the Confederacy, the Army of Northern Virginia and the Army of Tennessee, there is this to be said. The first was commanded by the incomparable Lee; and when Jackson was its spearhead, it was invincible. After Jackson's death, after Gettysburg, its power was lessened, but it was still a dangerous instrument in the hands of a matchless officer. The scales had not yet tipped irrevocably towards defeat and the South's ruin, for as in the beginning it would depend upon what happened in the heart of the Confederacy, specifically what happened to the Army of Tennessee. In a sense, if there could be any true comparison, the Army of Tennessee deserves more praise. It had not Lee but a Bragg to command it. Without confidence in its commander, time and again it had come up to the verge of success in battle, in marches, only to have its endurance and courage, its skill and devotion, thrown away by that feckless person. Not until after Chattanooga did its morale break and the units of its organization lose form. Even from this it quickly recovered when Johnston took charge. In the last act of the drama it had the kind of commander peculiarly suited to the kind of strategy which would offer the Confederacy a chance, if not of making good secession, at least of an honorable peace. This was the strategy of the defensive: delay the war until after the presidential election soon coming up. In spite of its reverses the South still seemed strong and hard to beat. Lincoln's popularity was at a low ebb. The peace party was strong in the North, and McClellan, who was to run on the Democratic ticket, seemed to have a fine chance of winning; but only if the South continued to seem hard to whip, which meant that it must maintain its armies in the field, drag the war slowly out. The obvious policy now was to wear down the patience of the North, and Johnston was the man to do it.

The two opposing armies faced each other in North Georgia, the Army of Tennessee slowly but carefully retreating towards Atlanta, waiting for the right moment to strike the enemy. This meant that Sherman had a long line of communications, back to Louisville, Kentucky, upon which his success would depend. It would depend upon keeping Forrest in Mississippi. This Sherman knew. As he advanced, his strength would lessen; as Johnston retreated, his strength would increase and he would come closer to his line of supply. He fell back with such skill that it was said he didn't leave a broken axe handle behind. Sturgis was sent into Mississippi to hold Forrest there and was overwhelmingly defeated at Brice's Crossroads in June of 1864. This was a perfect battle, although on a small scale. Forrest concentrated his troops at the right time; defeated the enemy; and pursued him until the enemy's organization was completely broken up. On June 15 Sherman communicated with the Secretary of War: "I will have the matter of Sturgis critically examined, and if he should be at fault he shall have no mercy at my hands. I cannot but believe he had troops enough. I know I would have been willing to attempt the same task with that force; but Forrest is the devil, and I think he has got some of our troops under cower. I have two officers at Memphis who will fight all the time— A. J. Smith and Mower. The latter is a young brigadier of fine promise, and I commend him to your notice. I will order them to make up a force and go out to follow Forrest to the death, if it costs ten thousand lives and breaks the Treasury. There will never be peace in Tennessee until Forrest is dead!" There is a note of hysteria in this document which leads one to believe the commanding general, as well as "some of our troops," just possibly might be under cower of that dread name, Forrest.

The drama of personalities, which was to have such a decisive bearing on the final outcome of the war, was fast drawing to a climax. Forrest's fine display of skill at Brice's Crossroads, his crushing defeat of Sturgis, served to bring in relief one of the greatest blunders ever committed by those who directed the Confederate war policy. On May 10, the return of Forrest's cavalry showed his strength to be 9,220. If he had been turned loose on Sherman's communications in Middle Tennessee with even half this number, he could have broken them so effectively that Sherman would have had to retire. The railroad guards were mostly negroes, and there were not a great many even of those. Never again in this campaign would Sherman's communications be so vulnerable, and Forrest was sent by his immediate superior towards this end but had to be brought back when Sturgis invaded Mississippi, because of a scattering of the other forces in North Mississippi. This was in line with

Davis' effort to protect every crossroads and creek bank. Davis, even so late, did not meet Grant's grand strategy with a grand strategy of his own. He abandoned his interior lines of communication to his dispersive departmental system. When it was clear to almost everybody else that all other interests should be subordinated to those of Virginia and North Georgia, Davis held to his departments with a fatal jealousy.

The month of June passed. General Johnston appealed through Bragg four separate times—on July 3, 12, 16, and 26—to have Forrest thrown into Tennessee. On the thirteenth he sent a request directly to Davis, and he made one final appeal to him on July 16. General Cobb, Davis's friend, and the Governor of Georgia added their petitions. "I regret," replied Governor Brown on July 5 "that you cannot grant my request. I am satisfied that Sherman's escape with his army would be impossible if ten thousand good cavalry under Forrest were thrown in his rear this side of Chattanooga, and his supplies cut off. The whole country expects this, although points of less importance should be for a time overrun in the destruction of Sherman's supplies. Destroy these, and Atlanta is not only safe, but the destruction of the army under Sherman opens Kentucky and Tennessee to us. *Your information as to the relative strength of the armies in northern Georgia cannot be from reliable sources.*\* If your mistake should result in the loss of Atlanta, and the capture of other strong points by the enemy in this state, the blow may be fatal to our cause, and remote posterity may have reason to mourn over your error."

This acid reply was flashed at once from Richmond: "Your telegram of yesterday received. I am surprised to learn from you that the basis of the comparison I made *on official reports and estimates is unreliable.*\* Until your better knowledge is communicated I shall have no means of correcting such errors, and your dicta cannot control the disposition of troops in different parts of the Confederate states. Most men in your position would not assume to decide on the value of the service rendered by troops in distant positions. When you give me your reliable statement of the comparative strength of the armies, I will be glad also to know the source of your information as to what the whole country expects and posterity will judge."

\* Italics mine.

Well, there it is, the outward appearance of that inner state of mind which historians can never reach, but only interpret. Brown was probably trying to tell Davis that Bragg was misleading him, out of hatred for Forrest and jealousy of Johnston, who was popular with his former army; but Davis, already at odds with Johnston and under the strain of defeat, was to lose his sense of reality and demand an offensive at any cost, when such a policy in the reduced condition of the Confederacy was highly imprudent, aside from the political implications of the coming presidential campaign which he failed to understand.

Forrest was finally sent in, too late, after the railroads were strengthened and after the corn got ripe. He did enough damage, but only enough to show the fatal misuse of opportunity and talent. Atlanta fell, and there followed the odd sight of two armies marching away from each other. Sherman was undertaking the campaign which won the war, with sixty thousand men marching against the civilian population of Georgia. Lincoln and Grant were highly nervous over this move, but they showed the courage to back him up. Hood invaded Tennessee, where the odds were even. If he had not thrown his chances away, Sherman's gamble might have lost. Forrest isolated the enemy cavalry for three days and gave Hood the chance of beating the separated forces of the enemy in detail, but Hood lay asleep in his tent; and when he awakened, he murdered his army at Franklin, when he discovered what he had allowed to happen at Spring Hill. Sherman's policy of total war triumphed and the Confederacy went down to its doom.

The American Civil War was, in effect, the first phase of the total wars we are now engaged in. (Bismarck understood this, pointing out Europe's mistake in allowing the American states to be welded into a central power.) Everything from the distortion of the Word to trench warfare found its pattern in the Sixties. There is a peculiar spiritual blindness which follows the deadening of words, too often spoken, which caused the politicians at Montgomery to think, after hostilities had begun, that they had just recessed there from Washington; that they were making only another political maneuver in redrawing the Constitution, when the torch was already browning the words. Later Davis, standing on the virtue of the defensive at Richmond, cried out States' Rights as a maiden might cry *virginity* while the rapist grasps her hair. And Lincoln, freeing a moiety of the population at the risk of reducing the whole to slavery, saw too late what he had done and tried to repair it with malice for none and charity for all. With humility he at least tried to repair the damage. But it was not he who would define the terms of reconstruction, that effort on the part of the Radical Republicans to make of the South a pocket borough and so disenfranchise Democrats all over the country, to the end of putting the spoils in their personal pockets. Materialism had triumphed in its most brutal form. They took Grant for their tool and elected him President. They did not miss the point that it was he who had asked for unconditional surrender, the very definition of slavery, that total sacrifice of the will to the will of another. Constitutions, phrases like States' Rights and Freedom, whether they are four or one, are verbal statements of hopes to be sustained or earned by reasonable action. They belong to that relative condition of rational order which failed even in the eighteenth century and has never yet controlled the conduct of affairs for nations or the individual. It is an effort to make weapons of words, either for good or evil ends. But war is the raw naked aspect of an action. It is our inheritance from the Garden which brought death into the world. And you have to be a man to face what it means. Restricted war was the eighteenth century's answer. Napoleon brought that to an end. Total war requires of man that he risk himself totally and in entirety. Forrest knew this as he knew he had no wife or child, no house or land, unless he could get rid of such an enemy. And the quickest way was to drive him out or kill him; and when you go out to kill, you risk being killed. That's why Sherman said there will never be peace in Tennessee until Forrest is dead. Total war, as we now know, means the murder of the defeated society; at best its enslavement. You cannot win it by purchase or default. The only other Confederate commander of power who understood this was Stonewall Jackson. The Puritan and the wilderness man by their very natures see things in their absolute condition. They are without compromise. It is either freedom or death. Once committed to war, their calculations are limited to means, not ends. The end has been accepted.

In the wilderness a boy undergoes a natural kind of initiation which does not leave him long a boy, and Forrest was the head of his

mother's family at thirteen. He knows legs are not something just to
hang a pair of pants on, that eyes are not only to see with but to see
with first. You don't often get a second chance at sight in those
wastes of trees and lowgrounds where the beast lurks. But to see the
beast first is not enough either; you've got to *become* the beast to
track him down for the kill. So it wasn't much of a transition for
Forrest to be able to do this in war, in the kind of war he had to fight,
where the beast in man is released from all constraint. The great
heroes are born of beasts or are suckled by their dugs. At the least
they go into the wilderness and live with them and become them (St.
John Chrysostom, for example). The great hero is too busy thinking
of the enemy's shortcomings and fears, the death blow he means to
give him, to think of his own danger. He is a devoted man, unaware
of death since he has already consigned himself to it; so when he
loses a division, he hasn't lost anything. Forrest lost his commands
through Bragg's malice. He was merely relieved of command, which
could have been his Shilohs. But there was that crucial difference
between him and Sherman. Forrest never saw a command as some
abstract power outside himself. His command was an extension of
his will to victory. His troops looked upon themselves as a multiplication of his will and person. While Bragg was calculating the
odds or else merely frozen in his terror, after he had refused the kill
at Chickamauga and so lost the siege of Chattanooga and his command there, Forrest, ignoring the low fortunes of the cause, raised
another force in West Tennessee and by fighting it in that area and
in Mississippi, showed that quality which is never defeated, if it
controls the policy of a state or an army. He had overcome odds and
the *fear* of death. That's why his name was synonymous with hope
and victory. At the very end, after Nashville, it was he, commanding
the rear guard in that retreat, who got the army safely over the
Tennessee River, in the dead of winter, in the face of overwhelming
odds. During Reconstruction he took the *Un* out of unconditional
surrender by heading up the Ku Klux Klan, to beat the carpetbaggers and scalawags and the radical wing of the Republican Party. It
was not the kind of fight he liked, but he always chose the strategy
which the occasion demanded. And he won again and, knowing the
danger of this kind of tactics, he disbanded the Klan after its work
was done. Then he tried to pick up life where it was. But his work
was done, and his mind disbanded his body which had obeyed him

like his troops, and freed from the passion of his burning spirit that had burnt it up, the body collapsed into the dirt it was. It is the Shermans, the Johnstons, and the Davises who live on, clinging to the husk, gasping in that last breath *washtub,* or with the final tremor of the body, *States' Rights.* But the ground opens just the same, and it closes; and anywhere you dig, you turn up dirt.

# A *Retrospect on* Bedford Forrest and His Critter Company

BEDFORD *Forrest and His Critter Company* is a young man's book. To have anything more to say about a book you did thirty years ago brings you hard up against the matter of time. The young author shows a familiar visage, as enigmatic as the portrait of a great-grandfather "struck" in his youth, gazing into the close air of the parlor. You know you are kin, but *that* youth belongs to the ancestors. Therefore to redo or revise in any real sense would mean to make another book. Thirty years can change more than the use and control of language. The world may go on for a thousand years and, outwardly at least, be always the same. Then something appears out of nowhere, so sudden does it seem, and a shattering takes place; as for example when the stirrup was introduced into Russia by the Sarmations riding out of Siberia. They stopped with the conquest of Russia, but the stirrup did not stop there. The Goths took it into Rome. It ended the stalemate between the mounted archers of Parthia and the Roman legion. It had its long history in Europe. It came to an end as an instrument of military power about a hundred years ago in Alabama.

Everywhere east of the Mississippi the Confederacy lay in ruins. The great Lee had surrendered, and the Army of Tennessee, constant in defeat, workmanlike always, was stopped forever at Goldsboro. But Sherman had reported that "There will never be peace in Tennessee until Forrest is dead." His very name, so long as his troops were intact, made all these larger victories unsure. Reports had it Davis was fleeing Richmond to join him, cross over into the

Trans-Mississippi department and there carry on the war with Kirby-Smith. And then the news. Forrest had *surrendered*. The Wizard of the Saddle had dismounted for the last time. He had been whipped in his last fight, the one general who always won and whose victories were always thrown away by others in higher places. The war was now indeed over. The Republic of the Founding Fathers was no more. A certain ideology used by a sectional group of new men and interests had usurped the name "Union" to undo the political union. The Numerical Majority, as Calhoun called it, had triumphed over the Federal system; and, since numbers never rule, indeed cannot, but are always manipulated by some active minority, such rule is never representative of the whole except in rare moments of pressure or emergency.

History has borne Calhoun out; it has also made his predictions seem too local and domestic. Wise as he was, it was not to be expected of anybody in the eighteen forties and fifties to foresee so quick an end to Britain's hegemony of the world. The tragic consequences of change, and so Calhoun viewed them, would therefore involve only the internal health of the union and not foreign entanglements. For the United States to be strong enough to intervene in the quarrels of Europe and emerge the dominant power in the West, would have seemed fantasy to those politicians who saw Senator Mason rise in the Senate to deliver the dying Calhoun's last words. And yet ten years later a war was fought and won, the ultimate consequences of which would be just this.

So in a very literal sense the Civil War was the first World War. It not only created a powerful nation of organized resources and potential military might, but the greater world wars took their pattern from the American one, even to the trench system Lee set up at Petersburg. These wars were internecine, all of them; but it was not in this that we find the crucial resemblances. In view of a common Christian culture wars within Europe would of necessity be internecine, but at least at one time there were Truces of God. What this country brought to Europe was unconditional surrender. The actual phrase was used by Roosevelt in the Second World War, but it was not his phrase. Grant had delivered it to the Confederate Command at Fort Donelson in February, 1862. Its implication is total surrender or total destruction, or slavery, or whatever. A strange alternative to be delivered by one Christian state to another; and yet it had precedent in Sherman's harrying the lands of Mississippi and Georgia, whenever Forrest was out of the way.

The result of these wars has been the self-exhaustion of Europe, the loss of prestige before the world, and another possible shift in power from West to East. We seem to accept this with a fatalism strangely foreign to us. The battle of Lepanto was fought and won by a Christian prince. Since that time Christendom, if we can still call it such, has been free of danger; but there is a strange resemblance between that time and this. The Christian princes were divided among themselves as in our world wars; they were threatened by their own invention, the firearm, which the Turk added to the first use of the disciplined regiment. We have only to remember Spengler's warning as to the folly of teaching the techniques by which the West had overwhelmed the world and wonder. Will the time come when we will pray for another Lepanto? There is no Christian prince today strong enough to take a stand. This country is presumably strong enough at least to risk a defense, but to stand always on the defensive is to prepare for defeat. It was Davis' great failure of policy to which he committed the Confederacy.

So the great change in the world this time is not technological, although there are plenty of new tools. It is obviously spiritual. Yeats' trembling veil is at last rent. The Nineteenth century abandoned God officially, and the faith of Christian communicants was absorbed into the powerful western will; and this will set out, openly at last, to know and control not only nature but the universe. In the late stages of any society there is always the aging form and the formlessness of the new *pistis;* but this is no new faith; it is a perversion of faith, the final and open acceptance of Machiavelli's science of politics, the politics whose end is absolute power, whose technique is reason without any theological restraint. This prince will do anything, assume any role, to bring about his ends. Certainly Stanton, Lincoln's Secretary of War, was the most ruthless and greedy of all the Machiavellians. There is strong circumstantial evidence that he had to do with Lincoln's assassination, when the Northern president set in motion a peace which would bring the country back to a status quo.* It took a while for this to dominate Northern policy;

* *Why Was Lincoln Murdered?* by Otto Eisenschiml, Little, Brown and Co. (1937).

but after Grant and Sherman took over the command, the entire strategy became Machiavellian; any means justified the end. In the Wilderness campaign and at Cold Harbor, Grant's slaughter of his own soldiers was not merely lack of imagination. It was the sacrifice of the individual, the humane, the personal to the force of abstract mass; for unconditional surrender, that is, absolute power was his end. And yet he was a kindly man. He almost pushed it too far, for excessive loss in an army's manpower comes in time to shatter morale. Forrest had all the energy of the western man, his terrific will; but he was fighting for the traditional element in our society. He was able to use against the enemy his own method. He, too, asked for unconditional surrender, and added or I will put every man to the sword. But he never lost the sense that an army is composed of individuals. Nothing threw him into a temper so much as the useless loss of men. It was his care of man and beast, the thorough inspections of harness and shoes and the possibilities of entry and exit, that turned his fighting force into the most efficient body of horsemen in the South. His soldiers would follow him anywhere and did, because they knew this. He always fed them, and he always brought them out, and usually stronger than they had entered the campaign. For this and other reasons he was the crucial figure in the crucial, the Georgia, campaign, and the Northern high command knew it.

Sherman said "War is Hell," and by this he meant total war, openly carried out upon the civil population, with the shrewd understanding that if the source of supply was cut off, the armies would dwindle and perish. Partly due to Forrest he was unable to lay waste sufficient territory to dismantle the army before him, but his subordinates' attitude toward the civil population, as is always the case, brought home to the people of the South the meaning of this un-Christian policy. It placed Forrest in the role of avenger, for he never failed to punish the enemy. The outcry in the North when Fort Pillow was so savagely reduced by him comes from the fear that the very forces the new Machiavellians had released could be returned in kind.

A circumstance in my own family bears out how this dangerous power acted in a specific instance. My grandmother as a little girl was playing outside her house with other children. A Union soldier up the street shot into the crowd of children and she was hit in the neck just short of the jugular vein. When she ran into the house to her nurse, the blood was in her shoe and covered an apple she still held in her hand. Nobody ever knew why the man shot into the group of children. He got on his horse and galloped out of town and was never seen again, and was certainly not apprehended by his own officers.

Of course this incident could have happened at any time, in peace or war, and for any number of reasons. The point to be made is the official enemy attitude toward the incident. Though she was obviously bleeding to death, a doctor was forbidden, since her father had not signed the oath of allegiance. A young officer from Kentucky took the responsibility of getting her one; but later a squad of soldiers arrested her father and took him away cursing to make him sign the oath, and later still in the night she watched the soldiers troop by her bed, staring, enormous and dark, as their bayonets scraped the ceiling. This was the image she kept as an old woman. She must have got it from her mother's helplessness before this invasion of privacy at such a time. This was the change that was to come over the world; the helpless made to feel their helplessness. "It is well," General Lee said at the height of his success, as Pelham's small battery was holding up the attack of fifty thousand men at Fredericksburg, "It is well that war is so terrible. Were it not so, we should grow too fond of it."

As the wars grew even more terrible and world-wide, and the results more abstract and inhuman, we began to feel the abyss below us. We cry for peace, not for a life of peace but from the fear of annihilation. Yet the Christian dies alone. The fact that millions may die at the same time is meaningless, for it was Christ's promise that at world's end each separate person would find his own body and rise up his complete self. And he would be judged as an individual among a neighborhood of individuals. This was the intrinsic meaning of Christianity; and it was new, the promise of immortality for everybody. Before Christ's coming the East looked to some world cataclysm as we do. They feared utter annihilation, as we do, for they had no sense of the Christian individual. We have lost, although not completely, our sense of it. As our high priests, the scientists, feel they are conquering nature, the mass of individuals grows more ignorant about it and, therefore, about human nature. The public does not really comprehend the meaning of a rocket to the moon. They've already been there in the comic strips. This public is Calhoun's Numerical Majority with a vengeance. And the minority of rulers has shrunk to the Supra-individuals or supermen such as Stalin and Hitler—or Roosevelt and Churchill. They have become the sources of destiny, if not of salvation, since they have had to assume, willingly or not, the power and will which was once God's. Believing only in Machiavellian power, Stalin starved to death some millions of his countrymen. Henry II put on sackcloth and ashes and walked across England merely for his implication in the murder of Becket. But he was a Christian monarch who believed in damnation.

The world over which Forrest's men rode and fought was closer to Henry II's than it is to ours. They are centuries apart; yet those centuries knew the orderly return of the seasons, saw the supernatural in the natural, moved about by foot, by horse and at sea by the wind. We have put our faith in the machine. This is the concrete showing of the nature of our change. We view the technology of its laws as if they were as automatic as nature's. But the machine is not nature. It is man-conceived but not man-controlled; hence the monstrousness in serving it. The machine was meant to ease and speed up man's business a little, not change the look of nature. If it keeps up, it will change the nature of man, for we are moving so fast nobody is still long enough to see what is before him. The highways which are supposed to connect communities are becoming the community. In certain states the wilderness is growing again, but this time it is owned by paper corporations. The one image to clarify and define our state of being is the tons of trees growing, to be chewed up, to make paper, to advertise Lydia Pinkham's female tonic. In the beginning was the Word. Is it to end a flux of printed matter offering nostrums at a price?

It may, for we are losing that immediate and substantial sense of our surroundings which remind us of our humanity. Our last frontier is the heavens. Our pioneers are already there, and the world looks no more familiar than it does on a map. In the old wilderness a man was sometimes by himself, but he was never alone. He made a slow progress. To camp on the wilderness trail, compared to our travels, was almost to settle. And he did indeed settle each night; his eyes made the flora and fauna about him a familiar hiding place. He might go astray or become bewildered, but he was never lost. He knew where he was, because he knew who he was and where he wanted to go. And this was always forward. Between stations he would "remove," as he said, further on. His descendant wants to leave the world altogether. What a man hanging to a ball in space will learn remains to be seen. But whatever, he will be the man quite without location.

Location is that other force in our inheritance which balances our need for movement. It is the family which represents it and maintains it. The family does not flourish among abstract ideas. It is substantial, concrete, sensible. There was no Augustinian here separating psyche and physic. Flesh and spirit moved the one in the other, confined by the internal mystic form of belief. It was the basic unity of the Christian community, and hence the state. It carried authority. No matter what talents an individual might have, the family was always greater than he. It was this kind of a community that Forrest surrendered in 1865, but it was not delivered over until a hundred years later. It was the community into which I was born and in which memory called Forrest the great hero.

The hero saves not only by his prowess; he saves by the divinity within himself. Indeed his prowess depends upon this divinity. The hero's most perfect image is, of course, Christ the man-god. There is no hero unless the odds are overwhelmingly against the thing he stands for, or the rescue which takes him upon his quest. They are the powers of darkness; they show in the brutal weight of matter, the seemingly irresistible forces of mass. Since fear and desire make all of us tremble, the first quest of the hero is triumph over himself; and afterwards he follows the quest, a selfless and devoted individual on the way of becoming an archetype. Indeed because he is devoted, he is fearless. We do not know all the circumstance of Forrest's triumph over himself. We know it only in his actions and because of one statement; he bought a one-way ticket to the war; that is, he had committed himself without reservation of goods or person. This is of the very quality of heroism, because it is a triumph over death. It is also the secret of his triumph over great odds. Never thinking of himself, he is free to think of the enemy; and so he finds the weakness which will topple all the weight and mass. There was never a greater half-truth than the statement that God is on the side of the biggest battalions. Moscow and Napoleon's retreat stand for refutation of this.

But in the end the hero always fails. He either dies as Roland dies; or the cause for which he fought is lost; or he wins the fight and the calculators who take over gamble it away, as with Forrest. Never in the world are the powers of darkness finally overcome, for they inhabit matter; nor, without the conflict of the cooperating opposites of light and dark, good and bad, would life as we know it be. What the hero gives us is the image of his devotion and selflessness and the knowledge that he can save us from the powers of darkness—at times. Forrest had shown himself to be the hero who could save absolutely, or so the young man thought who wrote this book.

# How Many Miles to Babylon

IT is not given to a man to know midways of the journey how many
are the miles, their quality and meaning. I take it the three score
miles and ten is a disguise, as is the habit of riddles, for the Biblical
number of allotted time; and a warning not to take the measure too
soon. But this warning is a further disguise to hide the actual
meaning from the pragmatism of the materialist, that ultimate
poverty of the spirit Christ said we would always have with us. (I am
assuming certain nursery rhymes are fragments of older forms of
meaning metamorphosed by time or Christianity.) In one sense
Babylon is the acceptance of matter as the only meaning, the source
of the mystery. That man could accept the shell for total meaning,
that his vanity could lead him to believe a probing into can control
matter and hence life, is the ultimate folly which brings on the
confusion of tongues: that is, the failure of communication which
returns society to the wilderness, the untended garden. Babylon
was sometimes called Babel and always understood in the Bible as
confusion. In the New Testament it meant Rome and hence the
symbol of its day for all world cities which grow like a boil on the
landscape; or they are like a disorder in nature, the head instead of
ruling feeding on the body politic until it bursts, too, from surfeit.
Babylon sprawled for two hundred square miles on both sides the
Euphrates, but who knows how far it made itself felt as the dominant presence? Because of the size of this country and other reasons
New York is the best image of such a city. It stands in only one
relationship to the hinterland. At least London and Rome retain
long memories of themselves as capitals, with physical and meta-

physical relationships to the surrounding land. But any one of them focuses the modern predicament. The Agrarians might be said, by exposing the synthetic mythology behind Industrialism, to warn that Babylon has returned. Twenty years is a short time as history goes, but I see no reason to withdraw the assumptions upon which the Agrarians based their warning. There has been a change but only of degree. It is apparent that the confusion of tongues is immeasurably increased. The pace of history varies. As it approaches crises, it goes very fast.

If this insight of twenty years back still seems valid, what of Calhoun's a hundred years ago? His term for totalitarianism, or Babylon, was the Rule of the Numerical Majority: that amorphous majority controlled by the small irresponsible minority, which in turn responds to variable pressure, and all deluded by the fiction of representation. Betrayal always comes about in the guise of the thing betrayed. The very meaning of language, that men and nations mean what they say (that is, words), was undone by the deliberate distortion which preceded the last war. Its after-effects are more dangerous than the threats of any atomic explosion, for even if the world blows up, each man dies by himself, which he is going to do anyway. But the confusion of tongues will destroy a civilization. This Calhoun foresaw, and how quickly his words showed their prophetic truth. The Constitutional Union came to an end at the hands of those who said they were fighting to preserve it.

The world Calhoun lived in was relatively stable. There was little of the confusion we know to point to. His wisdom diminishes that of all his disciples, and I take it the Agrarians were pretty much that. All he had to go on was his imagination and a care for the public thing, that final protection of private life; but he did know that ideas do have consequences, and he knew the meaning implicit in action as well. Before the clarity of his mind how glib now seems Webster's rhetoric, and one wonders how disingenuous it was. Webster is dead, along with Calhoun, but the rhetoric is not. It is the long undertone of history, rising like static when the will fails. It was first heard in the Garden. It is whispered by the mouths of present-day liberalism. It is the old evangelical tongue that renews its skin with the season. It is the tongue that was heard in the corridors when Hiss was on trial. It says publicly that property rights are hostile to human rights, as if one of the human rights, in American belief, is not the right to own property. It has many skins but one body. It casts off Abolitionism to take on humanitarianism. It is the lips of the man who says the idle pleasant word. It is the gift which costs the giver nothing. It is the largesse of spending another's money. Pierre Bezukhov practices it when he gave orders to improve his peasants' lot only to increase their sorrows. It is the fairweather friend. It undertakes the act but refuses the responsibility for it. It says in the nature of things all men are created free and equal. It is always assuming the prerogatives of the godhead and ends up cutting the Gordian knot. Perhaps as rhetoric its harm would pass, but somewhere behind there is always the box of Beecher's bibles. It is finally dangerous because it is in every man. It is compassion for man's lot, but it is also sloth and therefore self-betrayal. It wants the body of the world without the pain and effort of earning it, or caring for it. Babylon is its reward and its doom.

"Can I get there by candle light? Aye, and back again."

This question and answer exposes the other attitude towards man's predicament. Candle light is metaphorically the Agrarian admonition. The body of the world will remain mysterious and fearful, no blaring searchlights to make it seem immediate and reducible to man's will, for beyond the glare lies the dark velvet of space, which the great light barely pricks. The body is frail, the mystery irreducible; therefore the feet must be nimble and quick as well. This is the riddle, old when it was first made, older now. It makes a more modest assumption about man's capacity, but the man it considers is more of man. He is both good and evil, and he has a soul to win or lose. The defense against the evil within and without begins in a structure of a stable society. He must have location, which means property, which means the family and the communion of families which is the state. Otherwise, as now, the individual is at the mercy of his ego. He understands that awareness of limitations is as near as he can come to freedom. Without control of space he is lost in time. The discrete objects of nature make a treadmill. Lest he mount it again he must engage and restrain himself by ritual, manners, conventions, institutions (as opposed to organizations). He may explore and enjoy but at his peril possess beyond the flare of the candle light. An all enveloping institution, some Church, should guide and contain and suffuse the various divisions of society. But there is no need to walk over the tracks of twenty years ago, except to add one thing that seems clearer now than then. The South may well become the salvation of this country yet, both at home and abroad. Private property, controlled by the proprietor, may be the only restraining influence to remind us that the great corporate business has something private about it. The time will come, otherwise, when it will seem more efficient for the state to take over. In this sense there will be the change of tactics from twenty years ago: the enemy will become an ally of a sort.

And then we must remember that the South is the only section of this country that knows the meaning of defeat, that is, the nature of the world. Everywhere else there has been nothing but a rising triumph, a pyramiding of success upon success. It is a perilous condition. Here Babylon mounts to Babel.

# PART III

# THE
# LONG VIEW

# A Christian University
## and the Word

WE are here to bear witness and perform an act of piety. We honor as we revive in memory those men who established this university, that our days may be long in the land. Only the very young can live in Eden. Only they can begin each day afresh, without memory, their senses quickening to the objects as they appear, as if they looked out upon the first day. This is a wonderful view, but it will not wear. Innocence prolonged ignores experience; knowledge denied becomes a stone in the head. Psychologists tell us that the state of innocence is the state we chiefly regret; and yet every man who is a man survives its loss; accepts the necessity for knowledge and a responsibility for its use. But to do this you've got to know who you are, where you belong, and how to prosecute what talents God has given you.

Three bishops were our founders. Bishop Otey first had the idea; Bishop Polk gave it substance; Bishop Elliott became its image of learning and faith, the ideal made concrete in his person of what a Christian gentleman should be. Not that all three did not work in whatever way they could towards a common end, or that all three didn't share one another's virtues and courtesy. But it was Bishop Polk who finally made it happen. He studied universities at home and in Europe; he spread the need for a place of Christian learning; and he had persuasive gifts. He showed how in a short time of travel Sewanee could be reached from all the Southern dioceses; and by being maintained in common, the place would not strain beyond

*This essay is Mr. Lytle's Founder's Day Address delivered at the University of the South October 10, 1964.*

possibility any one community. The plan was good; it was unique almost. The university would begin, not haphazardly, but out of full knowledge of what a university should be, with a large endowment, not to be spent but whose interest would first raise buildings; then employ a faculty. Bishop Polk, having been a soldier, could distinguish between strategy and tactics. Since it would be founded to last, there was no need to rush in unprepared, at the mercy of improvised acts and decisions. The doors would open upon the full complement of teachers, halls, equipment, a library and of course a chapel. It was to be called the University of the South, a title as American as any, since the working parts of the Union have always been sectional. The university was expected to serve particularly the Southern dioceses, but it would open to all comers. A half million dollars was quickly raised, the cornerstone laid with thousands attending, coming by the trainload, by carriage, wagon, horseback and afoot. The South in all its parts, plain man, mountain man, planter, slave, man of affairs—all were here out of common respect for what was being done. The clergy and politicians spoke until the going down of the sun in praise of learning. This was October 1860.

In the spring of 1866 Sewanee was a wilderness again. The endowment gone, the few buildings burned down, the cornerstone blown up by enemy soldiers and carried away in their pockets as souvenirs. But they could not carry the land away, nor could they desecrate the idea for which the stone was laid. Men die and are defeated; an idea is eternal. In March 1866 Bishop Quintard with a few workmen entered this waste of trees, cut down a sapling and raised a cross twelve foot high, recited the creed, and sang "Gloria in Excelsis." In this modest way the university was redeemed and rededicated.

This was the sign, and the hope, that nature and nature in man was once again to be reduced to order, without which no society can survive or its members live in worth and dignity. Off the mountain, in the valleys and plains there was another kind of waste. The South was beaten, exhausted, and tromped upon. Whole counties in Alabama and Mississippi didn't have even a needle. Houses burned, stock and cattle gone, some women pulled plows while men pushed to keep their children from starving. For ten years the ex-slaves led by carpetbaggers and scalawags combed the South for anything left by armies, levying taxes, bonding states for their private gain, selling counties of plantations under the hammer, dragooning and humiliating the defeated population. But still something remained, intangible, incomprehensible. The South was still undefeated in spirit. So the second war of conquest was set afoot, the conquest of the Southern mind. Francis Wayland, former president of Brown University, regarded the South as "a new missionary field for the national school teacher," and President Hill of Harvard looked forward to the job for the North of "spreading knowledge and culture over the regions that sat in darkness." These fellows figured they couldn't do the old soldiers much good. They would concentrate on the young and "treat them (the soldiers) as Western farmers do the stumps in their clearings, work around them and let them rot out."

Well, there were a lot of those stumps at Sewanee in the form of Confederate generals and bishops, soldiers turned priests and priests who had been soldiers now turned teachers, and like walnut stumps it took a good deal of weather to rot them. They refused, like General Lee, to sell their names for fraudulent purposes; and with the sure instincts of an aristocracy, homespun though it may have been, turned to the true reconstruction of the South, the Christian education of their young men. It is very moving even now to read about these Cincinnati who once ruled in great affairs, living on short rations, in rough but beautiful surroundings, knowing however that the salvation of the South lay in the kind of thing they were doing. Out of the clear faith of a Christian view they knew that the Northern secular education relates to Christendom only in so far as it has for patron that old adversary, that fallen light which shines in darkness but does not illuminate. The lie we live today is that a secular society and a carnal world is the whole of life. It used to seem tedious to you gentlemen to come to chapel, but remember this. Only there could you feel yourselves belonging to a whole body, not just individuals engaged separately in a common end. I have seen in a large land grant university (forbidden by law to hold religious services) the small buildings of various denominations lurking around the campus like houses of ill fame, which indeed they are to a secular court which has decreed prayer to be a criminal act. Ideas do have consequences and the perversion of ideas perverse consequences.

The South was a Christian society, but an incomplete one. It had as many puritans as New England. And they were fine people, but communion between Heaven and earth is bound to be uncertain, so long as you have only a pulpit and no sacrificial table before which to worship. Yet Southern people were believers as are all people who are constantly at the mercy of nature and its laws. The seasons turn for a farmer (when there were farmers) and his welfare and even life depends upon this turning. The rough laws of nature may be defined, but nature is finally a mystery as it acts upon man. It is the very ground of a religious state of mind. When the formal religion of society knows less than the farmer about the mysteries of creation, then that society is likely not to know itself adequately and so suffer unneeded limitations. The great puritan heresy puts evil in the object, in a deck of cards, in a woman's hair, in dancing, in that great invention whiskey. The only time that church and state have got together in this country, since the Reformation, was to pass the prohibition law and create the most powerful and uncontrollable criminal class known in recent years. Evil cannot be in the object. It must be in the mind and heart. That's the only place it can be.

I'm not the one to say that the South would have been a more complete Christian society if the Episcopal church had been the only church. But it is true that under attack since the Missouri compromise, which frightened Jefferson like a firebell at night, all the sects were growing together towards one church. The South was struck down, unformed, before it knew itself. It had many diverse elements, but it had one institution which outlasted the destruction, which in this country and in Europe is the Christian unit, and that is the family. From the beginning here at the University the boys were put in boarding houses, so that they would have a home influence away from home. It was believed that without a woman's authority all manners would grow corrupt and all domestic virtues languish. The matrons in the dormitories are an extension of this and evidence of how an established practice must undergo outward change. As a basic part of society's structure the family has had to bear more than it ever was meant to. The recent attacks against the

South are actually against the family, for so long as it thrives a dictatorship will have trouble. A family must have location that outlasts a generation. Family farms and plantations are becoming unprofitable; the families are breaking up and drifting away. The towns and cities are filling up with rabbit warren slums and carbon dioxide. No family, no human being can stand such a plight long.

Now what are we going to do to be saved? How can the university help? I feel that both the liberals and the conservatives have lost definition. Neither one can make us know what a liberal arts education means. But a tradition might. The essence of the Sewanee tradition has been that of the founders, to graduate a Christian or a gentleman, but preferably a Christian gentleman, who will go back home, or out into the world, and be what he is. That's the only way anybody can be of any use. First of all he will keep private things private and public things public. This is the basis of order. He will not speak of poetry to the philosophers or philosophy to the poets, as if he had all knowledge. If he wants to preach, then let him mount the pulpit; if he wants to influence politics, then let him run for office; if he wants to bring about social reforms, let him behave himself and mind his manners. His mind will presumably be a trained instrument which can respond to any kind of experience. He will let information go through him like a flux, but digest his learning. Some graduates will become scholars, but we will make a great mistake encouraging our best students all of them to go to graduate schools and perpetuate themselves. Now there are mixed and legitimate reasons for this; nevertheless it's the monkey going around the mulberry bush. There is another thing that at least worries me. It's not that television is going to supplant the flesh teacher. What worries me is all this instruction and fiats, from loans to examinations coming out of Princeton. If it keeps up we'll be writing up there to find out what textbooks they'll be pleased to let us teach, and we will get a reply from the moon.

Now I am going to wind up. In a society fast becoming proletarian, in an age that will become known as the paper age, is it possible to graduate Christian gentlemen, even from a school founded to deliver a Christian education? For make no mistake about it, this kind of education is aristocratic. It can't be democratic. We've never had a democracy in this country. We once had a Republic. Since the Civil War we've had a plutocracy. It calls itself a democracy, but then it is customary to betray in the name of what is being betrayed. The Union, for example, was destroyed in the name of defending it. How can a gentleman function and be himself in an ochlocracy, towards which we are moving?

The image for a gentleman has been with us for a long time. It has survived from before the days when Christendom was rent. I think we have to go back to that. The world's plight is so precarious that we can not survive without a return to order and for us this can only be Christian order. Christendom was not a commonwealth; it was a god's wealth. The king was God's secular overseer; the bishop His spiritual. If you were the king's man, there was no doubt as to your place and degree, or likewise if you were the bishop's. Nobody mistook a man's function or place. The castle and cathedral stood forth for every eye to see, symbols both of physics and metaphysics. This entire order was held together, in the right order of relationship, by the Word, the eternal Word, for God said "Before Abraham was, I am," that is to say, I am pure being, pure creation, which is forever. The Word was God in His Creative function. There was God the Father, the lover, and God the Son, the beloved, and the Holy Spirit as the love which played between them. As the Holy Spirit this love came down from on high, in the likeness of a dove, to whisper into Her Ladyship the Virgin's ear the promise of salvation: to make flesh of the Word and the Wisdom that had created the flesh. Where else could the Word enter except by the ear, enter as the divine harmony of music, joining reason, imagination, the sensibility together to make the flesh to hold the spirit? Once before the dove brought to the ark a sign of reprieve. The doves were Aphrodite's attendants, symbolizing in their cooing her nature. Now at last with its fiery wings the dove as spirit entered invisibly matter, rendering not half man and half god but God incarnate. This is the mystery become the order Christians knew.

But this order fell (the world is much given to falling) and it fell first at the hands of priests, out of a lust for the total power of both rules; then Henry VIII usurped the authority which belonged to the lords spiritual. For both we can have but sympathy and charity, particularly for the priests who forgot the meaning of the sacrament and faltered as men. Ever since, the Word in Itself has gradually withdrawn into Itself, and the word as language without which man cannot know man nor get his business done has lost its divine form. Theology became partisan, but the divine glow was slow to leave language. The Spanish priests, not understanding that the imagination might be part of God's Word, spoke of *Amadis de Gaul* and *Don Quixote* as lying histories. Young soldiers too believed, which caused them to imitate Amadis and so hazard the lives of their friends who had to rescue them from heroic acts. The Word divine had become the word magical: this was the clear step away from meaning. After the sixteenth century decline was rapid. And now with few exceptions, the word is secular, legal, with no fixed definition. It serves to increase our appetites and to disguise the truth, and make us the slaves either to ourselves or other men. Whole forests are cut down daily towards this end. But there is hope. We were promised one thing; that the gates of Hell would not finally prevail. It is time to take the risk of judgement. A Christian university can begin to restore to language its meaning: first by definition which defines, makes more accurate the vocabulary of the various branches of learning, keeping them in their right order and relationships. This is the beginning of recovery, for without knowledge there can be no apprehension of the divine creative promise of the Word. There are words still with symbolic lustre, like sine and cosine, and honor.

Let us take the word honor, since it involves the whole action of man and not merely his profession. In Mississippi, Colonel Dabney, who had been a rich planter before the Civil War, afterwards found himself ruined. A white-haired old man, he did the family wash, because Sherman had said he would bring every Southern woman to the wash board. Also, in his prosperous days, in the routine of business, he had put his hand to a note, promising to pay. In the reversal of fortune, which any one of us might expect, he found his obligation increased a hundredfold. He paid every penny of it, working only for this, and then died. He did not bemoan the turn of fortune that made of a simple matter a heroic act. His name was on that note. It was the symbol to himself. It defined him, himself to himself and to others. That signature meant that he would deny himself, his total being, if the note remained unpaid. It also meant submission to another, so long as the promise to pay was not paid. To redeem his word was to make him free. About the same time Jim

Fisk tried to corner gold. When he failed, he said, "Nothing lost save honor." So, gentlemen, you have your choice.

That statement is the core of Yankee triumph over the South and its European inheritance. It means nothing matters but money. A man who so believes makes of himself a slave to an abstraction, his wife a fancy woman, and his children orphans. How could there be so many divorces if this were not the case, or so many children lost?

The University of the South maintains at least the rumor of its founders' intentions. In that is a moiety of hope: that it should turn out a Christian gentleman and today of necessity it must add gentlewoman, even though these words have become anachronistic. But the university still offers the disciplines of a Liberal Arts education, at least a sound education. We may take comfort in this.

# The Search for Order in American Society: The Southern Response

"YET once more, O Ye laurels, yet once more, Ye myrtles brown . . ." Once any school boy would have recognized the convention, if not the necessity for an apostrophe to the Muse. Now we address others out of the authority of our egos, relying entirely upon circumstances and our introspective autonomy. Today this attitude towards man and the cosmos is common to all occupations.

Such heresy would have appalled the Greek-Roman world. The classical poet, statesman, or general would have averted his eyes from one so recklessly defiant of the Fates—from one so publicly impious. Even centuries later, Milton, among other poets, felt the need to rely upon something beyond talent and skill.

It was more than a convention among the ancients. To tamper with the Fates, more powerful than the gods, involved the matter of hubris both in life and the arts. Greek tragedies, those that have come down to us, are dramatic renditions of what pride, concretely, can do to human beings, either by one human to another, or by the distant intervention of the Fates in their own ugly shapes or by the gods. There is no more poignant appeal than that of the child Iphigenia saying, "But what have I done? Whip me if I've done wrong." This brutal sacrifice of a daughter by her father to further his ambition would make even the keys of a computer sigh.

It is impossible to write a tragedy today. Man has become a

*This essay is a reprint of an address made by Mr. Lytle at a conference sponsored by the Foundation for American Education at Spartanburg, South Carolina in 1977.*

hostage to society. As hostage he no longer is responsible for himself or for his acts. Either the family or living conditions are asked to take the blame. Sometimes it is the mother's milk that has soured in him, and he never did no good. Or he becomes a criminal, since he has not gotten all the material things advertisement makes him feel are his birthright. Women often are his special victims. By the time the Press takes over, there are so many crimes and the details are repeated so often (always modified by the word "alleged") that, like a piece of music being killed, the crime ceases to have an actuality in the reader's mind. Through mass media we receive every thing filtered through distant views; so that vital actions are becoming more and more abstract, until one person suffers, and then it is too late to comprehend.

Without a tragic sense there is no moral sense, and without a moral sense, violence, uncontrollable and meaningless, rots what is left of institutional society. You can put two policemen on every street and a judge on every block, but without a sense of what is right or wrong, crime becomes the normal state and criminals walk the streets because the courts are crowded. In the crystalized stage of civilization, that of the world cities, to use a Spenglerian term, "forms harden, roots of the organic units of the state are lifted into the shallow pots of a Garden of Adonis, where they bloom shortly and die, removed from a rich continuous earth."

Richard Weaver's book, *Ideas Have Consequences,* makes a profound analysis of the predicament the Western world finds itself in. He picks the twelfth century and the Realist-Nominalist controversy as the time Christendom made the wrong decision. Occam's razor cut off the sustaining universals and put the truth in the individual mind, and that meant ultimately dependence upon experience. As Joseph Campbell says, "theology was abandoned in favor of psychology." I would like to add that without any absolute set of values to which action can be referred, and Weaver agrees, experience is largely that of sensation. There is the often-heard, "to learn from experience." That is the one thing you cannot do. We may suffer or delight in experience, but since we never have the same kind twice, that is, experience that is exact enough to permit generalization, we see at once how ideas have consequences. As a corollary to this, the word "Modern" replaces the word "Christian." It is like the elastic on an old woman's drawers. It will fit any shape. It is closely allied to Progress, that Whig word which makes an advance in time necessarily an improvement over the past, merely because it is the latest thing. Nobody seems to remember Queen Elizabeth's "progresses," those month-long visits to powerful lords. When she left their domains, she left them bankrupt and harmless. But to speak of modern man is self-deluding. There is no such being. At what time of the day or night does the natural man turn modern? At twelve o'clock? Two minutes after midnight? Now? Yesterday? I offer in our predicament a more exact word. The "momentary" man; that man who no longer has location, who is forever on his way, speeding from one inn to another, to the same bed that is not the same bed, to poor cuisines served in the same false ornament of supposedly foreign architecture. And because of the failure of our educational system, nobody recognizes the falsity of the Spanish rococo, or the French provincial bedroom suite.

I'm not going to bring coals to Newcastle and summarize Weaver's philosophical and learned argument. I am entirely in agreement. I am an artist, and it happens that I prefer the truths of mythology to those of dialectics, not in any way believing that they disagree, but that they occupy different parts of the mind. As a myth of pertinent relevancy for us today as in the past, I am going to explore a little the Garden of Eden. Many think that legends and myths of the ancient world come from Sumeria, presumably the first cultural kingdom to emerge from the mists of time. This is mostly speculation, and so must be the possibility that it is from the tales of Sumeria that our Garden of Eden derives. The J writer, to whom many biblical scholars ascribe the second account in Genesis of the Garden, left out a most interesting detail: Adam's first wife, Lilith. Now, she was a good girl. When she ran away, it took four angels to catch and hold her. She must have been a destructive part of the Mother goddess, until the masculine triumph in Heaven left her out of the Hebrew canon and she sank into oral legend. So, it came about that the Hebrew patriarchs, as well as Christendom, accepted the J writer's story of the beginning of things. Nor should the cogency of its meaning be lost to us now, especially one aspect of the Garden's drama. (I make this seemingly obvious point, since I find that one difficulty in teaching is the students know scarcely anything of the Bible or ancient history or the myths and fables of the classical world, as well as not knowing how to spell or construct a sentence.)

Let me summarize. The all-unknowable, un-namable, invisible power we refer to as God, for His ineffable reason, assumed a limitation. He became a Creator, that is an artist, and in six days made the cosmos within which we abide. Like all artists, at the end of a masterpiece He needed a rest. But to rest there must be a place agreeable enough to rest in. And so He made a garden where He could walk in the cool of the day. He made all the herbs and growing things. He experimented with animals, the crawling things, and those that had wings. Wherever He looked, up or down, before or around him, He saw that his artifacts were good. In the midst of all this brilliant performance, alas, the Creator got lonesome. Apparently He had not expected this. So He then made out of the dirt of the Garden an artifact in His own image and called him Adam.

All forms are contained in that part of the mind known as the imagination. All forms, when substantially completed, make an image, and this image is a symbol of a certain quality or act. This is the basic authority for the guidance of all craftsmen, and for the definition of what a craft is.

Naturally, all forms find themselves in the mind of God, else chaos would have persisted in its Quroboric inertia. Since man is made in the image of God, he has inherited this state of cognition, although no man can truly be said to create. Only God can breathe life into matter. All man as artist can do is imitate out of his private talent and vision the action and phenomena already established.

As Potentate of the Garden it was not God's intention to make Adam into an artist. What He needed was a gardener. Some will say that gardeners have many crafts. Be that as it may, the Garden needed to be tended by one with attributes sufficient to consort with the Landlord in his leisure moments. To be able to look after the flora and all growing things, Adam needed a limited power, with the emphasis on limited, that is a power sufficient only to his office. Anybody who has ever farmed knows that cattle and hogs can get in a cornfield and ruin it, or crows pluck corn deep out of the ground. So God called before Adam all the birds of the air, the beasts of the fields, the things that crawled, and had him name them. And what Adam called them, they were called. Adam also named Eve. Now, to name is to have power over what is named. Primitive tribesmen know this. They will never tell their true names to a foreigner. And nobody knows the name of God.

Notice that God, master of the cosmos and landlord of the Garden, its core, did not ask Adam to name the flora. The flora was there before Adam was made, containing along with the rest of the universe the mystery which it represented. To make clear to Adam his limits, God forbade him, as we know, to eat of the tree whose fruit contained a juice only the gods could digest: good and evil; those opposites whose balance ordered the motion of things. There was another tree at the center of the Garden God was careful not to mention: the tree of life. Be content, He was implying, with using and looking after all growing things, but make no effort to explore or investigate the secrets of life or of the surrounding firmament. All the while, Eve, standing at the side of Adam and a little back, with her eyes cast demurely upon the ground, was listening to the admonition. Now the ground is the natural habitat of the serpent. No doubt Eve saw him wink and crawl away, towards the trees at the center of the Garden. Else how would she have known which tree was which?

Now the artist must not only look at his artifact and see that it is good. He must also be surprised by what he has done, far more than he set out to do. This is the secret of the master stroke that pulls all of it together and sets it forth as the masterpiece it is. Such distinguishes the work of an artist from the formula. $H_2O$ must always be water and not occasionally carbolic acid. The very thing that makes the formula work for a science makes it inane and dull for fiction. Or verse. It leaves out, as John Crowe Ransom argues in *God Without Thunder*, contingency. Well, the Creator discovered that the juice of the apple had a most disturbing quality for the peace of the Garden. (This is always the risk the artist takes.) Concealed behind the smooth skin of the fruit were the laws of nature, more particularly appetite, the appeal of which to his creatures God forsaw at once, in the entire range of its implications. Indiscriminate appetite would replace the Garden of Innocence, or the suspension of life, however you call it, with a cannibal wilderness. Appetite is not only carnal.

That is vexing enough. There was also in the knowledge of good and evil an appetite for unrestrained power. This would change all the rules of the game. This was no threat to God's power. The threat was to the well-being of His creatures.

Not disobedience, but the sorrow of chaos's return is the lesson the myth of the Garden has for mankind. We of the West have rushed to misconstrue its warnings. The moment the European mind accepted materialism as the summum bonum, that is the dirt of the ground without the breath of God upon it, it initiated the repetitive catastrophes of Babel. The confusion of tongues is the prelude to downfall. It describes excessive specialization which reaches the stage where no master craftsman can interpret the disparate groups of skills upon which a state must stand.

We all think we know how it came out. Certainly the Garden would be no place where God could any longer walk in the cool of the day. In His quandary all he could think to do was forbid Adam to eat of that particular tree. He did not mention at first the tree of life. Now the subtlest beast of the field, the serpent with the speaking head, knew that Adam was obedient, and he spoke to Eve only in the most general terms about good and evil. He did emphasize what he thought she would like—to live in the highest fashion. The irony lies just there. She and Adam were already living as the gods, without any of the crushing responsibility and knowledge of what that meant.

The first result of this great change found the intimacy between God and His creatures diminished. He took to high places and spoke out of whirlwinds, and Adam and his family found themselves wayfarers in this world. But in the wilderness of their exile these creatures did not forget their genesis: they were made in the image of their Creator. If they had been cast out to suffer the laws of nature, they could take comfort in the knowledge of their heritage. No matter how disguised it might become, they partook of their Divine ancestry. The proof of this on the man's part was an innate need to make things. Nothing he could do would so nourish his spirit as working at some craft. This gave him a limited power over nature and freed him from nature's most pitiless law, cannibalism. With children, Eve discovered she had a family, and this made bearable the sorrow of birth. She also discovered that a family has to eat, and fairly regularly. No cook with many skills likes to keep moving about; so gradually, to skip eons of time, cultures and civilizations began to appear, and they mostly were based on the family as the unit of the community. Christendom's structure was just this. Every man was a craftsman from the lord to the peasant, and every person belonged to some kind of family. Manners and mores defined the forms and laws of society. Weaver reminds us that the French mark for civilization is etiquette and good food, which they limit to themselves and the Chinese.

It is not in the French nature to hide any light, no matter how dim, under a bushel. Be that as it may, a traditional cuisine, composed of culinary crafts, the basic ones inherited, does two things to stabilize society. It demands good manners, and this restrains appetite and thus makes for the etiquette of the table, which in turn makes for a respectful savoring of the dishes served, good conversation, and a celebration of a social amity among the diners. It maintains leisure, which gives pause for reflection, upon which the arts and, for the last four hundred years, history has depended. Memory, through recollection, into song, I believe is the classic inheritance the Western world has abandoned in its reduction of man to his physical dimensions.

But I can give you a more homely example. The taste and odor of the family victuals, which has the common taste of a province or region, binds the solitary to the family and the family to a place. Wander I don't care how far, or how well you eat exotic or strange foods, there will come a time when you hunger to eat some family dish or bread. It is usually bread. When I was a boy in Paris, I would have given a hundred dollars for a hoecake and a mess of turnip greens with two poached eggs on top and marinated onions on the side. But it was the bread I longed for.

A good cuisine does a second thing. It respects the fruits, vegetables and meats it uses. It does not take from nature these gifts for mere survival, which is the economy of eating today what you get today, with no thought of tomorrow. It receives these gifts ceremonially and, at times, with ritual care. That of course is the traditional society, one maintained hierarchically and hieratically. It accepts the curse, that we all live, man, beast, fowl, fish, and herb, in a cannibal world. Only by ceremony and ritual, a common respect for all living things, can we mitigate, make bearable, the knowledge of how we live. The Indians, the most religious and conservative of peoples, made peace with nature. In hunting they always asked permission of the deer or the bear before they killed it. And since their clans took the names of animals, there was no indiscriminate slaughter until we arrived upon the scene.

We taught the Indians our habits: make war on nature. Our retribution appeared in the form of the Momentary Man, who obliterates both time and space, living in the sensation of the moment or the suspension of every one but that of the monotony of speed. His table is the cafeteria, food without ceremony, where the solitary never dines, only eats.

I have a feeling I am stating platitudes. But when I try to elevate the tone, I wonder about the role of a male Cassandra. The eyes of thirty are not the eyes of seventy. At thirty the landscape looked familiar. It no longer does. Wherever you went, you were aware that families composed the community, in town or country. There were enough family-sized farms and private ownership of business to balance the abstract corporations of industry. Automobiles travelled the roads and turnpikes, but the roads were bad enough to restrain the disruption of families. The Agrarian position was this: if this country could only keep the equilibrium between capitalism, or the propertied state, and finance corporate industry (without which some foreign power might take us over) we would continue to lead a better life. It was business with actual owners in control *or* abstract corporations ruled by managers and dominated by what John Taylor of Caroline County, Virginia, called the paper and patronage aristocracy. This last was the genesis of all totalitarian societies, that is servile states, and it doesn't matter whether they are called Communism, Fascism, or Democracy.

But I don't want to go over the Agrarian proposals. These can be found in print. It was never a movement. We wrote with our backs to the wall by way of protest. It was the dramatic 1929 crash which made us seem to be prophets. Indeed, it has turned out that we were. None of us thought it could be as bad as it has come to be.

Richard Weaver was at Vanderbilt long enough to be influenced by the ideas generated there. His proposal for salvation—it is no less than that—is restoration of private property and the forms of language, and ultimately of Literature. Certainly he was one of the first to show the need of purifying language. Words mean what they say. When they do not properly express meaning, communion is on the way to being lost. In the nineteen thirties language was not so obviously threatened. More men knew then who they were. There was an eagerness to volunteer for the First World War. This was not so obvious in the Second World War, and the last one was advertised by its deserters. Men volunteer when they have something to lose, especially something they believe in and love.

The ingrained need for property is not yet totally lost, but without a proper understanding of language the proprietor will be hard put to defend it, and his enjoyment will be curtailed. And this is where a proper education comes in. A proper education would be as near like the old Liberal Arts as is possible today. It would introduce its scholars to the various areas of learning. It would discipline the mind, so that the graduate can perform in diverse circumstances. And the mind would flourish because it would be a poetic mind, that is, it would have a constant view of the wholeness of things.

Such a program would return us to an aristocratic education, literally the aristos Krateo, the rule of the best. It would take bold and intelligent young people to enter such a curriculum. They will have to learn how to restrain the mass media they were brought up on. It's been my experience that the best of the young are eager to learn, just as they are quick to despise and ignore the spurious. As graduates of such a training they would have a larger knowledge and a belief in something outside themselves. And it just might be that, returning home, they with their sense of order, would find those who are lost turning to them for guidance. The communities less and less are representing what a community should be. They may help them to recuperate. This all will take time, but in a crisis the effects of such an education would proliferate.

Literature can never take the place of a commonly accepted and practiced belief in religion, but we must not forget that the Word was a creative power of God, and that it was made flesh in Christ. To want to restore a lost faith will not restore it. But in a materialistic and secular world, language and literature, and the richness of language is literature, seems to me as the best if not the only way to rescue us from the rapid advance of a confusion of tongues. This knowledge will clear our eyes, allow us to see that we who have thought of ourselves as rich have only been profligate, and that our progress has been the progress of Hogarth's heir. Then instead of the habit of gluttonous appetite, safety and comfort, we may know again faith, hope and charity. But we will not know them until we correct our distortions by a sober reconsideration of the natural virtues; justice, prudence, temperance and fortitude.

# The Momentary Man

IT is the exceptional university student today who knows that the
sun god, Apollo, is the patron of artists and craftsmen; that he is
part of our inheritance from the classical world; that in the dim
reaches of prehistory he killed the python and so raised the light of
truth above the dark powers of the earth. The twining laurel is his
crown. From Greece with its mythology, although it is a metaphor
with us, the laurel signifies not only the discipline of the athlete but
all branches of learning. The funeral games to praise the illustrious
dead had races, athletic contests; but also poets and dramatists,
actors and dancers, sculptors and painters, competed for the myrtle
prizes.

The laurel shines out of the light of reason certainly, but that is
not all. Its spectrum holds the full light of truth, all the parts of
truth; and this includes the heart and the imagination, the necessity
for ceremony and the proper forms of matter. It demands that we
distinguish between what is public and what is private, else disorder
and darkness will return and, coiling, thrust its tail into its mouth.
Again then the serpent Quroboros will resume its inert circle about
the waters of chaos. Perpetual night will return that invisible state
before God set the moon and the stars in the firmament, as he
divided things from things. And made the cosmos.

As you see, I have joined two parts of our inheritance, the
Hebraic and the classical mythologies. The metaphor is not mixed,
but two legends whose images tell us the same thing.

It is these myths and legends and semi-histories which materialism is erasing from the common memory and the formal instructions in schooling and the church. I find one of the difficulties of

teaching students imaginative literature is their ignorance of the Bible and mythology, as well as grammar and spelling.

And this is because, I believe, the structure of the state has become predominantly secular. Prayers are forbidden in school. They will soon be forbidden in churches, as we set the computer upon the altar. The need for etiquette and ceremony grows less. Many young people are marrying behind the church rather than in it. These are couples who deny the very meaning of family by aborting. Very young children and babies, doctors tell me, are increasingly brought to hospitals maimed or tortured, some beaten beyond repair. They were in the way of selfish indulgence. And now in public address, instead of propitiating the Muse, we speak out of the authority of our egos, relying upon circumstance and our introspective autonomy.

To address the Muse, to thank the Muse, always in formal matters, that is to accept the divine mysteries behind our acts, is repugnant to us. We are independent. We did it all by ourselves. And so beset by hubris we are gradually losing the meaning of our institutions; we are even changing the birthdays of our heroes to suit the convenience of a week-end. At this pace no society can hold together. In the beginning God breathed upon matter and made life. Matter, unquickened by God's breath, is death. Without the acceptance of and belief in a divine order, how can we take this truth seriously. And yet the truth is the truth.

Happily, today, we come together out of the economy of the old disciplines of learning, somewhat less than they should be, nevertheless we can rightfully call them The Liberal Arts. If not quite the trivium or quadrivium, it is these arts which will mold the forms of your education. Some of you perhaps will learn to explore the mysteries of a craft, imaginative writing but not only that. Any craft involving an art makes visible the opaque ideas concealed within the mind. Later, in the hurly-burly of life it will be possible for you to demonstrate by actions this training you have received.

Let us say that a man is best defined, not by his amorous prowess (although that is not to be neglected) but by his work. It is a matter he spends most of his time at. Also he lives by his work unless he prostitutes himself. But the endowments essential to manhood are the talents given us at birth, as our genes give us the color of our eyes.

The perfection of these talents by craftmanship or, as we say loosely by working at it, shows the quality of manhood. I know that more and more we serve the machine instead of the other way round, but not to work towards the end of doing the best with what you've got is to neglect or mar the gifts of God. And that might be the unknown sin, although privately I think the unknown sin is the practice of puritanism: that is the will to power over man and nature, that is putting evil in the object such as a bottle of whiskey, the movement of the dance, or a woman's entangling hair. This is putting it where it is not. For good or evil abides in the heart.

All this puritanism is an effort to steal some of the power of God. God made us in his own image, but he reserved his creative power to himself. The temptation by the serpent with the speaking head, that Adam and Eve could live as the gods, knowing both good and evil, holds a devastating irony: our first parents were already living as the gods, without the burden of evil: that is they were not God. When expelled into the wilderness of life, they carried one divine attribute, and that was the sense of craftsmanship. But again no creature can create. Only God creates. Man imitates. All the multiplicity of substance and forms the world holds, the artist by his effort, may recreate out of his vision. This is unique to him. And it is this uniqueness which sets him apart from all other men. At the same time it is what all men, to varying degrees, have in common. Even when they debase or squander it.

By means of this bold claim, that we are made in the image of God, the structure of Christendom bound all men together, from king to peasant. Each made a living by what he did. Every man was a special kind of craftsman then. Today, under the exploitative idea and habits of the Industrial revolution, the craftsman has become a special kind of man. He is rare today, even in farming. We still hear occasionally such words as priestcraft and kingcraft, but I doubt if we examine these words in their full meaning, governors of secular and spiritual matters, as God's overseers. Bishop and king were craftsmen, as was a goldsmith, ironmonger, or tailor. (It is a significant change that ironmonger has become the steel industry.) In that economy each craftsman worked to produce something of utility, like a pair of pants, or a chalice. He worked for a fair return on his labor, as well as to the greater glory of God, the divine craftsman. By the quality of their artifacts they praised God as well as pleased man, the patron. And when you cease, in your mind, to please God, you become subject to pressure groups, such as the labor Union or, in John Taylor's words, the Aristocracy of paper and patronage.

Now this Christian economy may seem distant to your education. However, the Liberal Arts was the Christian education which in a lesser form has come to us as our inheritance. I have had complaints from good students that this kind of education did not prepare them for the world. What they mean is a world totally materialistic, secular, and carnal. It is a world with the habits of Puritanism without a belief in God. Without a belief in some form of a divine order, a belief in something outside and beyond you, you accept the falsehood of the will as supreme; and power, irresponsible and absolute, as the end of endeavor. This is the world we inhabit. Of course a liberal arts education does not prepare the student for this, nor in any way can the student accept it as the only good form for society to endure. When the university does accept this world, it ceases to be.

This is a question for the friends of the university to consider. There is no absolute answer. But truth is truth, even when it occupies a hostile environment. There is no pure state. But the discipline and values of the kind of a liberal arts education can save the graduate from being swamped by and distorted by (that is the human condition) a world which accepts the abuse of power and appetite as the ends proper to man. It is not going to be easy, because it is into that world that the graduate goes. There (or here) money and the getting of it is the common appraisal of success, whatever that means.

We too frequently hear a man explain himself by saying I am a business man. He doesn't really mean that, for every man has some business. Even farmers, although farming is a man forever making his last stand. But business is rarely any man's whole life. If it is, he is a monster. He belongs to a family, is a husband, a father, a churchman, a politician. He is all things a man should be who lives in and takes part in the life of the community. This kind of community has always been the strength of the South, not that it has been limited to the South. When it goes, and it is going, we will find ourselves in the servile state, a state wherein authority is no longer at home, but where we follow rules and regulations from afar, from bureaucracy, which increases like the amoeba by division. A real community in the western lands must by inheritance be a Christian community. And this condition looks to its continuance in after life. That last great Christian and statesman, Sir Thomas More, prayed for the dead as well as for the living. Even to his enemies he promised "we shall be merry in Heaven together." In preference to such an acceptance of life, we are offered Progress, which can be made to fit any shape or form.

As it is, we can't live without money, without shelter or food, but it is the far happier man who makes it by the pursuit of some talent, or an occupation that uses most of his gifts. He tends then to use all of himself in fabrication of an artifact, or as a professional man whose actions are like artifacts. One virtue: the expense of time and energy takes form before his eyes. The artifact is outside himself but it is the best of himself, and with it he can witness his perfections or shortcomings. He sees in a concrete way the end of his efforts. And when those efforts serve his fellow man and not only himself, a grateful community crowns him with laurel in life, and in death the brown myrtle.

# Semi-Centennial: An Agrarian Afterword

FIFTY years, half a century, does not come within the spiral of history. Although the years are fifty, it is not the years which mark it. Most of life passes as do the seasons; but a few events, public and private, remain. Things that count never seem ended. You do not look back; you look at—a kind of perpetual present tense. During the last half-century *I'll Take My Stand* has seldom been out of print. The royalties have been small, the publishers generally uninterested; yet it will not die. It is contemporaneous, not a historical document. Not yet. No better proof can be evinced than these essayists who celebrate its semi-centennial and make their statements—rather, their professions of faith (some of them)—about the South, what threatens it, what distinguishes it from the other regions of the country.

It gives me the occasion to consider how I think about it now. First of all, it seems obvious that the Agrarians were better prophets than they knew. Certainly we failed to get the kind of attention necessary to delay or modify the evils of Industrialism. But we did not think of ourselves as prophets. After the stock market crash of 1929 and the Depression, our hopes were raised for a time that we might be listened to. We were trying to stop something we felt boded no good for our kind of life, which once had been (and still was, to an extent) the dominant kind of life for the entire country.

Family and neighborhood made the world we inhabited. Travel through the countryside today and you will find it empty. People dwell there, but as individuals, except in certain stubborn and traditional pockets. They do not compose a community. Travel to the towns and small cities and they all look stamped out of plastic.

They differ mainly in size. The outskirts hold flat buildings of assembly plants owned from afar; more sinisterly, factories dealing in chemical poisons pollute the countryside. People as well as the towns are beginning to have an anonymous look. Underneath, not quite covered but crowded out of any meaning, like General Lee's house in Richmond, relics of the past stand. They will stand for a while, until the ubiquitous bulldozer or that flinging ball pushes them into some trash heap. I am mindful of the restoration in places like Charleston, Savannah, and New Orleans and elsewhere, but the life which built these dwellings and public buildings has not been restored.

So the Agrarians failed. We failed at least to make any practical impact upon the amoeba-like growth of the machine and its technology. Only recently has it come to me why this is so. No man can know why, but I will venture this: none is prepared for the violent revolution which changes the nature of the familiar. I feel that this is why the communities threatened with extinction only sympathized with the book's protest. They could not believe that *their* way of living would disappear. Well, it has.

I can wish now that *I'll Take My Stand* and the writings that followed had made it clearer that, in defending what was left of Southern life, we were defending our common European inheritance. Maybe the time was not right for that kind of admonition. I did follow Red Warren and Allen Tate in wanting the title of the book to be "Tracts against Communism," but this now seems inadequate. It was too political, as in other times were states' rights and the divine rights of kings. Rights are properties, not the thing itself. States exercise sovereign powers, not rights. It was a tactical error of supreme importance that Southern rights supplanted sovereignty. Nor do Christian kings possess divine rights. They are the secular agents of God.

It takes but one bad idea to ruin a man or a state. The idea that mankind can control nature, and that nature concerns only matter and energy, has lost us belief in the divine order of the universe. Materialism with all its accompanying isms is a sorry substitute. To put it in religious terms, we have lost the covenant with God; we perforce must practice magic. What is magic but the pretense and effort to control nature toward some private end. That end is inevitably power.

I've said it elsewhere, but I'll repeat: The opposite of love is not hatred. It is the addiction to power. Hatred is the eclipse of love, but under proper conditions love can be redeemed. But when the will fails, power can overwhelm love's beneficent properties. Magic in human intercourse manifests itself as lust, abusing and casting aside its object. This is a part of the universal human condition, and the victims can be rescued. But the magical incantation over nature is more indirect as to its effects. Of course, an office must have the power to execute its functions. It is the violation of this power that should concern us, for magic can seem to possess the ultimate secrets of knowledge. It is one thing when an Indian shaman, failing in his incantations to bring rain, blames his failure on the lechery of the young women never the young men and points to the flattened bean patches as evidence. If the drought persists, such an excuse fails him, and the tribe puts him to death. But what can we do when our shamans have tampered with alchemical discoveries and released the cataclysmic genii from the jug? The side effects of this malevolent power we cannot neutralize, not even by burying them in the ground. They reappear in mysterious diseases, miscarriages and malformed children, and in the foods of life. They even threaten life itself with sterility.

Because of the loss of the covenant with God, those who rule us at home and in foreign affairs are at a loss as to what to do. These scientists, these economists, these politicians make one incantation after another, but none can agree. None can agree, for they all accept that the trouble is only a matter of managing the machine of state. We have forgot that we are made in the image of God, and schoolchildren are forbidden to pray together.

Those who rule us, wherever they come from, are the inheritors of that power which destroyed the Confederacy and with it the idea of the federal republic, which at least gave lip service to the divine in Deism. I don't see how we can be too hopeful of a Christian regeneration of any institution. Magic obfuscates any enlightenment of present or future ways, but there is solace in the fact that these essayists exhibit belief in the persistence of what we think of as Southern.

We might take further hope from another consideration. There is a north and south the world over, with distinctive characteristics. Provence is different from Normandy. The south and southwest of

England which had the only English king called Great is not like the Danelaw. It would be to little purpose to discover whether it is the climate which makes the people or whether the climate draws distinctive natures to flourish as the weather, the seasons, and the land determine. Certainly our geography nourished the family, without which no Christian state can stand. After the physical places which fix a people in its customs and belief are gone, can the family function as it did when it belonged to a community of families? We know the answer to this question. The family is the most ancient of institutions.

In mythology and history old families carry the drama of human needs, as they watch with jealous interest the safety of the res publica, even when they undermine its health. Of course, no one family is older than another, but the families who think of themselves as old nourish their history, their pride, their fortunes, all qualities which they feel set them apart and promise longevity. To them the once-familiar debate between inheritance and environment is an academic question, brought up no doubt by those who had no family. Only the bloodlines hold the truth.

As proof from nature, they will point to the thoroughbred. This prince of animals did not just happen. At the source is always an Arab horse, and we know that in battle the Arabs carried in a saddlebag the horse's bloodlines, in case of the rider's death. I had an old cousin who, writing down parts of his descent, in a moment of absentmindedness shifted an ancestor to the line of a Lindsay Arabian. It didn't seem particularly humorous to him when he discovered his mistake, nor indeed much off the point. His interest was merely a part of an old habit of calling a family after its farm. The farm was not only the land; it composed all the creatures inhabiting it, and all the things that grew. Even Brother Rabbit. This connection is no idle matter, or the sentimentality of pride. It is finally metaphysical. The identification of man through family with physical nature measures the state of religious belief. This induces a respect for and concord with all of God's creation, and a more practical knowledge of what to expect from the world. It teaches that you often eat your meat with sorrow and that you can lose in vital ways all that is dear. This is the supreme historical admonition we should accept from the downfall of the Confederacy. Everywhere else in this nation's "progress" there has been a succession of triumphs, until now. I would hazard the guess, when the true crisis comes, as it will, that a Southern-born man will step forward and meet it. This because he has known defeat of his society, because he has eaten his bread in sorrow—in effect, because he knows what the world is, that it is not all teatty.

This is not said in pride but out of common sense, which depends upon the hard learning from experience. Let me extend it and say it will be someone or many from a republic of families as he or they oppose the abstract state, usually referred to as the government. This kind of individual will know himself because of his love for the family. This is not to say that being a member of a family is one long love feast, but it does involve a freedom of intercourse among its members, a hierarchy of order, and the will to defend it or any part of it when threatened. Today the abstract state is totalitarian; that is, the power state, Calhoun's rule of the numerical majority, always controlled by a minority with partial and selfish interests. The Agrarians called it industrial, as did recently the news media in denominating the summit conference of the Western states as the "industrial nations." But whatever we call it, it opposes power to charity, the rule of man to the covenant with God. To repeat, its processes move by the incantations of magic; whereas the family, because of its love for its members and its surroundings, is instinctively religious. It knows that in great stress it must pray; that to bind together, to harmonize the opposites of public and private, it must cherish and sustain ceremony, ritual, the formal conventions which fix the eternal truths in poetic language. (By "poetic" I mean the only language which can translate the eternal mysteries into a simple understanding.)

Manners are the means of discipline and intercourse between members of the family and strangers. Good manners are not only charitable; they also protect us from the world's intrusion, and the world from us. Because of the family's fixity to place and loyalty to kin, it is harder for an absent power, either domestic or foreign, to traduce or manipulate it against its true interests. The proletariat or any group dependent upon wages and social security alone is more easily threatened. But the family has its weaknesses, too. Its innate conservatism and its antipathy to change make it acutely vulnerable to dramatic innovation. This can be from a failure of vision, a rigidity of habit and mores, and too often from an isolation from that which will undo it.

The South, particularly the Old West of Tennessee and Kentucky, experienced an influx of Scottish and Scotch-Irish before and after the annihilation of the Highland clans by the Duke of Cumberland, that archetypal Sherman. This bloc of people brought with them an adherence to the clannish feeling of family, as well as its inboned history of defeat. Their presence gave a distinctive quality to our sense of behavior of the region. The Scotch-Irish were said to keep the Sabbath and everything they laid their hands on. I don't know what bureaucrat so defined them, but the very understanding of themselves was through the family and clan. Clan means children. The chief or captain, as he was earlier called, was kin to everybody under his authority; this is the rule of blood. It had and has its blood feuds and other sins of pride, but I propose it to be more durable than the rule of purse or sword. Even now, when the clan is a sentiment only, our particular sense of family still derives from it. It is the lasting inheritance of the tribe. When it ceases to rule, the state changes its nature, and this usually means into a rule of irresponsible power. During and after its imperial days Athens strained the tribal democracy beyond its capacity. Power to rule others supplanted the will to rule themselves, and brought the Peloponnesian War and ruin.

Although history reveals to the present rulers how the past rulers lost a war or a state, few seem able to learn anything from history. There may be a good reason for this. For four hundred years or longer the West has come to look to history for its truths and judgments: that is, it has looked to man as the judge of mankind's acts. (I am not talking about some objective record, say the history of the Hapsburgs.) I mean the gradual displacement of God by man, or the divine order of the universe by its physical properties. This was clearly under way in the Renascence, surely an inadequate name for the squandering of Christendom's inheritance.

To make a brutal summary I will name three names as evidence of the ambiguity of this period: Sir Thomas More, Machiavelli, and Luther. Luther in protesting the corruption, at least the secular usurpation in the Church, *The Prince* by Machiavelli usurping the Christian office of princes, and Sir Thomas More's *Utopia* revealing indirectly the political crisis of Europe, either the unity of Europe or its fragmentation in the National state. Luther threw out the baby with the bath. *The Prince* taught princes that their selfish interests and wills were paramount to Christendom's understanding of a king's office as God's secular overseer, as the bishop was His spiritual agency. More defended the whole, knowing that the defeat of a part was the end of Christendom. When More lost his head, he took the king's challenge to speak shortly at his execution by saying, "I die my king's good servant but God's first." Cromwell, who by lies brought More to the scaffold, could only say, "I have offended my prince and therefore I die." This is a paraphrase. Incidentally he had a copy of Machiavelli's book in his hand during More's trial.

When More's head tumbled into the basket, the purification of the one Church and the unity of Europe were doomed. Machiavelli's interpretation of what was already afoot, the discrete struggle for power lacking any divine restraint, introduced in the Renascence the beginning of the so-called Modern world. The paintings of the period for a while had for subject the Court of Heaven and the Passion, but soon we find portraits of men, such as Titian's man with the glove, in secular dress. In a steady decline we reach Sargent's portrait of Woodrow Wilson, where only the eyes, according to Yeats, are alive. The eyes should be instruments through which the imagination and spirit seek, select out of the multitudinous forms which God has created in nature, that which can be studied as learning and loved as the enrichment of life. This use of vision inevitably leads towards the ultimate mysteries and desires for salvation. The will alone, fed by the ego, only wants power, power to use and devour others. Woodrow Wilson's eyes are pure will. His skin has the pallor of a corpse.

In the Renascence not only the skin but the entire body is alive. The release of the senses from a monastic ideal comes like a rush of the blood to the body politic. The body of the world becomes mankind's desire. In Christendom's high noon it was ground for the drama of the soul: salvation or damnation. The vision of God's son emphasized the man in the man-God, but usually what a sorry appearance of a man he was. A dead man wrapped in a diaper being taken down from the Cross, a man who in life would have driven no money changer out of the Temple. This is the body of the world, not so much the image of a man-God who died for the sins of man's nature, but dead. Then look at the ikons of the Eastern church. There is little flesh, but every eye is open on eternity. Ceremonial robes hide the flesh. No eye wavers. All look out of some inward unshakable absolute of belief.

There is a later episode which is a clear instance of acceptance of the world as the end in itself: Ponce de León's search for the fountain of youth, in anguish at his failing virility, looked not to his soul's salvation but to some magical place and its pool of waters to restore him.

To bury God in nature is alchemy, and it has turned all of those who instruct and rule us into alchemists. By learning a few of the secrets of nature they have made God obsolescent. The acceptance of history in place of metaphysical belief has obscured the meaning of what has happened, but when Hitler said, "If you lie enough, it becomes the truth." Where does this leave history as guide? Or where does it leave us all in our present plight, if we do not by some miracle renew the covenant with God?

There is always a remnant. When General Lee was about to surrender The Army of Northern Virginia at Petersburg, a young colonel asked him this, "What will history say, General, if you surrender this army?" Lee thought before he replied, "If it is right for me to surrender this army, I will take the responsibility." There was no blaming Northrup for refusing fodder for his cannon and wagons and cavalry, no blaming Davis or the Confederate Congress, or that Squire in the Valley of Virginia who threatened to empty his army by writs of habeas corpus, none of the excuses we hear today, shifting blame and responsibility to the state or to others. General Lee gave a Christian answer. He took the risk of his act. He was willing to be judged, perhaps by those who did not have his responsibility, but with charity, for he believed that the ultimate judgment lay elsewhere.

# A Myth in a Garden

BORN the day after Christmas, 1902, like a wet firecracker, as my mother remarked, I entered a world that lived with and by other creatures. My grandchildren and their ilk are unaware that they are creatures. I am closer to the 12th century than to their world, for that world has money, not salvation, as its ultimate desire. College graduates study jobs to get, not occupations to risk.

As I grew up in Murfreesboro, the town easily joined the country. There were horses to hitch up, cows to milk (and that twice a day), often gardens to make. In town and country both, communities had the same kind of family life, with kin and connections, the connections by marriage, not blood. Because of this, people of the same station had the same social life and, frequently, the same marriages. Farming had not lost then its prestige as a way of life, and you could live well by it.

My mother was a town girl. My father lived 10 miles in the country, but he kept fast horses. He would dance all night and drive the 10 miles, throw a blanket over Lunette's back (she was a Hambletonian), and go straight to the fields. I spent my childhood mostly in town. Coming home at the end of the day, tired from play, I could smell roasting coffee beans down the long street to my grandmother Nelson's house, where we lived for a time. The odor sharpened a boy's appetite, but chiefly was reassuring. I breathed it as

*This essay is the text of Mr. Lytle's speech given at the 1986 Ingersoll Prizes Awards Banquet where he received the Richard M. Weaver Award for Scholarly Letters on November 21, 1986.*

comfort without knowing why. I felt the invisible link between all the houses on the street, filled as they were by families I knew or knew about, who had children I played with, or special associations.

Mr. Dee Smith striding to the Square and Miss Luly, his wife, trotting behind like an appendage trying to catch up. He was a cousin of my grandmother's, whose dwelling meant love and discipline, food and sleep, where grown people always looked the same and never had to be measured for growth. Across the street lived Miss Katie Fowler, who sang in the Presbyterian choir. A suitor, Mr. Peter Binford, Sunday after Sunday sat enthralled, watching her bosom rise and fall in song. One memorable Sunday he saw the sack of love break about her heart, and the heart leapt two feet towards him. Her mother threatened to put him in the asylum, and he threatened to pick every pinfeather out of her old hide. He had a good cousin lawyer whose defense was: A man in love is naturally insane. The case was dismissed. Not long afterwards, Mr. Binford asked my father to go in partnership with him in selling frog legs. He said they were bringing a good price on the Chicago market. "How will we get them there?" my father asked. "Hop them," he replied.

Further down the street lived my other grandmother. They had thought it best to sell her farm, where she lived alone, and bring her to town. One night a storm had come up and she went into the garden to look after some small chickens. There was a loose paling in the garden fence through which she by habit went. The wind blew her lantern out, and all night long as the rain fell she wandered trying to find the loose board. As I went to school, I passed her house on the other side of the street. Bending under a load of books, I hurried along, but she would call across the street, a thing my other grandmother would never do, "Hold up your shoulders, grandson," and I would straighten up. This was in front of Mr. Rufus Hayne's house, who conjured some warts from my hand. He just took out his pocket knife and ran it over the warts, mumbling words I didn't catch. In a few days they were gone.

Half a block towards town lived Miss Carmine Collier. She was a miser, and she dressed well, in a mustard-colored coat suit, a big hat with a bird of paradise roosting on her head. I looked hard to see what a miser was. Any difference from other women was in the eyes. Round-like glass eyes, they were steady as a hawk's. She never married. One lover said, "Carmine, I'll put down two dollars where you put one, if you'll marry me." He said later a glassy film closed down her eyes, just like a chicken's. With that he gave up. I was playing on the hearth when Miss Carmine came to thank Mammy for the posey her mother held in the coffin. Mammy said, "Now Carmine, you can't live in that big house all by yourself. Buy you some hats, go to Florida in the winter and the springs, in the summer, and get you a man." "Miss Kate," she replied, "I've thought about it. But suppose I was lying in bed with that man, and he would want the window up and I would want it down. They will have their way, and I'd freeze to death." "Get cold in bed with a man?" Mammy said. "I had to take a fan to bed with Robert."

Country boys were usually tougher than town boys, not in mean-ness, necessarily, but just better-natured. A cousin once told me about his little brother Micajah. He said he was hard as a pine knot and tough as a horse mule colt. He didn't waste no time. He came into the world a-bouncing, hollowed once, and then made for the teatty nighest him. Looked like Ma never could wean him. She complained, "I can't git my washen and ironing done. Ever whar I go it's teatty this, and teatty that. A body can git too much teatty. A woman needs to dry up like any creature. He pulls so hard, and now he's got teeth, I declare . . ." Aunt Marthy said to her, "I'll tell you what to do, Sister. Look at Othel. I weaned him in the dark of the moon, and look what a man he made." "Dark or light, it don't make no difference to Micajah." "Do this then. Go to the storehouse and git you some quinine. You've got cayenne pepper and lard. Mix them ingredients good, grease yourself good, and when he comes in, offer it to him." She done it. She and pappy were settin' on either side of the farplace when in he bounced. Right off, "Mammy lemme have it." "Well, here tiz, son, come git it." He squared himself, grabbed it like a snapping turtle, and jumped back like a snake had bit him. "Pappy," he called, "Gimme a chaw of tobacco. Mammy's been eating bitter weed."

As a child, I don't remember any fears or real distress. I'm sure there were the usual threats to innocence, but there were plenty of warnings from that back room where all authority was. There were Gypsies of course. They were given to stealing away boys from their families. It was a dreadful thought. Once a year they came from all over the country to bury their dead in Nashville, at which time a shiver would run through the galloping herd of boys. Any dark-featured stranger would get covert glances. L. W. Coleman, my playmate, and I were on the Square as a contingent of Gypsies passed in their wagons. L.W. had stolen a quarter out of his mother's sewing-machine drawer, and we were loaded with all-day suckers and chewing Long John Wax dusted with powdered sugar, molasses popcorn, and holding each a sack of goober peas. Fearing to take it home—and we were instinctively headed that way, for Gypsies had mysterious ways of conjuring children to them—he gave me what was left. I knew I had to hide it, or there would be questions. I went to Daisy, our cook, and she obliged. She and I already had a criminal record. I took one of my grandfather's cigars, and she and I smoked it. I learned quickly that crime doesn't pay, while Daisy went off with the cigar.

In my childhood, most human creatures, as they set forth to work or play, dance or love, touched hallowed ground, a pond, an everlasting spring, an old elm, a farm that generations had known and lived on and by. Children know these special sympathies for places, where they can hide and pretend. There can be no greater delight in privacy than the tunnel made in bales of hay, leading to a fragrant hollowed-out and usually itching place in a barn loft, which most little girls instinctively suspected. This pretending is child's best play, that ineluctable moment, just east of Eden, when eyes are still shining from the afterglow of the Garden, just before sight dims in the light of the world, and pretending trembles upon quickening knowledge. And there was the common knowledge of the long history all creatures shared. The rat, the skunk, the fox that set out on the chilly night had most of the instincts, needs, and faculties humans shared. At Cornsilk I once set two Domineka hens. They hatched about the same time. One was a poor mother and began losing her hatch. The other hen scratched, chuck chucked, and the little chicks ran to her. I put the Lib hen in the stockpot (she wasn't fit to eat) and gave her chicks to the good mother. She now had about 25 to feed and raise and tell what that shadow from the sky meant and what to do. One morning as I went to let her out of the pen, I saw the oddest-looking creature. She did not have a feather down her front, but she had all her chicks under and around her. During the night she had fought off a mink. That was over 50 years ago. I've got close kin I rarely think of, but when I think of all those batteries of Leghorns dropping their eggs into a slot like squatting robots, mules and horses disappearing as work stock, and cows milked by metal hands, I wonder what we have done.

We have been told that we were made in the image of God. That no doubt is true, but so are all creatures, a hummingbird, a jackass. We are all artifacts together. We were made, not begotten. It is true, Adam was given the power to rule over those he had named. He named Eve, too, but perhaps he chose not to exercise the power in this instance. At any rate, it was a delegated power.

We might do well in our present plight to look again at Eden, that myth in a garden. In the beginning of things, the creation of the cosmos, why did the Creator make that little garden, some say of Innocence? First, the invisible power we refer to as God, for his ineffable reason, assumed a limitation. He became a creator, that is, the First Artist. The next thing, he looked about him and saw that what he had made was good. This is the surprise all artists know, for in the heat and stress of the work, the maker cannot know for sure just how the artifact will come out. In Louis Ginsberg's *Legends of the Jews,* he states that "God made several worlds before ours, but he destroyed them all, because he was pleased with none until he created ours."

At this point there must be some query into the forbidden mystery of the Creator's mind. Simply what limits had the All-powerful One put upon Himself when He created Himself Creator? Without pause he split the void with his lightning stroke. After the explosion he must have seen that he had not done away with the dark. He had merely scattered it. And furthermore this startling discovery: He who had only known Eternity found Himself in Time. The moment there are opposites, there is motion; there is Time. Perhaps at this moment we can conjecture that he made the Garden of Innocence, outside Time, into which he could withdraw as landlord and, without being rushed, decide what to do next.

Obviously he had intended to restore a small fragment of Eternity in this place. He entered the garden royally, only to discover he was no longer a free agent. He had become an actor; a creator, but now a prejudiced creator. He found it pleasant to walk there in the cool of the day. He was perfectly satisfied at first with the flora and fauna. All the artifacts in the garden had one thing in common. Each was perfect in its seasonal way. But since there was no Time, there could be no aging or seasonal change. Each plant stood in the perfection of its moment of creation, but did not grow. And so it was with the fauna. Indeed there could be no action. Although they seemed to move, their motions were the motions of angels, visible but without body.

When the Creator-now-turned-landlord saw that his artifacts were good, the more he looked the more he felt the power of possession. Herein lies the drama of the Garden. According to the Haggadah, the legendary part of the Talmud, the landlord saw that Adam, unlike the other creatures, was alone like Himself. He had not yet begun to say the Lord thy God is a jealous god, but lest the other creatures should take Adam for a god, too, he told him to pick a wife. Adam by nature was biddable, but he could find no female he could claim kin with. Most were four-legged, or they had tails. Some crawled, some flew out of range. Not for an instant did he consider the fish, but he looked long and hard at the sheep.

Now the plot thickens. It concerns Adam's first wife, Lilith. It is not said where she came from, but she brought one thing the garden did not have. She was full of flesh. The dictionary of angels counts her as one of the four guardian angels of whorehouses. She ate children. She had other uncomplimentary habits. But she was no threat. She took one look at the creature who seemed painted air and fled. Four angels pursued and caught her, but they could not drag her back to the garden. The landlord was relieved. He wondered why he had not seen the solution before. There was Adam, a hermaphrodite, a whole creature, male and female in one form—as Plato would later say, looking like two people embracing. The solution was simple. He had done it once on a larger scale. He would do it again.

He put Adam to sleep, and we know the rest. Adam called her Eve. She was two-legged and a great hand at giving advice. The landlord was not entirely pleased. She almost looked as if she was made of matter. She had the air of disobedience, and that was a certain threat to power. In His angelic garden, hidden at its very center, stood two trees of a greater density, the same kind of density the female Eve had. They had appeared, unordered, in his emanations. When power is uncertain, it threatens. He called the man and woman to him but addressed Adam as the head of the house. "At the center of the garden is a tree. It grows a fruit only the gods can digest: good and evil. If you eat of it, you will surely die."

Not yet brought to full life, to die meant nothing to Adam. It was like telling a child, "Don't go near the fire, you will burn." All the while Eve was listening with her eyes demurely to the ground. At first she thought it a beautiful tree trunk—maybe the very tree Adam was told not to touch. But nobody told *her* not to touch it.

Its golden scales shimmered in a round undulation as it grew out of itself, coiling upwards. Her eyes were dazzled, and there leaning towards her was a head with lapis lazuli eyes. They winked. How strange, to wink without a lid. She waited enraptured, bewildered before the tree's luscious fruit, the mandala swollen into a sphere, dirt come to its miracle. At the very topmost bough, now russet, now golden, hung the most tempting object of all. Saliva moistened her mouth. She reached to touch it but met instead the flickering tongue, gliding towards the shell-like ear, saying softly, "sicut eritis dei" ("you will be as the gods"). She bit: Her five senses throbbed with appetite. Her eyes opened, and there was the world, and she and Adam were in it. She offered him the fruit. He bit and they rushed together. And he bit again.

Not disobedience, then, but the sorrows of knowledge, of good and evil whose end is death, that is the lesson the myth of the garden has for mankind. The loss of innocence is no fall. You cannot fall from innocence. You quicken. You enter the motion of life. In spite of himself, the landlord and his creatures, now carnal, must reckon with Time. Adam and Eve with their increase will now be wayfarers in the world. The Creator either had to withdraw into his invisible omniscience or follow his creatures into their predicament. This he did, but no longer a landlord. No more walks in the cool of the day. No conversations. A thunderer now from high places. A patriarch bereft of all but power. An archangel whirling a left-handed swastika before the garden gate, humming forbidden, forbidden, a hollow hum, for there was no garden. Once lost, innocence is gone forever. It was hard for the landlord to give up his garden, his artifacts, and there was Cain cultivating the wilderness, insolently using Time and its seasons to imitate His own creations. Sweating but bringing forth fruit from the ground. To be blessed. Not to praise his creator, but his produce.

So it seems, and so it seems that the power of the Creator as artist was displaced in the divine omniscience by the power of possession. One of the faculties of creation puts the essence of the artist into his artifact. It was out of this that Cain, the inheritor, acted, that is imitated. Man cannot create what is already there. He can only imitate what his vision discovers and what by form he can render. All the artists in Time cannot exhaust one created artifact, for in it is the fullness of the divine intention. But the landlord of the garden in his shift in roles mistook imitation for the thing itself. Now the god as patriarch was a jealous god. He saw imitation as an attempt to deny power, and so brought death and disease into the world.

The divine problem seems to be the stress between Eternity and Time. To summarize much, that the Creator's human artifacts become carnal gave Him a great vexation. So much so that he drowned nearly all of them, along with the innocent animals who had done nothing but be animals. When the land dried out, he made a covenant with mankind. As the sweet savor of Noah's sacrifices rose to the divine nostrils, He understood how frail He made the flesh. He foresaw the inescapable part appetite (and the most dangerous appetite of all, power) would play in his creature's long history; and his heart, if one can speak of the Creator's heart without blasphemy, softened. He put a colored bow into the clouds as a covenant between Him and man, promising never to curse the ground again. He came to understand better his role as Creator as He transferred into all creation not his appearance but the world's forms now made visible by the transaction. In the High Days of Christendom, all men as craftsmen accepted this. What they made they did to make a living, but they did it also to the greater glory of God.

But to quote Coomaraswami, no longer is every man a craftsman. Today the craftsman is a special kind of man. The power we suffer now is not God's wrath. It is man's pride. In deleting the "as" from the "be as," it is we who offer the affront, not Cain. What poor grammarians. Only one word. As. How could its deletion do such damage? Christianity supplanted by Progress, a religion without a god, carnal goods its prayer book, its hope of salvation the perfectibility of man, all Puritan desires. There has been a fall of man, but it is the fall into history, man judging man. But man dies.

What we have lost by this is our sense of a common creaturehood with living beings, and that includes ourselves; and we have lost our tools. Nevertheless, there is still man's deep need to make things, in spite of technology's grim effort to deny him its practice. Few men now are craftsmen, that is, few men are now Christian. No longer artists, we serve the autonomous machine. For a long time the machine as tool aided the craftsman to make. A divine inheritance withers when the tool becomes the master and the Word is drowned in words. If we can hold in mind that the Word is the creative power of God, we will take to heart that it was made flesh in Christ. Only in this way will we become again good grammarians and restore the "as" to the admonition.

But to want to restore a lost faith in a secular society will not of itself do so. We've got to have some luck or by some miracle rescue language from the surfeit of half-truths which confuse its authority. Again it takes only one word to betray. We have witnessed temperance turn into prohibition, that blasphemous theft of God's own tool, the Word. And debase it. If language in all its proper usages is not restored, the confusion of tongues whose advance is rapid will grow more so. The care of words as it guards meaning can reopen our eyes, allow us to confess that we who have thought of ourselves as rich have only been profligate, and progress the progress of Hogarth's heir. Then instead of appetite, comfort, and safety as ends, we may know again faith, hope, and charity.

But not without the cardinal, the Roman, virtues: prudence, temperance, fortitude—these three defining Justice, as prudence disciplines the will, temperance the sensibility, and fortitude that moral courage which makes it possible. Else Justice will have no more meaning than a case won in court.

If a miracle could happen, every man as craftsman would know again he has only one contemplation, the mystery of God, made manifest in the natural order. Remember: Any divinity we have is imparted. It allows us by craft to make things, because we were made, not begotten. Both as artists and actors, human creatures may again try to turn the wilderness of Time into a habitable garden, as did Cain. And, this time, growing the foods of life and building creature shelters may not seem to the divine Essence a threat to a god's power.

# A Journey South

I was a freshman at Vanderbilt when Allen Tate was an upperclassman. I did not know him then. I met him later when I was at Yale studying playwrighting under George Pierce Baker. Our teacher, John Crowe Ransom, wrote us both and brought this about. Allen and Caroline and their daughter, Nancy, were living in the Village on 27 Bank Street. They had the basement apartment, Allen as a sort of janitor in the sense that he got the quarters free for firing the furnace. Writers liked to live and congregate in the Village. It still had the virtues of a village. It was fairly cheap and for artists free of restrictive conventions. Not all but many felt very Bohemian. These were not the best craftsmen.

Those were the days of speakeasies and Italian restaurants where you could get an ink-like red wine with your meal. But first you had to be peeped at through a hole in the door. Usually this was a formality, particularly if you were a regular customer. Prohibition had its own mores. For example, if you were short of funds, you took the subway to Hoboken, bought a beer or two, and ate for free, slices from an ample roast beef, cheeses, sauerkraut and other foods. If the joint was raided, the proprietor just moved next door, with scarcely a pause in his service. There was a string of these houses, looking all alike.

Allen and I were soon talking about the Dayton, or "Monkey trial," in Tennessee. We were in entire agreement about this, as had been our philosophy professor, Dr. Herbert Sanborn, almost alone at Vanderbilt in exposing the fallacy in the argument that the trial was about academic freedom. I've forgotten our discussion in detail, except that we were in agreement that scientism's position was a Liberal attack on our traditional world. Now I see it in other terms: Reconstruction's breach of the citadel. After the economic exploitation of the South, this attack in the name of knowledge on a belief in a literal Genesis denigrated us before the world and made us laughed at; but the real aim was more insidious: a forced acceptance of faith in a secular order for guidance rather than in divine authority. Practically this would mean a total, instead of an economic, dominance by the Northeast. There had been a partial seduction of the Southern mind, but not yet of its spirit. The soul is not so easily traduced, especially of a people who live by the land. Such are naturally religious. Even though the tactic of defense was inadequate at Dayton, depending as it did upon a strict construction with its literal fallacy, so was the Liberal attack equally fallacious. Darwin's theory was only a partial truth, not the whole understanding of the mystery of the universe, which only God understands. Along with this came H. L. Mencken's journalistic description of the South as "the Sahara of the Bozarts." This is like the thief who robs a house the second time and complains that the owners do not eat with silver.

This was felt but none of it was entirely clear. It was a common habit for the young men in the South and West to go East to thrive. Allen would complain later that a gifted young man had to go to New York and do well before he would be accepted at home. I once got a prize in Nashville for a one-act play, to be put on by the little theatre. Jesse Beesley, former playmate, a known wit, and later editor of my hometown paper, printed "Local boy makes good at home." Progress was the word, and it was like Dorian Gray's portrait. Out of victory's euphoria in the European war, it was easy for the young to believe in progress and that the South was taken back into the Union and that the great metropolis of New York was as much ours as anybody else's. It was also easy to say that the arts rarely prosper, but there was always the possibility that any artist could. There is no telling how many thousands were sacrificed for the making good of ten. Allen lived as a free lance writer, joining no cliques and respected in that role. He wrote a great deal for *The New Republic* and became friends with the editors, certainly Edmund Wilson and Malcolm Cowley and the one Southerner on the staff, Stark Young. But this was precarious. Once he wrote an editor for an advance. This was at Benfolly in Tennessee, so the problem was not fixed by location.

What you going to do when the meat gives out?
Stand in the corner with your chin poked out.

What you going to do when the meat comes in?
Stand in the corner with a greasy chin.

He put a footnote to this. "My chin," he said, "is perfectly immaculate."

His mother-in-law arrived one day from Kentucky. She casually remarked that she had had no breakfast. When told there was no food in the house, she and Caroline went out and replenished the larder. Being a Meriwether from Kentucky, whose family had held large holdings in land and slaves, and still had much land, if under different circumstances, it must have been incomprehensible to her not to have food in the storeroom. When her visit was over, she took her grandchild home with her. Only for a while of course.

I don't want to overemphasize the effects of either the Dayton trial or Mencken's journalism, or even what his purpose was, for he was a sound scholar. Nevertheless it was about this time that Allen began his research on Stonewall Jackson. Actually it began the unfolding of his history. I add this, because too much has been made of the letters crossing in the mail between brother Agrarians concerning what came to be the symposium *I'll Take My Stand*. In fun we later addressed ourselves as Generals. I called John Ransom's wife, Major. My most pleasant memories of this later time were the seven years we enjoyed one another socially as well as treading in the vineyard of the cause. Allen was working on the Jackson when I met him. That was in 1927, as it came out in 1928.

I don't remember when the Tates moved into the Cabinet of Doctor Caligari. This was an old building on Hudson Street, once a Revolutionary inn and more recently the headquarters of the Hudson Dusters, a modest association of gangsters before the great explosion of crime engendered by the Puritan law against drinking. There were bullet holes in the ceilings, but the proprietors were very sensitive about the place's respectability. Each floor had a toilet fallen somewhat into desuetude, but there hung in plain sight a warning not to throw rags down it. And a well-known writer and a better-known banker for his help to artists were thrown out after a too riotous party.

This I was told, but I can speak with more authority about an experience of my own, which will indicate the cosmopolitan tone of the apartments; perhaps more succinctly demonstrate the relevance of its name, *Caligari* being an action in the mind of a madman. I had come down from Yale to spend the weekend with the Tates. Having other guests, they put me in the apartment of a friend who had gone to Long Island for the weekend. I had a cold and was getting ready for bed when I heard a knock at the door. I opened it and a young lady came into the room. She said, "Are you living with Della?" I replied that I did not have the honor, whereupon she said her name was Marguerite and she wanted to borrow Della's victrola. I told her it was not mine to lend. She sat on the bed beside me, and we talked until I knew her better. Later, on another floor, I stood with the records and music box in my arms before a door behind which a party was obviously going on. As the door opened, a cloud of Russian cigarette smoke puffed in our faces. It was stale and larded with greasy odors of foreign food.

Two women confronted us and barred the way. One of them, a tall pale woman with marble eyes looked me over and told me I couldn't come in. If she had had a red cap on, she would have looked like a *Révolutionnaire*. A year later she ended up in a sailor's dive in India. I met once her husband, a forlorn painter, dressed in shabby Pre-Raphaelite clothing and beard. I met once also their son, a nice boy working for a reformed fur thief. He is on my conscience. I could see he was hungry and intended to invite him out to dinner and see what I could do. But I didn't and he turned on the gas, leaving a note for his employer's wife, complaining that her husband would not pay him and he was hungry.

The other woman came to my defense. She had sandy gray hair out of control and a combative manner. She was Margaret Sanger's sister, the woman everybody knew once as the girl who went to gaol defending birth control. Miss Sanger won, and I was allowed to come in, I must say with diminished cheer. Somebody poured me a drink, but even as I was reaching for it, another hand was quicker than mine. And so it went. There was a gangster there with a gold tooth, and the general conversation was about being beaten up by Irish policemen, with a tone of boasting about it. Near me leaned a striking woman from the Isle of Man, with lovely but not quite clean hair, and it bristled over her face, and her eyes looked out of it like a fox. She was saying, "He invited me to tea, and when I came, he put his hands upon me and said, 'I would like to rape you.' And I said, 'Why do you not rape the Virgin Mary? You would get more satisfaction.' And with that he hit me."

All talk finally settled upon one subject, somebody called Harry, who they believed was in a bar nearby. It soon became clear that he was a gangster, too, and furthermore the intimate friend of Marguerite. At once my position became ambiguous. I rose to leave, but was not allowed to. I began thinking very hard when Miss Sanger and Marguerite went to fetch him. They were gone a long time. Once more, about to escape I was urged to stay. At some point the door opened and there stood Marguerite, disheveled, bruised in the face and with a dry hysterical sob only a woman can make. It came out that she and her friend had found the bar and Harry was there. But right away Miss Sanger began picking up beer mugs and tossing them at the patrons. It was a confused story, ending with Harry rising like the gentleman he was, to the lady's rescue. They fell to the floor together, whether in defeat or amnesia I did not learn. But I was learning cunning. As the comforters crowded about Marguerite, I slipped quietly away. Next morning I recounted this adventure to the Tates and Katherine Anne Porter.

It was from these portals that we set out for the Eastern battlefields. Allen had bought a second-hand Ford for fifty dollars. Its name was "Old Ninety-Seven" from that ballad, "The Wreck of Old Ninety-Seven." We had got into the habit of singing old songs we had heard at home and telling family stories, a thing none of us did at Vanderbilt in the flush times after the European war. This was the beginning of an awakened interest in our common familial past. The trip was ostensibly for Allen to go over the battlefields in a more thorough way than he had had to do for his Stonewall Jackson; actually, instead of research for his biography of Davis, it became the quest for our common historic past. I have a picture of all of us taken in front of the Ford just at the moment of departure: Allen and Caroline, little Nancy about three, Katherine Anne, and I. We already looked a little travel stained.

We set out in high spirits and spent the night at a rock farm house in Pennsylvania, where we dropped off Katherine Anne. I have forgotten the name of our hosts, nor do I remember exactly the sequence of events or an accurate time table. Of the battlefields I remember best Gettysburg, still haunted by Jackson's ghost. Jackson was still much in Allen's mind, but at Antietam his presence became almost visible. We stood behind the rail fence behind the cornfield through which the enemy charged at the crucial moment of the contest, as Lee referred to the war. Allen turned to me. "Two thousand of the enemy fell here," he said with lowered breath. Caroline laughed aloud. She had never seen such glee, she said, in two men's eyes. But it was not only glee. The intervening years had fallen away and the imagination surcharged by the heart revealed the action as if we had stood there. In action there is no past, only the moving present tense. I felt then, as I'm sure he did, a tradition and its history quickening.

Red Warren joined us at Harpers Ferry, where John Brown's madness released the greater madness. Three of us were writing or about to write biographies: Red on John Brown, Allen of course on Jefferson Davis, and I about to begin on Bedford Forrest. Since Forrest operated in the middle of the Confederacy, miscalled the West, I would not have felt the necessity to examine so thoroughly the Eastern theatre. And yet my book would have lacked much, if I had not gone on this trip with the Tates. We camped at Harpers Ferry for several days. When Red arrived, we spent a night in a house. He was fast on his way to Kentucky. The minor irony was discussed: the first person that Brown's men killed was the Negro guard at the bridge. Colonel Washington was awakened in the night and asked where his slaves were. He told them they would have to do what he did when he wanted them: hunt them up. One of the raiders took the Washington sword.

It is the journey itself that is clearest in my mind. From Pennsylvania to Alabama we passed over no superhighways or interstates, only country and state roads, much of it gravel, some paved. Nor was the silence of the countryside afflicted by tires humming through the dirty smell of gas and oil. Old Ninety-Seven sped along with Allen at the wheel, his eyes sealed to the road. If he weren't driving, his head and lips dropped with the most excruciating look of pain, his usual expression of boredom. Sometimes, if we thought we could afford it, we stayed at a tourist home. There were no Holiday Inns; occasionally in towns there would be a small hotel called somebody's House. We had pup tents to make camp with, and frequently some farmer would let us stay where there was water and pick turnip greens free. I sometimes cooked these with the hoe-cakes. Meal was cheap, but I don't remember much about the food. Caroline is a good cook. The small town restaurants charged thirty-five or forty cents for lunch. If we were tired or hungry, we splurged. We never saw but one tourist camp, and it was just that, a place outside Richmond, Virginia. It had a common washroom with the usual facilities. It was very public. Here we pitched our tents underneath a great oak. In the evenings we dressed up and went to town, as guests to friends of Allen. The bookstores were still selling his Jackson. I got the taste of what it could be to see your words in print. There is no excitement, barring none, quite like that first sight. Once, returning late to camp, we found the great oak blown down upon our tents and scattering our belongings. The night watchman was the grandnephew of John Bankhead Magruder; the camp manager was the grandnephew of General A. P. Hill. Hill, you remember, was the general whose name was on the dying lips of both Lee and Jackson.

We would never again, nor would anybody, pass over and take in this world, and that is as true for Pennsylvania as for Tennessee. Pennsylvania had its heavy industry, but we did not see it. The suburbs of Philadelphia ended gradually in fields. Today from Trenton there are only buildings and a blur of light at night. We parted at my parents' house in Huntsville, Alabama. Little Nancy exclaimed, "Is this Uncle Andrew's camp?"

The Odyssey was under way; but if we had called up the dead to lap blood, it brought Allen finally home to Ithaca.

# The Abiding Mystery

FOURTEEN generations from Adam's exile, Ham discovered his father without clothes, a natural man just like himself. He thought. Without shame or profound speculation he stared at that member which begat him, but it told him little of the mystery of his birth, for he saw no further than the carnal appetite. But the mystery remained, the private, forever unrevealed source of creation. He would have been equally obtuse as to the public aspect of the mystery: how Noah had been set aside to replenish the earth, lest mankind perish.

Hoping for support, or at least sympathy, he told his older brothers what he had seen. But Japheth and Shem rebuked him. Out of respect for their father and his office, they took the garment and, going backward into the tent, covered their father's nakedness. Such acts of piety sustain and represent the traditional society, sacramental and institutional, whose manners depend on distinguishing between what is private and what is public concern. Unlike his brothers Ham was the first modern man. Unless you say that there is no modern man. At what time of day or night does the natural man turn modern, now, yesterday, two minutes from now? Perhaps we should say instead that Ham is a momentary man, immersed in the whirl of immediacy, with no sense of the past nor any of the future.

The momentary men crowd our common life. The sure sign of

*This essay is a condensed version of a talk given at Hillsdale College for a Center for Constructive Alternatives seminar on "Images and Imagination: Man's Search for Identity" in November of 1976.*

their presence is the declining family, baby sitters and senior citizens. The care of the child, instead of being a family matter, becomes adventitious. To speak of grandfathers as "senior citizens" is a travesty and a misuse of the language. There were no senior citizens in the town I was born in. The old men were identified with their families. We took them as the sign of a persisting inheritance, something stable, the repositories at times of wisdom.

Often they restrained folly and advised the young, so that the young would not have to begin each day afresh, without historic or personal memory. And when advice failed, they would foregather in front of the fireplace with black hats on their heads. They spoke of eternal and unknowable matters such as the weather, the crops, family traits, and sometimes recollecting action, the follies of their children.

There are few hats today, black or otherwise, those articles of dress which stand for sovereignty, as they cover the part of the body which rules. Certainly our "senior citizens" don't need them. They don't go out. We more often send them to "nursing homes," those ante-rooms to the morgue. Primitive societies where nature is hard, cast out their old onto the ice or onto barren land. This is understood by the old, as they no longer contribute to the family welfare, but to cast the old into nursing homes is to separate them from the family communion, each a solitary among strangers. This is death-in-life, for it is the death of habit and the mind. It is the withdrawal of familial love, for the old have become merely an inconvenience to comfort.

Love or its absence concerns all our actions. The artist who deals with the essence of action knows this, discovers the proper union between form and subject which shocks us into a proper understanding. The inherited mythologies contain the recurrent actions, both natural and supernatural, we are doomed to encounter. An archetypal myth may almost always be traced through international tales such as Cinderella, which are found in every culture. But there is one myth that, for the Western mind, underlies all others. It is the myth of the Garden of Innocence.

I do not think that we in this country think too often about Eden, except in jest. Yet the sense of it is everywhere present in the Orient. In the arid landscapes surrounding green oases, and in their rugs. The rug pattern almost always depicts the garden and the wall around it. Since some thirty thousand tribes make these rugs, the universality of the pattern becomes obvious. To these craftsmen the oasis and the garden, green, with succulent food and cooling water, is a familiar desire. I'm afraid our landscapes were too rich and varied to make us dream of the garden. I say "were" intentionally, for sadly enough we've depleted the land. Improvidence may yet instill in us what nature has done for the East.

Now the myth tells us that after the six days of creation, God took a rest. But to rest there must be a place, and so he made a place and called it Eden. And then he looked about him, as any artist would, and saw that what he had made was good. In this garden God liked to come and walk in the cool of the day. Only divine inspiration could have forseen the design and plantings which gave Eden its appearance. The fauna were as diverse and many as God deemed fit, but neither the fauna nor the flora was enough. After a while, in the play he had reduced himself to, he got lonesome and made a creature in his own image to share this paradise. We are no longer innocent enough to imagine our ancestral likeness to the creator. Indeed there are those who believe man has made God in man's image. And yet it is this very likeness which allowed for the intimacy between the creator and his warm-blooded artifact, Adam. For the myth implies that from the beginning, by his divine craft, God created a living human being, apart from himself but into which he had put himself, as every master craftsman puts himself into his work. To this extent, as it was to be with his Son the Word, God suffered a self-imposed limitation.

Adam was made in God's image, but he was not God. God had given him an imagination and to test this he allowed Adam to name the fauna. To give a name is to have power over what is named. God had named him Adam. To this extent was Adam the creature given power, but it was a delegated power. Only God creates. Man imitates. He imitates by recognition of the qualities in every creature which make each creature unique. Also, to imitate is to recognize that God is always and everywhere Himself. This describes man's severe limitation.

And it was this human limitation that Adam forgot. We must assume that at first Adam was hermaphroditic, that is the complete form, the cooperating opposites of all possibilities within one whole. Since the first creature was both masculine and feminine, confined in one body, it could imagine things but not act. And the masculine part imagined Lilith, which legend calls his first wife. I suppose Doctor Jung would call Lilith Adam's anima. But the trouble was that Adam didn't quite know what disturbed his perfect balance, for there was no female object in the garden to compare her to. God, again like a good artist, realized that what had seemed good and whole and perfect in its way had a flaw (always thinking of God in His self-imposed limitation). Human nature can't stand wholeness. So he put Adam to sleep and took the woman from his side. She wasn't called Lilith. But that didn't help much. Eve was a great hand at giving advice, and this resulted in the man and woman's expulsion from the garden. As we all know.

In the exile there was a subtle rebuke sometimes overlooked. The two innocents had yielded to an empty temptation. Satan, that old dragon, always lies, but his lies always imply the truth. He didn't promise Adam and Eve that they could be gods, only that they could live as the gods, which they were already doing, without the responsibility of divine knowledge. What they lost was their perfect situation, their innocence. What they gained was the knowledge of good and evil, but without any power to control it. And saddest of all they learned the nature of their humanity, that humankind would suffer and was mortal.

We all know the curse, that man will earn his living by the sweat of his brow, and that the mother of all living things shall bring forth young in pain and sorrow. Birth itself was the imitation of God's creative power. Lest the woman mistake it and think that she had done it all by herself, the pain was there to remind her that she was only the vessel. Nor is the man given any reprieve. In the process of bringing forth bread from the ground brother was set against brother in mindless competition. The result was murder. This time the reproof was not subtle. Man had seemingly one power of the godhead, death. By naming the beasts of the fields and the birds of the air and the deep-down fish he had a legitimate power to kill. But he had not named his brother. In either case he was only the instrument, not the power itself.

After the garden the wilderness must have looked bleak indeed. And all for an apple. But just suppose Eve had said, "Look Adam, here's another. The tree of life. I wonder now what that is? Nothing was said about eating that." No doubt at that moment Adam had discovered they were naked and were in need of an apron. But perhaps the property of that tree was such that one only had to move in its shadow to know it, for it was life that our first parents brought into the world.

And life, of course, is composed of good and evil. Without the stress between its multifold forms we would not know that we are alive. It has been said that the experience of evil is the one way to maturity. And that the experience of good makes it bearable. Nature fell along with man. To put it another way, the death of innocence brought the turning seasons. So death was in the garden all along, quiescent, waiting for the drama to begin. The flaming sword hummed "Keep out" for the protection of the evicted tenants.

Adam must keep in memory that garden where his creator walked in the cool of the day. And greeted him, or gave orders about trimming bushes and cleaning out the bitter weed. Deep within his consciousness he would remember that he was not begotten. He was made in God's image. He was an artifact. This knowledge he took with him beyond the wall. It would give him the fortitude to withstand the variable weather on the outside. Also fresh in his mind was the lesson he had learned. If he could not create, he could imitate. This would allow him to simulate, by substantial means, the garden. And so mitigate the curse.

He began to till the ground. His first born, Cain, became a farmer and his second born, Abel, a shepherd. They were well on the way to re-establishing a semblance of what had been lost, but we all know the outcome of the fable. The odor of Abel's burnt offering was sweet to God's nostrils. But he refused Cain's sacrifice. At first this seems unjust and willful, until we recollect that Adam was allowed to name the beasts of the field and the fowl and fish, but no flower. The garden was in full bloom when he arrived. So to make a crop and not mind too much the sweat and work was not exactly carrying out the curse. Certainly this attitude showed no impenitence. Indeed, God who read Adam's mind saw what he was up to, a matter of restoration, the sin of pride. To punish Adam he punished his first born, and this brought murder into the world.

Now the all-powerful, all-mysterious, and all-knowing God, the creator of all things in Heaven and earth, by assuming the role of potentate of the Garden, found the limitations of that role. When he drove out Adam and Eve, he found he had to leave, too, or withdraw

into his usual invisibility. As the garden vanished, so did the potentate. He found himself a patriarchal god. He had the world to walk
in now, but he preferred the high places. He still spoke to the
creatures but at a distance, like thunder. But Adam and his descendants were not hard of hearing. A sensibility had taken the place of
lost innocence. By such means men could discover what the world
held and respond to people of like kind. Fortunately the potentate
of the garden, out of the logic of the change in roles, assumed a
sensibility as well. The burnt flesh of the lamb smelled sweet to him.
He understood instantly how frail he had made the flesh. He had
given it appetite. Still the master craftsman, he foresaw the inescapable part appetite would play in his creatures' long history. This
induced a sympathy for man's plight and allowed him to propitiate
Cain, who had complained that his lot was too hard to bear. When
Cain wandered east of Eden, into the land of Nod, he carried with
him a safe conduct, the mark of Cain, that ambiguous sign which, as
it protected, announced his crime. Murder, public and private,
would now be a part of the world's action.

Then there is the complex drama of human appetite. But Cain
did not kill out of a desire. He killed from jealousy, because what he
had grown was rejected. Jealousy and craftsmanship, two attributes
of the Creator, identify what the potentate had imparted to creatures made in his own likeness. Abel's simple communion between
man and animal nature was not, obviously, the plan. The myth is
clear: it is Cain's descendants who will populate the earth.

Adam saw, let us assume, the futility of trying to restore Eden.
Unless something was done, his descendants would forever be way-
faring strangers in the world. By settling them in communities he
could give them the illusion of fixity and stability. It would take
crafts to build cities and keep them supplied. Memory of our likeness to the Creator has placed in the very sump of our being the
necessity to make things. Imitating the Creator of Eden, mankind
learned that a craft not only gives form to matter, it induces love for
the thing made and recollects God's love for us and admonishes us to
love our neighbors as ourselves.

In the beginning Adah's son Jubal invented the harp and so the
formal composition of music. Tubal-Cain became an artificer in
brass and iron. Cain himself built the first city and named it after his
son Enoch. Adah's other boy, Jabal, was the father of such as lived in

tents and raised cattle and sheep, a necessary but subsidiary occupation, made so by murder. Life on earth therefore took its design
from Cain, whose heart we must accept, in spite of the fratricide, as
both good and bad.

But it is not my purpose to explore the fulness of Genesis, but to
say that the loss of identity has recurred before, and in Genesis.
Babel is the archetypal instance of this. The Jewish writer and
others who, inspired in writing down what has become for us the
first myth, set forth all its attributes. And these component parts
pertain to what is forever true. In spite of their momentary eclipse,
the crafts, which are the servants of the arts, persist. The technology
of the so-called industrialism has perverted the proper relationship
between man and his work by making man the servant of the
machine, which in effect makes him the subject of an abstract
power, which the cunning of certain men control.

Two things have always been opposed: the crafts and the destructive forces of war. To make things of utility and beauty transformed
the wilderness into the community, and so mitigates the curse. War
destroys and scatters these artifacts, as it brings death and famine to
the community. China is an example. It has had many societies.
Superior craftsmanship describes all of them. On a worm they built
that rare harmony of many skills which is the silk industry. Its
persistence is a kind of domestic heroism, for beyond the Atlas
mountains and the Sea of Azov came the rider to destroy and loot.
North China built a wall, but it did not deter them, nor did caravans
of tribute buying peace. Over their stinking clothes the horsemen
put the silken robes embroidered in gold and silver and complained
the cloth was no good. The briars and brush tore the garments to
shreds.

These horsemen were terrifying because in their way they were
devoted craftsmen. They understood the arts of breeding and they
knew the arts of war. They spared neither themselves nor their
victims. They were devoted to unrestricted power. They rode and
slept and ate and defecated in the saddle. They rode until their
clothes rotted. Part of their terror, if the wind was right, was that the
victim could smell them before he saw them.

Whole cities were burnt to the ground, the inhabitants put to the
sword. There is an instance in which a hundred thousand skulls
made a pyramid to mark the spot of what had been a human

habitation. A few craftsmen and a few beautiful boys were spared. And yet the excess and repetition of this violence and death did not destroy the need in man to make. As soon as some order was achieved, the looms worked, the potters turned their wheels. Bridges were fixed, fields resumed their cultivation. Belief in the divine order of the universe returned, not always through the old religion, but the temples were rebuilt and worship, ceremonial and devout, continued.

To draw nearer to our own past, to go no further back than the middle ages, Christendom was a God'swealth, not a commonwealth at first. Its essential structure and daily living depended upon many crafts. Things were made for utility but also for the glory of God. The divine inheritance still made itself manifest through the works and acts of men. Every one, from King to subject, from Bishop to monk, was a craftsman. We still hear, if without understanding, such words as priestcraft and kingcraft. Such words once defined the very operation of the secular and spiritual authority of Europe. If a man had no craft, he had no place, and might have to cry with Cain, my lot is too hard to bear. He would be beyond the pale, that is outside of the protective fence, at the mercy of man and beast. The usurer could not be buried in holy ground. I used to think he violated his nature by getting something for nothing. But now I believe it was because he made nothing; he had no craft; therefore he denied that essential thing about himself which showed his likeness to God.

Most craftsmen were attached to a Guild, that is most men were identified by what they made or did. The source of this impulse is finally metaphysical, for why one could make best a pair of pants, another shoes, another a silver chalice or armor, nobody knows really. Today if a teacher asks a student why he wants to follow a given profession, he will give a reason; but usually it will be specious. We still feel we have to have a reason for an act, in this last gasp of rationalism as a *modus vivendi*, in extreme instances as the definition of man.

Recurrently in the past civilizations, if every man was known publicly by his talent, domestically he was known by his clan or family. Our inheritance is of course Europe, largely the north of Europe. Europeans held a universal belief in a divine order, hieratic and hierarchial. Open discussion and doubt had to do, especially in the 12th century, largely with the institutional interpretation of truth. It was repressed by the arbitrary dicta and acts of Rome. This began the schism which resulted finally in the separation of the sciences and the arts, the Church and state, ending in the confusion as to an individual's identity.

But it is not only identity which is lost, but our inheritance, which manners embody. Manners have a two-fold purpose. They derive from that command, love your neighbor as yourself, and this makes for the complete sense of social identity. And they always protect one from the world. Formality always denies a too ready familiarity. Today we too soon address a person, on a first or at least second meeting, by his given name. Primitive tribes, those close to the whirling sword, never give you their real name until you have been taken into the tribe, for addressing you by name gives the same power as naming. Only your intimates should use a given name, for such speech is as intimate as touch.

The manners of personal behavior are one property of a formal, ceremonial state. This is always the traditional state, composed of families as the units of society. There is no family older than another, but when we speak of old families, we mean families who are aware of a continuing inheritance from past time. It gives the illusion of permanence. In Highland Scotland, although the McMillan lands are long gone there is a famous inscription on a sea rock, "McMillan's right holds good to Knap, So long as wave beats on rock." And once when the head of the McGregor clan failed to gain his place at the head of the table, he pounded it and said, "Where McGregor sits, is the head of the table."

Klan means children. One of the names of the McGregors was "sons of the mist," because they lived in high places. The Chief of the clan was the head of the family. In the beginning literally he was kin to all members of the clan. His authority was based not on power or place or riches, but on blood. In crisis he looked after his own as fathers do when their children or kin get in trouble. And the klan responded in like manner. This tribal order must have been one of the earlier social forms, going back of our myth of the garden to pagan times. The permanence of the family, the illusion of this permanence both here and beyond the grave, was strengthened by the belief of its descent from the gods. Greek mythology is full of this. When the name lyon is attached to a Scottish coat of arms, it means king for progenitor, who himself was descended from a god.

Of course all things pass away, families as well as civilizations. But the traditional man, unlike the momentary man, will feel he is attached to something lasting, and he is never in doubt as to who he is. In a basic way place helps sustain this belief. A farm that has been in a family for generations adds a substantial comfort and self-assurance. It gives substance to memory. Ancestors lived and tended the very fields the present generation cultivates or wastes.

It doesn't have to be a family of kingdoms and power. It doesn't have to be a farmer. I knew a poet whose family had been shoe-makers in Germany for five hundred years. I don't think he quite understood the greatness of this inheritance, for he thought being a poet was an improvement on the family's occupation. But at any rate, whether it was king or simple craftsman, there was never any question as to identity. The question never arose. The man knew what he was doing, he was making something indeed. This gave him a place in society, and this place gave him the sense of belonging and lasting. The fact that his family had been doing the same thing for a long time helped sustain this sense of himself. This view was not historical. It was genealogical. And genealogy, if you push it far enough, will disperse in the mists of the beginning of things, and such is necessarily metaphysical, where any act is carnal and supernatural at the same time. Where the worldly city is an imitation, slim indeed, of the heavenly city. But no matter how poor, the imitation indicates a belief in a divine origin.

Our trouble today about identity depends upon the acceptance of the world as the end in itself, not the stage where the drama of the soul, salvation or damnation, is played. This is particularly western and Christian. I once in an essay spoke of the second fall of man, the fall into history: that is, man judging man as final truth. This was particularly relevant to the Nineteenth century, where people asked the question, What will history think of this—not was the act a good act. History made no answer, but man made a-plenty. I must now correct myself.

It is not the second fall of man. It is the same old tumble. To live as the gods is the same old promise of absolute power, that is power as an irresponsible wish, not the necessary power limited to the fulfillment of an office. The old wish of reunion, the two opposites brought together in a perfect whole, is no longer our wish. We have forgotten Cain's solution. Whatever we have of the garden has become myopic. We do not see Adam, the one form separated into two, nor the yearning of the two to be one again. We see a strange hermaphroditic shape of man as God and man as man.

We, especially our practical scientists, have fallen for the same old temptation, not only control of the laws of the universe but eventually the creation of life, without any of the fun of doing it. It was a while before this attitude became so explicit, but it showed itself as the beginning of what we call the Renascence. Slowly the crafts were doomed to extinction, when the profit system was substituted for making for the needs of man. The craftsman was slow to give up or in. So long as he owned his tools, he was a relatively free man. When he tended a machine he did not own, he ceased to know who he was. Coomaraswami, that learned scholar and curator, said that once every man, east or west, was a particular kind of craftsman, but today a craftsman (he said artist) is a particular kind of man. And that is hard, to be apart from the doings of your fellows.

The antonym of love is not hate. It is power, irresponsible and selfish. Pushed to extremes the choice is either love or lust; in politics, ochlocracy or the ceremonial state; in economics, private or absentee ownership, in religion, the mansions of God or the secular slums of humanitarianism.

Instead of worrying too much about identity which is lost, I would ask another question, What can we do to be saved?

# They Took Their Stand: The Agrarian View After Fifty Years

THIS title is for me ambiguous. Of the twelve agrarians who wrote the symposium *I'll Take My Stand,* only three are alive: Robert Penn Warren, the poet and novelist; Lyle Lanier, a psychologist and former executive vice-president of the University of Illinois; and myself, a writer and reader of fiction. I don't presume to speak for either Warren or Lanier, and I don't know how to address myself to myself in the past tense. Perhaps I am not here at all. Secretly I've had the feeling I was killed at the Battle of Brice's Crossroads, taking the bullet meant for General Forrest. You understand it was Forrest who, if he'd been let, could have been decisive in winning the war of the Northern Rebellion. Too often Confederate forces won the field only to retreat later on. Brice's Crossroads, fought in Mississippi, was a perfect battle. It should be an example of such in the textbooks of war colleges. Forrest combined his forces at the right time, defeated an enemy with odds of two to one against him, and then pursued the enemy and drove him out of the state—not to speak of the seizure of supplies, which was large. So perhaps it will be all right to speak of myself in the third person, along with my companions in arms who must of necessity be so addressed, if what you see here is not me but my ghostly presence. But if I am a ghost, what are you?

And what then are all those good men and true who find their beliefs disembodied? For as there is God, no idea, principle or belief

*This essay is Mr. Lytle's address originally presented to The Philadelphia Society meeting in New Orleans in October 1979.*

is ever defeated. Men are. Except those men who continue to believe and take the proper risks. I cite you Thermopylae. As military science and tactics are never either defensive or offensive but both, so no surrender need be final, not even unconditional surrender. There was a moment when the agrarians thought this, a particular moment when the country suffered the 1929 stock-market crash. The book coming out after that made us seem prophets. We did not so see ourselves in the writing of it. None of us was a politician or intended, I think, any pragmatic action. We were protesting an unhappy condition of Southern affairs and a continuing conquest. Today it is clear to me, at least, that we were better prophets than we knew. I don't feel that any of us at the time could have imagined that the conditions we protested could become so rapidly worsened.

So, after the crash, for a while at least, we had hopes of making the word flesh. It was a lot of fun. We addressed one another as generals, I hope you understand facetiously but not entirely. The depression was upon us, and it was heavy. People were stealing corn in broad-open daylight, and my father turned his head. I know of a fireman in Trenton, New Jersey, who rode his bicycle into the country and stole apples to keep his family from starving. William Dodd, historian and ambassador to Germany, tried to persuade Roosevelt that he might do well to listen to what the agrarians had to say. He got the dollar-a-year men. I spoke to Senator Bankhead. All he could come up with was forty acres and a mule. (There were mules then. They are curiosities now.)

Before I go on, I must remind myself how pervasive was a growing acceptance of the new materialism we attacked as industrialism. The South had prospered during the First World War. In the euphoria of victory there was a general feeling that we were back in the Union. The New South propaganda of progress everywhere said as much, and most of the media of news and public information took it for granted. Farming was looked down upon. Tired of poverty and honest work, the young began to desert the land and go to town, and in town the ambitious youth took the train to New York City, as did many young men from the West. The educational world began to change its curricula. The Chancellor of Vanderbilt University announced at a crucial moment of an agrarian fight that he wanted to graduate bankers, not writers or farmers. Rumor had it that the English building, ordered by him, was to be as much like a factory as possible, and the architect obliged. It was not the Church's Thanks-giving that we chanted. A New England holiday was universally celebrated as the national Thanksgiving. This salvation of the Puri-tan fathers after their hard winter was instilled into the minds of Southern children as the salvation of their founding fathers. One of my projects in kindergarten was cutting out and painting turkeys and tall-hatted men with bibs to paste in front of a log cabin made out of twigs. At home *Uncle Remus* was read to me, but in public it was John Alden, why don't you speak for yourself, John? that we were read. We were not told that Captain John Smith, sailing the Atlantic coast, brought smallpox to the Indians at Plymouth and so let the Puritans land in safety. Always it was the New England story which concerned the genesis of the nation. Not the other John, John Rolfe, who courted the Indian maiden, Pocahontas. Their subse-quent marriage made an elevating and romantic story of amity between races. No teacher knew enough to reveal the historic mean-ing of this incident. It was the first instance recorded in English of the Indian woman's preference for the European. The betrayal of her tribe for the white man's favors was a constant element in the pattern of Indian defeat. Nancy Ward, a beloved woman of the Cherokees, saw nothing wrong in sitting in council while living with one of the enemy. Her betrayal indicates the complexity of the Indian mind, for she never left the council and remained beloved and respected.

Whoever wins an internecine war writes the history of that war. And the textbooks as well. Lost in diaries and obscure histories, there yet survived many stories about the settlements in Middle Tennessee, both of Indians and of Americans, which would have told our young of stamina and courage. The attack on the stations around Nashville, the skillet and the kettle at a bend in the Tennes-see River, or an account of that one man Spencer who lived in the arm of a hollow sycamore, alone during the hardest winter that country had known, with only half a skinning knife for protection and food. It must have been some tree, for he was so big a man that a French trader, seeing his footprints, jumped into the Cumberland River and swam away. He thought he was fleeing a monstrous bear. Later at a militia muster Spencer intervened between two young men who were fighting. One tried to get rough with him, where-upon he picked him up and threw him over the nine-foot fence surrounding the stockade. The man called back, "If you will just throw my horse over, Mister Spencer, I'll be getting on my way." There are a number of these tales which, along with more formal documents, carry the truth about a history, the quality of a tradition.

It was not long before some of us, at least, suffered a disillusionment: it was not clear that we were back in the Union. There were two incidents which had a good deal to do with this; at least they gave some propulsion to reforming our opinions and informing our judgments. One was the Dayton or Monkey trial in Tennessee. The trial concerned a law forbidding the teaching of evolution in the schools of the state. This law was loudly proclaimed as an attack on academic freedom. Almost alone at Vanderbilt, our philosophy professor, Dr. Herbert Sanborn, a New Englander, exposed the fallacies in scientism's argument. I first met Allen Tate in New York City. We at once began discussing the trial as a liberal attack on our traditional inheritance. Now I see it as an advanced phase of Reconstruction. Maybe they are one and the same thing. After the economic exploitation of the South, this religious attack on the Southern spirit seemed to have a double purpose: to denigrate us before the country and the world and to make us laughable as backward and ignorant. But the real aim was more insidious, a forced acceptance of belief in a secular instead of a divine order of the universe. Practically this would have meant a total, instead of an economic, dominance by the Northeast. But the soul is not so easily traduced, especially of a people who live by or close to the land. These people are religious by nature because they enjoy and suffer nature, or they starve. Of course the defense at Dayton was inadequate, depending as it did upon a strict construction of the Bible with its literal fallacy. But the Liberal attack was equally fallacious, that scientism (there is not science, only sciences) was the only truth about man and nature. Along with the Monkey trial came H. L. Mencken's journalistic description of the South as "the Sahara of the Bozarts." This is like the thief who robs a house the second time and complains that the owners do not eat with silver.

How far such calumnies influenced the twelve I won't try to say, except for myself. One of the dangers of this kind of a discussion is inflicting your own responses upon your fellows, who certainly spoke for themselves. It set me to studying American and Southern history, about which I knew little to nothing. I kept at it for seven years, with Frank Owsley to guide me. One of our professional historians, Owsley's life work was to replace biased or inaccurate accounts with the truth. Soon Tate was writing the biographies of Stonewall Jackson and Jefferson Davis, and Warren a biography of John Brown. I was at work on Forrest. At any rate all the writers were Southern and most of them, by accident, were associated with Vanderbilt University. These men were already known or were to become distinguished in their proper occupations, whether it was history or psychology or literature. Their agrarian writings merely displayed their common cultural inheritance, which was Christian and European. Let me quote a paragraph from the statement of principles in the Introduction to *I'll Take My Stand:*

> Opposed to the industrial society is the agrarian, which does not stand in particular need of definition. An agrarian society is hardly one that has no use at all for industries, for professional vocations, for scholars and artists, and for the life of cities. Technically, perhaps, an agrarian society is one in which agriculture is the leading vocation, whether for wealth, for pleasure, or for prestige—a form of labor that is pursued with intelligence and leisure, and that becomes the model to which the other forms approach as well as they may.

Surely, then, it must be taken that a poet, a farmer, a banker, a historian, a schoolteacher, must live in a certain place and time and so exhibit the kind of belief and behavior defined by the manners and mores of that time and place. It was not necessary to be a farmer to be agrarian. It was merely the basic occupation of a commodity-producing society. The Liberal cartoons attacking us showed us with our heads under a mule's tail, or a lone privy, or Necessary as George Washington called it, with a half moon cut over the door and the door closed. It left to the imagination what was behind the door. Allen Tate remarked that he preferred an indoor commode so long as he didn't have to kneel down and worship it before using it.

Only the Liberal mind could confuse equipment with the thing itself, but then the Liberal is always promising to relieve us of our common ills at somebody else's expense. He is the propagandist of the power we opposed. It is an old fight and the agrarians were not the first to enter it. This is no time to reargue the case. The books are there to be read, and read in light of our present circumstances. I do want to emphasize that agrarianism was not an effort to reconstitute an ideal state, a utopia, unless, in the sense of Sir Thomas More's *Utopia*, an allegory criticizing his king's English and European policies. An outright statement would have lost him his head much earlier. The agrarian effort was towards the preservation of an inherited way of life, a way which was threatened but still in existence. I said it was an old fight. Napoleon tried to restore the legitimacy of kingship, but London, the center of international banking, defeated him. At St. Helena, he told Las Cases, "Agriculture is the soul, the foundation of the Kingdom; industry ministers to the comfort and happiness of the population. Foreign trade is the superabundance; it allows of the due exchange of the surplus of agriculture and home industry; these last ought never to be subordinate to foreign trade." This country's policy has reversed the order: foreign trade first, industry, agriculture a poor third. Each day news reports witness to the folly of this order.

Shortly after the American Revolution the cogent opponent to what he called the paper and patronage aristocracy was John Taylor of Caroline County, Virginia. His question was: Why set up in this country the same power we fought a war to be free of? He was speaking against banking and central government. He was a Jeffersonian but more agrarian and more lucid than Jefferson. He refused to put any hope in men themselves, but always in principles. In 1813 he published *Arator*, a collection of essays on farming and politics. The thesis was this: agriculture and politics are the sources of wealth and power. Both contain good internal principles, but both are subject to practical deterioration. If agriculture is good and the government bad, we may have wealth and slavery. If the government is good and agriculture bad, liberty and poverty. We must remember that at this date nearly ninety percent of the American population made its living by or on the land. From 1940 to 1974, the number of farms in the U.S. declined from approximately six million to a little over two million, 62 percent of our family units. Since the Second World War, thirty-million people have left the country for the city. You don't need more than one wrong idea to destroy a state.

I am not talking from statistics, but this great acceleration of such widespread loss of farms and families sustains my argument, which is this: at the time we wrote there were enough families living on the land and enough privately owned businesses in small towns and cities to counterbalance the great industrial might, which was a fact and had to be reckoned with. If our proposal had been listened to, this necessary industry might have been contained, might not have grown into the only idea of the kind of life everybody must be forced to accept. A family, and I mean its kin and connections, too, thrives best on some fixed location which holds the memories of past generations by the ownership of farms or even family businesses. Not only sentimental memories but skills passed down and a knowledge of the earth tended. And a knowledge particularly of the bloodstreams, so as to be warned and prepared for what to expect in behavior. Industry today uproots. It's like the army without having the army's raison d'être. Promotion, except among the basic workers, means pulling up roots and being sent elsewhere, with the promise of a better car and another room to the house. The children, just as they are making friends and getting used to school, must begin all over again. This is a modification of the Spartan state, which reduced the family to a minimal role.

The most irresponsible of our critics accused us of the self-indulgence of nostalgia, of foisting on our readers a myth, and by myth was meant something that never existed. All societies are sustained by a myth. Such a myth is of necessity metaphysical, but it was not this kind of myth the critic had in mind. He had mischosen his word. He meant fantasy, something that had no grounding in fact. It was unfortunate for this kind of argument that many of us were historians, and in Frank Owsley we had the best of professional historians. I speak of Owsley rather than Nixon because it was he and his wife, Harriet, who exposed the alien "myths" about the South—that it was composed of large plantations with Old Marster sipping juleps while the slaves sang; and on the fringe were the one-bale (if that) cotton farmers called "poor whites." He simply went to the census records where the facts were. Also to diaries and county records, but the federal census carried particular authority. One instance of this: Presumably the black-belt counties would be the area of the large plantations. Now the census taker went down the road, stopping in order at this farm and that, as he went along. The Owsleys discovered the greatest diversity in ownership, large plantations by moderate-size farms, small farms, a plantation of

two-thousand acres with no slaves, a man owning slaves and no land.
I won't go on, as the authority is here to correct or amplify me, if she
so wills. You see the South was never solid until after the war. Defeat
made it solid.

The misunderstanding, even among the most sympathetic critics,
like Louis Rubin, have assumed that a commodity-producing society, such as the South and West, had not a chance of sustaining itself
before the successive triumphs of the financial corporate role of
money. And this kind of money is always international. They were
vague about this corporate rule, but they accepted as absolute the *ex
post facto* assumption of the relative poverty of the Southern farm
and its ultimate doom. The confusion lies just here. The communities composed of families with real property and private businesses still existed. The fight was on, but the outcome was uncertain.
The depression was a heavy blow. Cotton cost seven cents a pound to
grow and it brought, on what is essentially the world market, five
cents. The only answer Roosevelt's government could give was plow
under a fourth of your labor, cotton, corn, hogs, and cattle. This is
the most immoral fiat ever handed down from afar: destroy your
handicrafts and life for an abstract stock-market purpose. Where
was the Joseph to talk of lean and fat years, store away instead of
destroy.

The communities were the shape of society, even after the First
World War. I was there. I lived in them. Most of the towns in the
South, and cities, too, lived by the country. My argument in two
essays was this: the small farm upholds the state. I didn't give any
number of acres. What I meant was a family-owned and operated
place. If the place has no mortgage, you live in a dwelling-house
without paying money for rent. If you plow with a team, you grow
your own fuel. You grow most of your food. You do grow crops for
money, but you are not completely in the money economy. You live at
home with security. And you are part of a living community, with
other families in your situation, some better-to-do than others, as
will always be the case.

Now witness the county seat. I'm speaking from experience
again. All the roads radiating from the seat were privately owned.
They had tollgates every five miles, and to pass through cost so
much, a buggy, twenty-five cents, so much a head for sheep. I used to
go with my father to collect toll, and the money, all coin, would be

stacked in order, silver dollars, halves, quarters, on down to dimes and nickels, and they all smelled of snuff. There were very few paper bills. This meant that you didn't leave home idly. You lived in a community with a radius of, say, five miles. This lasted almost until I went to college. The automobile was in its infancy. It was a toy for those who could buy. The ladies wore veils and everybody wore dustcoats when "the machine," as it was called, took you out for a short spin. People would call and ask if you were going to bring it out. It scared their mettlesome carriage horses. And rightly so. It was the horses' doom. But it took some years before it broke up the community. Thirty miles an hour was fast. The roads were not fit for speed. It took the greater part of the day to go from Huntsville, Alabama, to Guntersville, forty miles away. Punctures were frequent, or a mud-hole with brush in it would delay you for maybe an hour, until you could find somebody to hitch up his team and pull you out. Of course unless the team was obviously nearby and the hand out. My father had a Ford tractor. It could break four acres a day, but so could a good team. He used it for disking, as broken ground is hard on animals. This was for Cornsilk, a twelve-hundred-acre place, which the T.V.A. stole and covered up with water.

This family farm I talked about earlier (here I am not referring to Cornsilk) was dismissed as a "subsistence farm." In the first place, there is no such thing as a subsistence farm. That is an adjective used by a voice who thinks milk comes out of bottles, or a term that applies possibly to land so poor that no insurance company would give it a mortgage. But even land such as this is no subsistence farm. Even this has its place in society. If it has little money and no credit to buy advertised products, it still has a life of its own. When the T.V.A. began to build all those dams, making of the best land a permanent flood to control floods, it had to buy a little place near Muscle Shoals. This place was so poor it had no mortgage against it, but the shack did have a chimney whose fire had not gone out in a hundred years. "Eminent domain" or not, the T.V.A. had to move that chimney, the coals covered and hot, to its new location. The point is not that the move cost more than the price of the farm. The point is that from the mirage of history, fire on the hearth has been the symbol of the home. Neolithic man "identified the column of smoke that rose from his hearth to disappear from view through a hole in the roof with the Axis of the Universe, saw in this luffer [*i.e.*, louver] an image of the Heavenly door, and in his hearth the Navel of the Earth." The man who cherished that chimney and forced a sovereign power to preserve it was not a man who thought much of comfort, that euphemism which disguises the perfidious intention of turning man into an appetite, to be perpetually bloated by some new appeal of an expanding economy, expanding until the resources on the earth and beneath it are exhausted.

In 1928, Allen Tate, his wife, and child, and I travelled in a secondhand Ford from New York to Alabama, going over the battlefields. There were no Interstates (maybe the Pennsylvania Turnpike), but many narrow paved roads and roads with gravel, all rough in places. The outskirts of Philadelphia ended easily in the country, with its farms—and not just Amish either. (Today, from Trenton to Philadelphia there is a flow of houses which obliterates the state lines, and at night becomes one long blur of light.) Through Maryland into Virginia we camped by the side of the road or in a farmer's lot and picked his turnip greens and cooked them in a pot with sowbelly. I knew how to make a hoecake. The water and greens were free, as was the campground. If we felt we could afford it, we would stop in a village or at some courthouse with buildings about it and eat a lunch for thirty-five cents. If it was forty-five, we might drive on.

There was only one tourist camp the entire way, no buildings but a common washroom and commodes. This was outside Richmond. We pitched our pup tents here. Sometimes we washed and dressed and went into town on invitation, which was always welcome as a change of diet. The night-watchman was the great-nephew of General John Bankhead Magruder, late of the Confederacy. The superintendent was the great-nephew of General A. P. Hill of the Army of Northern Virginia, whose name was called by both Lee and Jackson in their dying speech. This was the familiar world all of us were born in, and I hope I am making it clear that now I am not speaking only of the Southern terrain.

Later, I went on alone to Mississippi, where Forrest often rode. I can't believe it had changed much from war days. Going through the backcountry to Tupelo, I stopped to inquire the way. Teams were hitched about the courthouse fence; a political meeting was afoot. The patriarchs, in black hats and with white beards, sat on the platform with their hands on hickory sticks. It was obvious that little of folly would take place in their presence. I was asked to "take-out" and join the crowd. I was not asked to park my Ford. I thanked the man but told him I was running late. Could he direct me to Tupelo. I was told to go down the road, and he pointed which way, until I came to a widow-woman's house, where I was to turn left. I thanked him and went on. I had no trouble finding the widow-woman's house. It had no stovewood stacked in the yard.

I've often asked myself: Why was it that so few people listened to us, although most were sympathetic. The kind of life they knew was at stake. I think the reason of their seeming indifference is this: Nobody could imagine the world they were born in, had lived in, and were still living in could disappear. Well, it has.

As my final word, I think we should have found a larger word than agrarian, for it was this whole country's Christian inheritance that was threatened, and still is. But let there be no misunderstanding. We still are subjects of Christendom. Only we have reached its Satanic phase. I can't believe that any society is strong which holds physical comfort as its quest. There is only one comfort, and it is the only thing that has been promised: the gates of Hell will not finally prevail.

# PART IV

# TWO
# INTERVIEWS

# Monteagle—1983

*A 1983 interview from* The Review of the News *conducted by James B. Graves, associate editor.*

Q. Mr. Lytle, you've spent much of your long life as a teacher, not only of literature and writing, but also of history. How do schools and students today compare with those of a generation back?

A. Students, I suppose, are always the same, but their learning can be no better than the instruction they get. And the public-school system has gradually worsened not for one generation but for three or four. Entrance to the University of the South is very competitive and we enroll the best and the brightest. But that can be surprising. For instance, we once accepted presumably the best student from a Middle Western high school only to discover that he'd been made to do very little writing; had not been taught the fundamental principles of spelling, grammar, or syntax; and, had been assigned very little reading. Soon he was failing with us, and wrote his high-school teachers to tell them how they had failed him. He was a gifted boy, the University instructors gave him help, and he overcame his lack of preparation. But it was not the University's business to do the work of the high school.

Q. The recent Report of the President's Commission on Excellence in Education has suggested that what is needed is across-the-board pay raises for teachers and a general increase in educational budgets. What are your thoughts on that?

A. More money isn't the answer to every problem. Suppose the curriculum is at fault, or the administration, or the system itself.

Q. Then you think the difficulties of the public schools lie on some deeper level?

A. Yes I do. If you can stand a little history of it, consider:

After the internecine war of the 1860s, along with the "Reconstruction" of the South, there was fairly general school reconstruction. For four years young men on both sides had been deprived of schooling. Because of the defeat and widespread destruction of the South, General Lee as president of Washington College introduced into the curriculum courses to train the young to rebuild the civil state. That is, lest it go under. At the time there was no intention to do away with Latin and Greek or the idea of liberal education. But the softer elective courses appealed to certain students and in time began to compete with the more rigorous arts and sciences.

The symbol of the change was the dropping of Latin as a requirement. Latin, it was said, buttered no bread, nobody spoke it, it was a dead language. It was overlooked that more than 52 percent of our mother tongue was derived from Latin and that Latin had been for centuries the universal language of Christendom. It was in fact one of the things that united Europe culturally and religiously.

The pragmatic result of dropping Latin has been the decline of public and private speech through the use of a semiliterate journalese for a model. You see what this means when you remember that the great men who wrote our Constitution were trained in the orations, literature, and history of the Roman state.

Q. What are some of the other problems?

A. We increasingly fail to put first things first. That is, as I have suggested, we neglect to obey those basic laws of language and rhetoric by which we reach others and are able to impart our understanding of the laws of nature and man. The schools now tend to rely too much on mere facilities and even mechanical devices. There is actually the suggestion that we will be able to do without teachers altogether and can simply throw the lessons on the electronic screen. One wonders who will inspire the students to work.

Q. When President Reagan visited Tennessee recently and advocated that the pay level for teachers be made commensurate with teacher performance in the classroom, the National Education Association, a labor union for teachers, raised a hue and cry against the President's proposal. No doubt there are some thorny problems associated with determining who is and who is not a successful teacher. But do you think the N.E.A.'s objection arose out of anything other than a desire to protect the mediocre teacher?

A. I think it was not so much a desire to protect the mediocre teacher but to protect the small minority who run those teacher organizations with their dictatorial control over education. One of them recently said at a public meeting that, if the President's plan went through, it would destroy the educational system. What that educationist meant was it would destroy his (and their) control over it.

Q. What about the teachers' colleges? Are they part of the problem?

A. Our educational failures were institutionalized by the normal schools, as teachers' colleges used to be called. They were founded out of a true need, but quickly fell into the hands of a small bureaucratic body that today dominates the teachers' organizations, the Parent Teachers Association, and directs education policy in the state legislatures and in Washington, D.C. This group sets the requirements for teachers to teach in the public schools, causing them to spend much time studying abstract courses purportedly designed to teach how to teach. These courses represent method without imparting solid subject matter to give them shape. The "method" is supposed to serve all disciplines equally. Of course, that's nonsense. Every legitimate academic subject develops its own method of presentation, modified by the teacher's capacity to teach.

It's a waste of time and money to force a teacher to study what the good teachers never use. Only those who shouldn't be teaching anyway rely on these abstractions. An abstraction that never finds its concrete incident is far too easy to substitute for learning. It can never be put to the test, and when it is established as the standard it becomes a Procrustean bed. Whatever doesn't fit is subject to having its feet or head cut off.

Q. Have you noticed public-school attitudes carrying over into the private schools?

A. Yes, some of this has insidiously crept over into the education associations of the private schools, and many have foolishly agreed to certain of the rules dictated by the educationist bureaucracy. They allow the word "accreditation" to be held over their heads like a club. The private schools should stand upon their own record. The best do.

Q. What about more aid from the federal government? Can that help the public schools, or help anything else for that matter?

A. Thomas Jefferson thought the government that governs least governs best, and our national government is not a sovereign power. We forget that. It is a *creature* of sovereignty. It represents us in foreign affairs and protects our domestic privacy from intrusion. (That is, it should.) But it is the *people* who are sovereign. When some branch of government invades our privacy, as is so frequent today, it is performing exactly like the tyrants of old. The Supreme Court has ruled, alas, that what the government subsidizes it *must* control. Hence the use of federal monies in the misuse and perversion of the public-school system.

Q. What are some of the problems in our colleges?

A. When you spill even a little buttermilk in the well, you spoil *all* the water. On every level of schooling, students suffer from the secularization of education. There was once no distinction between secular and religious education. Belief in a Christian order of the universe informed all institutions. Each had its own function and need, but the separation of church and state was an impossibility. They were already separate but serving a common end. Then the prelates of the Church of England made the mistake of becoming politicians, and the reaction against that produced in our culture this ambiguous separation of church and state.

All the fuss about prayer in the schools is part of the old confusion. The President, when taking his oath of office, puts his hand on the Bible held by the Chief Justice of the Supreme Court. The Congress has chaplains. In ordinary courts the witness puts his hand on the Bible to swear that he will tell the truth, only the truth, and nothing but the truth. These are all institutional offices. The schools belong to the institution of learning. Prayer has the same purpose there as the President swearing by the Bible that he will uphold the purposes of his office.

The problem of secularization has gone so far that one can witness it in the fact that small buildings of various religious denominations now lurk around the edges of public-university campuses like houses of ill fame, which indeed they are to a Court that has declared prayer in public schools to be a criminal act. But the religious colleges are mostly secularized, too. The word *Progress* has been substituted for the word *Christian.* Of course that is satanic. The notion is to replace God by man with the aim and end of human perfectibility. As if a human being could perfect himself in some far-distant future; as if a father could pass on every experience and all he knows to his son. This business about Progress is the old delusion first pronounced in the Garden of Eden: *Sicut eritis dei, You will live as gods.* Except that gods never die.

How can colleges do what they ought to do where the atmosphere is largely secular, carnal, materialistic, and atheistic? The answer is that they cannot.

Q. What should be the purpose of a college education?

A. I am going right down to bedrock here, and again the answer applies not just to the colleges. The guidance and restraint of formal learning discipline us to endure the loss of innocence. Only the very young can live in Eden. Only they can begin each day afresh without memory, their senses quickening to the objects as they appear, as if they looked out on the first day. This is a wonderful view, but it will not wear. Innocence prolonged denies experience. Knowledge tends to become a stone in the head. Every man who is a man accepts the responsibility for knowledge and its use.

Q. Does everybody need a college education?

A. Everybody needs to read and write and cipher, know some geography and the truthful history of his country. But to force learning on a student beyond his need or capacity—and this goes for the lower grades, as well—has brought about the anomaly of passing a student whether he has made it or not. This is generally corrupting. It also impairs the minds of the best students by assuming that *all* students fit an average age group. All children, the educationists think, should receive equal treatment. This delusion forgets that our country is not a democracy. What is it then? It once was a republic. Remember how John C. Calhoun replied to Jefferson's famous half truth by pointing out that men are not equal, for children are the most helpless of all animals.

Q. Are there still good teachers around today?

A. The truths which the disciplines of learning disseminate are hard to pervert finally. This is because the truth is true, and there are still teachers who are committed to the discipline which attracted them to the profession, no matter how bad the educational system has become.

One of the false assumptions of the educationists is that a teacher can teach any subject. But he can't. He must be committed; he must love what he teaches so as to be able to stand the weariness of learning, resist the constant temptation to sustain easy prejudices, and endure every day in class the face of smooth and shining ignorance.

Also he must love his students, and they will return this love by studying. They do it to please him. For out of respect they conclude that what he knows and feels to be important must be worth their knowing and exploring. The true teacher's love for what he does, and for whom he does it, is going to be the salvation of this country.

Q. Mr. Lytle, what kind of graduates should a college hope to train?

A. The old English idea of a university as a training ground for those who would guide and protect the state remains valid today. But I am not talking about a curriculum that attempts to impart "skills." Some of our religious schools still keep faintly the idea of educating a Christian, or a gentleman, or a Christian gentleman, who will go back home or out into the world and be what he is; that is, what the school trained him to be.

What will such a graduate do? First of all, he will keep private things private. How hard that is today! And public things public. That, too, will be hard, because the Leftist strategy is to destroy the state by confusing the two, and our shoddy journalists go along with this. But the distinction between public and private is the basis for order. If the graduate wants to preach, let him mount the pulpit. If he wants to influence politics, let him run for office. If he wants to bring about social reforms, let him mind his manners as an example to others. His mind will presumably be a trained instrument which can respond to any kind of experience. That's what it is supposed to do. A university cannot teach him everything about any subject. But it can show him where all of the subjects are, and which are important and in what degree. Such graduates will let information go through them like a flux but digest their learning. They will by character and understanding offer hope and recourse.

Q. You've written a great deal about the place of the family in society. Will you tell us what you mean by family and why the family is so important?

A. By family I mean not just parents and children. I'm talking about the whole thing with all the kin and connections as a unit of society as it once existed in this country. The families made up the county seats and finally the states and overlapped the state lines. A family has to have location. It has to own something, either a small business or a farm, preferably one that's been inherited and will be passed on through the generations. The land or the small business which this family uses to make a living will pass on the intimate relationships between the members of the family who are involved with it.

In the South, at least, one sense of the family that has been so strong is the Scotch-Irish or Scotch clan. The head of the clan was kin to everybody in it, so he would take a familial attitude towards those dependent on him. This is entirely different from everywhere else in Europe where the power was separate from those who were controlled. Families in this sense take on characteristics that everybody in the community recognizes. In the South, again, it used to be that when you met a stranger you asked him where he was from; meaning, if you tell me where you're from, I'll no doubt have kin or connections there and can learn from them who you really are. Now we ask a stranger what he does. In other words, we inquire about his economic status. The difference is obvious, and it measures our decline.

Even a mediocre person in a traditional family has more

behind him, and those dependent on him, than the most brilliant man who goes out into the world alone. To oversimplify a
little, in one sense it comes down to this: You've got to have
somebody to go your bail in time of trouble.

Also, families have something to lose. So they'll be very careful how they vote. This is why the Communists want to destroy
the family. No monolithic state, no tyranny, can exist unless it
has control of all units of society, and families are much harder
to control than individuals.

Q. In view of climbing divorce rates and the prevalence of working
mothers and such, does the upheaval of American family life
show up in problems in the schools?

A. Divorces and the other problems families are experiencing are
more symptoms than causes. But to answer your question, it's
true that some children nowadays come to school already de-
praved. I don't think that's too strong a word. The problem is a
lack of love. Living the way they do now, many people just don't
love their children enough to raise them the way they should.

Q. Mr. Lytle, you have written a history of your own family in
Middle Tennessee, calling the book *A Wake For The Living*. Why
did you give that captivating and inspiring book such a gloomy
title?

A. I don't think of it as gloomy, for I intended two meanings. At
every traditional funeral there is a kind of wake to which people come to pay their respects. In Ireland, you know, they put
the whiskey bottle on top of the coffin. That's an old inherited
way that is alive with nuance. And I was also being ironic,
suggesting that the wake in this case should not be for the dead
but for our present society. The society described in my book
was a much sounder, stronger, society than we see today.

Q. Along with Allen Tate and John Crowe Ransom, you were one of
the 12 Southern Agrarian writers who in 1931 published the
famous collection of essays called *I'll Take My Stand*. That book
recommended to Southern farmers that they would do well to
stay on their land rather than going off to the cities to take jobs
in factories. What advantages does the hard life of a farmer
have over city conveniences?

A. Our idea was not just to keep farmers on the land. Nor were we
addressing only Southerners. We were trying to defend, using

the word agrarian, the whole inherited European world of which our society was part. Our idea was to keep the other professions and livelihoods sensitive to the agrarian way of life so that the institutions, the form and intent, and the ultimate meaning of a traditional and conservative society could set the tone and values for everything else. We wanted a society not only of farmers but also of agrarian teachers, agrarian businessmen, even agrarian bankers.

To get to your question, you can see that those city conveniences you spoke of have largely turned into nightmares, as we foresaw they would; whereas the kind of farmer we were talking about, who was not wholly immersed in a money economy, was able to live securely and at moments dramatically. In farming there will be a time when you have to make crucial decisions. You are dealing with nature, and know that you are dependent on it.

It was an attitude toward nature, among other things, that we were defending. Nature has contingency, and if you can appreciate nature it will show you that life is finally mysterious and inscrutable. It is a lesson we have forgotten to our great loss. Life can be very strenuous for the farmer, but it is sometimes very leisurely and there are periods when you do nothing more than mend the fences and other catch-up chores. Leisure gives opportunity for reflection, which you don't find in the monotony of industrial work. It is reflection upon which the arts and, for the last 400 years, history have depended. Memory, through recollection into song, is the classical inheritance the Western world has abandoned in its reduction of man to his physical dimensions.

Q. I believe that you and two of the other writers of *I'll Take My Stand* wanted to call the book *Tracts Against Communism*. What did you mean by that?

A. The family is the source of the traditional and Conservative state, and the Soviets were and are destroying families. Take the situation in the Ukraine in the 1930s where those millions of farmers known as *kulaks* wouldn't go along with the tyranny in Moscow and were intentionally starved to death. We saw Moscow-style communism as a force that needed opposing and there were few who were then opposing it.

But we were also aware of another kind of communist threat that we discussed in the preface to *I'll Take My Stand*. There we were concerned with the fact that the leading notion of the day was that the evils of industrialism would disappear as soon as bigger and better machines came along, and more of them. Among the advocates of that idea there were influential people who wanted to find superengineers in the shape of boards of control that would have the purpose of adapting production to consumption, regulating prices, and guaranteeing business against fluctuations. In other words, state planning was very much in the air. We called the people behind this trend *sovietists* or *communists* because they would have the government set up an economic superorganization which would in turn become the government.

Q. Mr. Lytle, to what degree have subsequent events vindicated the forecasts of the writers of *I'll Take My Stand*?

A. I don't think any of us could have considered that things would be as bad as they are today. Those who laughed at our position— the Southern "Liberals" and others—don't laugh any more.

The idea of the supremacy of the applied sciences had already saturated and infiltrated every area of life. People were being asked to make sacrifices for some halcyon days in the future when men would become perfect and be as gods. Now I ask you if that promise has materialized?

It has occurred to me that the reason more people didn't listen to us then was because nobody can believe that the society he was born in, and expects his children to be born in, can just disappear. But that is largely what has happened.

Q. You have said that you and your colleagues did not see yourselves as political activists when you published your manifesto. But it is now widely recognized that your efforts constituted perhaps the first concerted effort in America to elaborate a defense of Conservative principles opposed both to industrial cartels and the monolithic state. Did you have any sense of being an intellectual pioneer in 1931?

A. No, it's just that we felt that our backs were to the wall. We were protesting a bad situation, but we were not politicians. It was the Great Depression that made us seem prophets by showing that we were not alarmists.

Q. Why have the rural areas of our country always been so patriotic, and why does radicalism have such a hard time taking root in rural soil?

A. Farmers own something, don't you see? They've got something to lose. They still have some sense of community; their patriotism is natural; and, despite the leisure they have, farmers don't have much time for foolishness. At least they don't waste their free time on foolish undertakings.

Q. Back when you and your colleagues were publicizing traditional American conservativism, your voices were among the few then being raised against industrial pollution and the reckless pillaging of our natural resources. That was of course long before the fashionable Left discovered the ecology as a political cause. Will you comment on today's radical ecologists?

A. Our attitude towards nature was part and parcel of the kind of life we wanted to preserve. You would naturally not destroy the things by which you made your living or the things by which you accepted the world. You preserved. Those who didn't lost their land. Our feeling was that nature should be enjoyed, explored, used—and conserved. It was mysterious and to be respected, and we took time to examine it in the world and in ourselves. Mystery and respect now seem to be old-fashioned words. But we knew that land is built up only slowly, and it can waste away in no time at all if not properly tended. So you preserve.

We had no sentimental attitudes, for example, towards that little darter fish. But the ecologists are sentimentalists. If they really wanted to fight pollution they should be opposing the monopolistic institutions and their collectivist allies that cause it at root. Instead they seem to think that the answer lies in more government. It does not.

Q. Your answers all seem to come back to the same point. Can you sum up for us?

A. If I must do so, let it be this: One bad idea, which is materialism and the acceptance of materialism as the sole end of behavior and desire, is all that is needed to destroy a man or a state.

# A Conversation with
# Madison Smartt Bell

*Madison Smartt Bell is a novelist and Tennessean. His most recent work is* Soldier's Joy.

BELL: I wanted to ask you about a term you've used from time to
time, in letters and in print: "the hovering bard." What is the
hovering bard, exactly?

LYTLE: An extension of Henry James's "central intelligence," that's
what it is. It's somebody who sees everything from above and
can bring it together. Just as you have in a real country community somebody who knows something about what happened.
Every country society has one, who doesn't do anything,
doesn't work, just listens to everything, tells tales, tells what
everybody's doing, you know. A sort of disappointed or incom-
pleted artist, who gathers it all together. And—he would hover
over it all.

BELL: So it's a person inside the story that that voice comes from.

LYTLE: Yes, he can be a character. Jack Cropleigh would be it in *The
Velvet Horn*. Someone like Jack Cropleigh, who doesn't dominate every scene, but could have. Everything could have taken
place in his mind, you have to assume that. So it's rather tricky,
but it's not an omission, it allows the comment to come through
this particular hovering bard to become a choral effect, along
with the action.

BELL: Can the function of the bard move from person to person in a
story?

LYTLE: Yes, but you can't just move it briefly. You can't do it just for
several paragraphs or a page or a short chapter. It has to be a

244

whole section which comes to some kind of conclusion, but which is part of the general, ultimate conclusion. But it's never stated. As long as you say, "I remember," then it ceases to exist. Because nothing exists in the past. So what you have to do is make the past into a moving present tense, joined to this one. It took me months to work it out.

BELL: How long did you spend on *The Velvet Horn*, altogether?

LYTLE: Seven or eight years. I had started a book that I thought was going to be about a society that is dead. And then I realized that nothing which is dead ever moves. So what you really write about is people and a given condition. I spent two years on that before I realized you never write about anything dead. And at that time I happened to be reading Jung and Neumann and Zimmer and mythology, and that gave me my enveloping action.

BELL: Could you say what the enveloping action is?

LYTLE: Enveloping action is the universal, the thing which is always true. The simplest example is the triumvirate: two people in love with one person. You can have a million circumstances there. So what you do is envelop the whole action, as a particular action representing that universal. So the present action will also represent the other.

BELL: Would you say what it was in *The Velvet Horn*?

LYTLE: I don't know. Incest—spiritual and otherwise. I wouldn't say absolutely.

BELL: Well, I wanted to get you to talk about shifting point of view, which it seems that you don't much approve of. I am wondering when it can work and when it can't.

LYTLE: Oh yes. It's a weakness for two reasons. On the reader's part, he gets identified with a person and a point of view—you do that, certainly, in James's central intelligence. Well, if you use that and then shift it to somebody else, then it puzzles the reader. He doesn't know what to believe, finally. That's the effect.

BELL: And a book can't get resolved if the point of view shifts?

LYTLE: It cannot, there is just no way for it to.

BELL: What about the couple of Faulkner books that work that way, such as *As I Lay Dying*?

LYTLE: Well, the dead woman holds it together in *As I Lay Dying*.

She's there. Think about it. She's always present, as if she is not dead. That's how it's held together; the presence is there, and that's why the voices work.

BELL: But in *The Unvanquished,* for instance, it's all told in the voice of the boy. So you don't have the problem of separating voices.

LYTLE: Yes. It's in the first person; that's the most dangerous point of view of all. With first person, I say you've got the limitation of prejudice, and then you don't get the whole truth because the actor is involved, and then you've got omissions. But if you can have that attitude and still indirectly show the whole truth, then it works.

BELL: Then that would make the narrator the hovering bard?

LYTLE: It would make him the bard, don't you see?

BELL: You've written that dialogue is not enough to make fiction, and that summary is important.

LYTLE: Summary is fiction. Because the summary includes scenes and also the implications of scenes. You've got to have the scene, the scene is the center, it's drama. You have to have it because it's concrete. So you hear people speaking in terms of the action, but summary comes out of the enveloping action, I suppose. I think that fiction is a summary—summary of scenes leading up to the scene which you need.

BELL: Did your acting career contribute to that understanding? What did you do in the Yale Drama School?

LYTLE: I went there to study action, scene, really, what it comes down to, and I learned that.

BELL: What sort of parts did you play?

LYTLE: Different ones. I was not a matinee idol. I wrote a play that was put on, a one-act play. Made a big hit in Nashville. Called *The Lost Sheep.* It really went well, for three weeks.

I was in one play on Broadway, ran for four months. It was called *The Grey Fox,* about Machiavelli. Henry Hull played in it, Crystal Hull was the female lead. I was Machiavelli's clerk.

BELL: You were in damn good company.

LYTLE: Oh yes, that was pretty good company. And I got a $50 bill and a $10 bill every Saturday night. You could live on it then.

Onstage, you see the actors physically moving, and they arrange their movements, acting together, and you get a sense that you never can in the written word. But you've got to try to get that sense. Your problem is how, by the use of the five senses, to make the reader see what he would see in the theater. That's how it seems to me.

Everybody uses the five senses who writes. But Flaubert is the man who almost made a law of it. He said the more you use the senses, the more sense of being, of the reality of living people, you get. You've got sight, the sovereign sense, and hearing is awfully close. The mortal senses, smell, taste, and particularly touch: you can't reach the world, you can't love, you can't do any of these things without touch. And the more of those you use, the more imitation of life you will get.

That's why you've got to have the scene, but you've got to have behind that all the enveloping action, all the summary leading up to it. And scene is very extravagant. Hemingway can make a scene, his is nearly all scene, some of it. His panoramic summaries are stage directions, certainly in "The Killers." But he can take dialogue and not only make the action advance, but the understanding of it. Well, you can go through the whole of "The Killers" and just see what the summary will do with the scenic directions.

BELL: Do you have any ideas about ways of living that would allow a person sufficient time to write?

LYTLE: There's no one way. I think you've got to have a little luck, for one thing. You can teach in these places, they help. You might farm. I tried farming. Now if you own the farm, and have some cows, and want to go and milk, and do those things, then you might do it.

BELL: Except it ends up that takes most of your time, doesn't it?

LYTLE: Well, don't try to do too much. You've got to have some help, you know.

BELL: I've heard you say it from time to time that you couldn't farm even with help and write at the same time.

LYTLE: I mean, really farm. But you can do, say, one thing. Cows, you can have something to live on. You can make a garden, I do that here, you can do certain things. You cannot really farm and write.

I'll tell you what I did, I had a man do over an old log barn on one place, and I ought to have been out there watching. But I was trying to write, and I wrote four pages, I thought it was perfectly beautiful. When I looked at it, when I got through, I kept one sentence.

BELL: You were watching him out of the corner of your eye, then.

LYTLE: But you've got to do something. And if you own the land . . . but if you've got to pay the mortgage, you've got to grow things you don't want to grow, like tobacco. That's 14 months a year, tobacco. And there it goes. Now I think you can do it, but in comparison to teaching, you've got to teach too. Even writing: there's just no one solution.

Here's what I do, and this is the ground on which you begin: sit down at the same place every day at the same time, and put yourself away from yourself, and enter the imaginary world. And then do the day's stint. And if you've got the strength left, then you can do whatever else you have to do. The only trouble with that is, that always has its own measure and its own rules.

When I was working on *The Long Night*, there was a hill behind the house, you know, and I would go up and put a board across a stump or something and stay there all day. And when I came in my father asked me how the muse had treated me. "Well," I said, "I saw a snake chase a frog to a tree. And the frog got to the tree and the snake crawled slowly behind the brush and then he turned and looked at me."

BELL: That's in the book, isn't it?

LYTLE: Yes. I was just another creature out there, and nothing could intervene.

BELL: Have you seen that book, *Nashville: The Occupied City?*

LYTLE: I've got it here, but I haven't read it. I just don't like to read about the Civil War anymore. It's not always miswritten, but it is so sad. There was no reason really there, at the end . . . they were as exhausted as we were. And they'd got all the people they could out of Europe. And Grant had thrown away 10,000 men in one attack; the men put their addresses on their backs.

BELL: Cold Harbor?

LYTLE: Yes, Cold Harbor. And Jefferson Davis wouldn't let Lee retreat to the mountain, and if he had, then Lincoln probably would not have been reelected, and McClellan would have been, and we could have brought the war to an end. That's a possibility, but it didn't happen, and so that's what we've got to live with.

BELL: Where would we be if that had come to pass?

LYTLE: Well, I think the Industrial Revolution would have been slowed. But I don't know how far. They might have rejoined the old Union, I don't know what that would have been. Or you could have had the Confederacy by itself. Then they probably would have taken Mexico and Cuba. They had an army, and the Austrians were done for there. The Yankees wanted to do it, too, so you just can't tell. I think they would have moved in that direction.

BELL: What would life have been like?

LYTLE: Country people would have made a living again, that's what they would have done.

BELL: You think there's a way we could have avoided having McDonalds and K-Marts all through here?

LYTLE: I don't think that's the farming interest. [laughs] We've got as many stupid people here as they've got anywhere else, of course. It's true. But they weren't that stupid before the war, because everybody was well-informed on politics, they loved to hear people debate.

You know, I figured finally, after 60 years, that that was one reason why nobody paid any attention to the Agrarian position: nobody could think of his own society disappearing. They couldn't think of it.

BELL: It did, though.

LYTLE: Right underneath them, yes. But you can see how that would be. Because this is the greatest revolution that's happened, certainly, in our time.

BELL: Well, it's the most destructive.

LYTLE: Yes. Well, they put this car plant at Smyrna, they ruined that beautiful country over there, for 3,000 jobs, not two million. And you're not going to control them, and it's going to go bankrupt finally, because people don't have the money to buy that many cars.

You know, it doesn't take but one bad idea, that's all you've got to have, to destroy a man or a state. That's what you've got: materialism, that man can finally be eternal, or immortal. You know, Allen [Tate] used to quarrel with Edmund Wilson, he believed in that: the perfectibility of man, Wilson did. But you know what the question is: *When? When?* And in the meantime

you've got to make all these sacrifices at somebody else's pleasure, or interest, toward that end.

It's a kind of satanic thing. They deny the nature of things,
that there's dark and light, pain and pleasure, day and night,
male and female. . . . They deny all that, to say that there's just
goodness, what's wrong is some mechanical difficulty. That's
what we're confronted with.

BELL: What do you think about Lyle Lanier saying we might come
back to a more agrarian type of society?

LYTLE: I think it's going to blow up first. I don't think it can come
back now—the grounds for it have been destroyed. Particularly
in the South, the smaller farmers, people like that. You take
Murfreesboro, Rutherford County, when they bought out the
old Lytle house and tore it down and put a Carnation milk plant
there, then there were 30,000 milk cows in the county. Not any
there now. The plant has been torn down, itself, don't you see? I
just think we have gone mad with this technology, and just
making things.

BELL: Even in dairy farming now the cows are milked around the
clock, they're never out to pasture, they just feed them.

LYTLE: Just like the chickens. That's a horrifying thing. What we
have done is violate nature. You make war on nature, you use it,
you see. And when you do that you yourself become a kind of
monster. It's a monstrous life, and in a way, you see the results of
that in these people.

A family farm cannot be torn down to the money economy.
We were at Cornsilk here in 1925 and '26; we had mules and
horses to plow, and we grew our own fuel. We had one tractor to
disc with because loose ground was hard on the workstock. But
then, you didn't have any rent to pay. And you grew a great deal
of your own food. But you just cannot be dependent on the
world market. Just to be on the money economy, no way for a
farm to do that and survive. In the first place you've got to
consider seasons. You can have drought; you can have too *much*
water. You pay $80- or $90,000 for one of these big tractors and
have a 300-acre farm, why, there is no possible way not to go
under the hammer like they do out there in the West.

And when *I'll Take My Stand* came out, it was about 50–50,

the chance was possible for some kind of restraint, by slowing down the speed of change.

BELL: Did the down side of it all turn out as you expected it might in 1930?

LYTLE: Oh no. We couldn't imagine it being as bad as it is now. You know, we were just protesting. The only thing that brought us into the public view was the Great Depression. And it came out about that time, so we seemed prophets. At least, not prophets then, but they think we were prophets now.

BELL: When did you get involved with the *I'll Take My Stand* project?

LYTLE: Well, that was the year I graduated. Red [Robert Penn Warren] was at Oxford. I was around Nashville then. . . . That's the first writing, really serious writing, that I ever did, and I did it right on that table yonder.

I was interested in it, and there was a good deal of talk done, among Don [Donald Davidson] and John [Crowe Ransom], and they corresponded with Allen [Tate] in Europe. Allen got back and said, "I can get a contract with *Harper's* while I'm here."

I just took it for granted I was taken into it—they didn't know that until they had seen what I could do. We talked, and Don didn't want to sign the contract. I don't know why—Allen felt that Don would never bring anything to a conclusion, though they were great friends. So John and I went and sent a telegram to sign the contract. And I came and wrote my part here.

That's how I got into it. I was very bumptious—I sort of confronted Don on that. It was the time when if you didn't do it, it would never have been done. That is what, certainly, John and I felt.

BELL: Was Davidson a professor at Vanderbilt then?

LYTLE: Yes. He was also John's student, did you know that? They were at war and came out. . . . I don't know when he was a student. He was a good teacher. He didn't think I was much of a scholar. I took that sophomore class in English, and Davidson always shook his head at me. I was a dancing man in those days, fooled around. He only gave me a C. And I never took a class with him again.

BELL: When did you first fall in with Allen Tate?

LYTLE: I can tell you exactly that. He was a senior when I was a freshman at Vanderbilt. And he and Red roomed together, they met in Curry's office, there. I didn't know him. I was a dancing man in those days, didn't think about writing. John Ransom wrote me at Yale and wrote Allen at 27 Bank Street, and that is where it came about; I came down. Allen lived in the basement floor of Bank Street, and got that half rent-free for keeping the furnace. So we got to talking about the monkey trial, and we agreed about it, as did our philosophy professor, Dr. Sanborn. We saw each other for the first time there.

BELL: So you didn't know him from *The Fugitive*?

LYTLE: No, he wasn't there, then, you see, he was gone. I went to *The Fugitive* my senior year, but I didn't write verse, although I did try, and John Ransom was good enough to publish some, rather poor verse, which Allen accused him of. Allen of course had left, and he went up to his brother's. Ben Tate had a coal business. See, Allen's father bought all that coal land up in Kentucky and West Virginia, and Ben developed it. And Allen shipped a car of coal in the wrong direction and Ben fired him. And, of course, it was an unconscious kind of movement. Allen had no business fooling around with coal and all. Any kind of business. He couldn't even see those 12 tomato plants drooping at Benfolly—he would go right by them and never see them.

BELL: You've done a good deal of teaching here and there. Do you think it's a good thing for writers to be absorbed into the colleges the way that they have been?

LYTLE: I think you've got to be with people who are doing the same thing. I don't think you ever talk about what you're doing while you're doing it. If you did, you would never do it. But you have to talk around it, don't you see, and like that.

BELL: Was it in Florida that you taught Flannery O'Connor?

LYTLE: No, that was in Iowa, she was out there. Paul Engle brought me out there for two spring terms. I ran that place the second term.

BELL: What was she like as a student?

LYTLE: Oh, Flannery, she was a fine student. She was already working on a novel; I worked with her on that, and she would listen. I think I learned more than she did. I was given her stuff to read when I came there because they knew I could pronounce "chitlins." There I discovered that you never let the student read his own work. The friends will say it is good; the enemies say it's bad. So when I taught I always read their work myself.

I enjoyed it out there. I remember Flannery was such a puritan, she was one of those Catholic puritans. She had in that story ("A Stroke of Good Fortune"), remember, this woman who was pregnant, walks up the stairs—just a wonderful scene. In that, she put the boy in bed with the woman at first. And I tried to say, "It's not done that way. You can't get away with it." So what she did: she put a hat on his head and made a comic scene of it. I remember that.

We talked. I didn't know anything much about how to teach then, and she talked about it, that helped.

BELL: There isn't any love in O'Connor's work; do you think that's a limitation?

LYTLE: Yes, it's a limitation—it's her limitation. But with her use of the grotesque, the enveloping action is clear; this is what happens when you have only materialism as the common belief of society.

BELL: I read where you said that a writer has only one true subject—what's yours?

LYTLE: I don't know. But I think your writing of it is an effort to discover it. Some who have written about me think it is the fall from innocence, the Garden of Eden myth.

We have lost the sense of when every man and woman was a craftsman. That was the Christian inheritance. My sense of that now theologically is that that's why man has something divine in him. It's not that he is made in the image of God—a mosquito is made in the image of God. Such diverse images. That's a poor theology.

So my feeling is that an artist puts the best part of himself—I don't mean his personality, but his very being—in his work. In his artifact. And I think that God, if He made man (He certainly didn't beget him), then He put the best of himself in. And so that's the only divine thing in human creatures.

So the writer of the Garden of Eden failed in a sense—he brought Adam and Eve alive. Now, two naked people can't live together and not know what they're doing, you see; there is no possible way to do that. So I think they were like angels, they were emanations, else there's no point to eating the apple.

Because when they ate the apple, they became knowledgeable of themselves, they came alive. Their eyes opened. That is, they were no longer innocent, they took on the body of flesh and then, the garden of innocence, they were out of it. They were then wayfarers in the world, you see. So my feeling is—*it seems so ridiculous that the beginning of the world is based on disobedience.* It just doesn't make any sense at all.

BELL: People think of the story of the Garden of Eden as a tragedy. You're saying it isn't?

LYTLE: It's not a tragedy, it's just the beginning of life. In the beginning of life you have comedy and tragedy too. But it seems to me you cannot fall from innocence, no way to. You quicken into living, and you fall into, you enter, the wilderness of time.

That's a mighty broad subject. I'm going to make some biscuits, if you'll cut the ham. Can you all eat some ham? The turkey is, well, not deliquescent, I hope it's not, but we might best avoid it.

# INDEX